i

Gratitude.

J. Thomas Hetrick

Pocol Press
Punxsutawney, PA

POCOL PRESS
Published in the United States of America
by Pocol Press
320 Sutton Street
Punxsutawney, PA 15767
www.pocolpress.com

Publisher's Cataloguing-in-Publication
Names: Hetrick, Joseph, 1957-, author.
Title: Gratitude / J. Thomas Hetrick.
Description: Punxsutawney, PA: Pocol Press, 2021.
Identifiers: LCCN: 2021935687 | ISBN: 978-1-929763-94-8
Subjects: LCSH: Hetrick, Joseph, 1957-. | Hetrick, Joseph, 1957- --Family. | Hetrick, Joseph, 1957- --Travel. | United States. Air Force--Biography. | Hetrick family. | BISAC BIOGRAPHY & AUTOBIOGRAPHY / Personal Memoirs | BIOGRAPHY & AUTOBIOGRAPHY / Military
Classification: LCC UG626.2.H48 H48 2021 | DDC 358.40092--dc23

Cover Photo: The author, age 3.
Rear Cover Photo: The author in Nashville, TN.

DISCLAIMER: This book uses the names of real people to recognize, respect, and honor them. Under no circumstances is it meant to denigrate or call out the behavior of others. Many of the circumstances herein relate to self-deprecation of the author. He alone is responsible for its content.

For my daughters

Alicia Jiyong Hetrick

Amelia Jisun Hetrick

"When you arise in the morning think of what a privilege it is to be alive, to think, to enjoy, to love ..."

— Marcus Aurelius, *Meditations*

Let joy arise.
Let it bubble up
as fermentation
gives rise to the golden
lightness of champagne,

let it burst forth
and drive away the darkness
we too readily embrace.

All that is calls us back
calls us home
calls us to joy that has us dancing
in the streets
even as we sit sipping our coffee.

Our hearts can dance even
when our feet do not move,
so let us turn, turn, turn,
in the waltz or in the *sama*.
The name of the dance does not
matter, what matters is the music we dance to.

-Steven Riddle

TABLE OF CONTENTS

Employment, Family Life, and Miscellaneous

Hetrick Family Biographies

ACKNOWLEDGEMENTS

This volume could not have been completed without the expert editorial suggestions of Ray Bugay, a native of western Pennsylvania. I'd be remiss without also thanking the Stained Glass Writer's Group, helmed by Jane Murphy. On several occasions, I attempted to read a few of the stories to the group. Their kind words are welcome criticisms provided a unique impetus to continue.

PREFACE

The jottings herein serve as a legacy for my daughters. Overall, the book contains four distinct writing periods and/or themes; Letters written to Steven Riddle about my military service time in Japan and the Philippines (1980-1983), Writing Assignments from George Mason University's English classes (1993-1998), and Recent Writings (2020) to fill out the narrative.

A final section details short biographies of the four most important people in my life; Grandfather Emery Elwin Hetrick, Grandmother Freda Miller Hetrick, and parents Joseph S. Hetrick and Rachel A. Perri Hetrick. To avoid excess sentimentality, all of these biographies are written in the third person.

The writings in this book are mostly autobiographical.

In retirement, I decided to take stock to document portions of my earthly existence, good and bad. I began to think about just how blessed I've been in relationships with family and friends, global travel, and my passion for books, sports, and history. After stumbling across some old papers in the garage, the ideas for this book began to take shape. Rather than create a dry narrative, my focus became short stories related to people and events I'd experienced. "Charles Ricks: Teacher Extraordinaire" and "Don't Look Down!" served as my springboard tales on my journey of self-discovery. A handful of these tales are written in the third person.

My modest goal is that this book can be enjoyed and spur others to create their own life narratives.

This and what follows is my story of gratitude.

Military Brat

When a United States Military enlisted man is assigned to an overseas post, there is but one option: go. Commonly known as "orders," the enlisted man reads them carefully, noting date of departure, current unit designations, and arriving unit designations. He then begins to pack his bags. Unless under extreme hardship circumstances, neither spouses nor children are allowed any opposition. School years are not considered. Questions to officers are not entertained. As the young son of an Army soldier, together with my mother, we were assigned to Stuttgart, West Germany, specifically Patch Barracks. In February of 1964, I was pulled out of first grade.

Uprooting wasn't new. At nineteen months old, I departed with my parents to Italy, living there for two and one-half years. My grandparents on my mother's side of the family came from Italia to Ellis Island in New York at the turn of the century. They assimilated, living the rest of their lives in Punxsutawney, Pennsylvania. Grandpa Gennaro Perri served in the United States Army and later became a tailor and dry cleaner. So, even at a young age, I became used to moving away, leaving friends behind. By 1964, you might say I was a veteran at being a "military brat."

Patch Barracks comprised of several three-story apartment buildings. The apartments housed military enlisted and their families exclusively. The complex featured a steep hill and forest behind our building with a gravel road leading to the top of the hill. For the next year and a half, this became my home. That gravel road and the surrounding treescape served as my playground. Weather permitting, my buddies and I spent nearly every waking minute when we weren't in school, or sleeping or eating, in that outside paradise. If it was hot in Stuttgart, my mother dressed me accordingly. I wore t-shirts, tennis shoes, and short pants. It seemed like my mother had her hands full tending to my frequently scraped-up knees. Staying clear of scrapes and bumps and bruises didn't seem to be in my makeup. However, I became more careful when father reached into the medicine cabinet for merthiolate. "This will sting just a bit," dad would say while applying the medicine. Yeah, right! Conversely, for winter days, my mother bundled me tightly in sweaters and coats and boots. When you're six, you believe you're indestructible.

To satisfy my appetite for outside adventures, and contribute to my daily injuries, my father bought me a green scooter from one of the German stores. The vehicle came equipped with pneumatic tires. Before any of us heard of Evel Knievel, I'd take that scooter to the top of the hill and race downward, dodging trees like a downhill skier. The entire ride took a few seconds, but we'd take turns zipping down on that little green scooter. If sheer speed was the desire, we'd haul the scooter up the gravel road, and race straight down. The scooter did not possess brakes. To slow it down or stop it, one's leg had to suffice. Yes, there were more chances for injuries as a result.

Winter did not deter me in the least, as I plowed my way down the hill in snow. My other buddies did not participate in this endeavor, probably believing that the snow and ice would be a bit too dangerous.

In the winter of 1964, having turned seven years old and in 2nd grade, I eagerly awaited the arrival of one Kris Kringle at Christmas. The teachers in the school brought in large, illustrated cardboard calendars. Per German tradition, each day on the calendar contained a tiny door, opened only when that school day commenced. On occasion, the door indicated a surprise awaited. Amid squeals from the children, the teacher passed out chocolates to all her charges. As the weather turned colder and the time lurched forward, Christmas day loomed. My father told me about the legend of Santa Claus originating in Germany. Taking off at the North Pole in his sleigh, Santa Claus would deliver presents to all the children on earth. Thanks to elves helping to make and wrap the presents, the gifts would be loaded into Santa's sleigh, pulled by eight reindeer flying through the sky.

Christmas Eve was the busiest time of year for Santa, with all those worldly stops to make. And, I believed every word. With Christmas Eve fast approaching, I was beside myself in joyful anticipation. Every night, in my pajamas, I'd prance around the house, questioning my parents about when would Santa be coming.

"On Christmas Eve," they'd say, over and over again. Three days, two days… one day.

Now, it was Christmas Eve! Mom helped me pour a glass of milk and leave cookies for our guest. My parents then insisted that I be snuggled in my bed early to allow for Santa to work his magic. That night, I had an extremely difficult time falling asleep. I'd need to go to the bathroom, get a drink of water, have a bedtime snack. Anything to avoid going to my night's rest. It must have driven my parents crazy. Besides, they'd be busy that night also. Restless, I looked out the window of my third-floor room. My view was perfect. Lighting up the night sky, a series of blinking orbs twinkled in the darkness. Without a doubt, Santa Claus was coming to our town! I flew to my parents' bedroom. "He's coming! Santa's coming!" I shouted. Was I a lucky kid, or what? My parents capitulated. More water and snacks and bathroom visits followed. When I finally calmed down, my energy leveled off and I plopped into bed, asleep at last. When morning broke, I bounded into the living room to see all of the presents underneath our shining Christmas tree, proof of Santa having been at our house.

At the conclusion of my 2nd grade school year, over the summer of 1965, my sister Gina was born. She was a preemie, and had to be kept in an incubator for her first few days. This difficult time for our family was compounded by my father receiving orders for his new assignment in Germany. Due to the circumstances, Gina would not be able to travel. When she was healthy a few weeks later, we moved to Rothwesten Kaserne, or Kassel.

If living in Stuttgart was a toe dipped in the water, the Kassel experience proved to be a full body immersion. In fact, more opportunities arose to learn about German culture, language, and history. Leading this effort was my father, who by now had grown enamored of German clocks and medieval castles. He began to study and collect German clocks of all types. Castles could not be collected as they did not fit inside our tiny apartment. I too discovered new interests. Our living quarters in Kassel, in apartments reserved for American soldiers and their families, did not contain the proper geography for barreling scooters down steep hills. Instead, my new obsessions became collecting comic books, shooting marbles, and playing soccer.

Comic book collecting and trading them with friends fascinated me and jump-started a lifetime of reading curiosity. Some of my comic heroes in this era included Superman, Batman, Richie Rich, and The Archies. I delighted to know all their stories while awaiting next month's adventure. New issues cost one dime.

Shooting marbles with other kids to win their marbles became a brief pastime and even induced some rather odd behavior. Entirely new vocabulary was needed for glass marbles including clearies, catseyes, and solids. Two silly incidents stood out in my pursuit of marble excellence. Once I asked my father to drive me to a German store to purchase marbles. He did, but I was sorely disappointed that German marbles were made of clay instead of glass. Real marbles, like the ones I craved, were all made of glass. Another time, because my brain was so full of marble thinking, I spied some loose marbles on the floor in the living room. Excited to find new toys, I grabbed one and began to position it in my fingers, ready to propel it across the carpet. Unfortunately, these were not marbles, but perfectly globular granules left behind by my now-crawling baby sister Gina. Didn't smell like a marble, either.

Then, there was soccer. Called *fussball* in Germany, I played this game in the grass behind the apartments with all the neighborhood kids. We played soccer beginning in the morning until dusk. Even German kids hopped the fence separating our apartments from Germany proper, to participate. For the first time, I learned a few German words and some trick kicks in soccer. Once, while dribbling the ball a significant distance, I blasted a shot toward the net. When it dipped past the goalie, I became somewhat of a neighborhood hero, receiving plaudits from the German kids. It was my fifteen seconds of soccer fame.

Our family time in Kassel amounted to my 3rd grade school year. The teachers made a sincere effort to teach their students some words and phrases in German. We also learned some history and cultural lessons, including wearing *lederhosen* and *tanzen* (dancing). I always enjoyed these lessons, but was not old enough to process the fact that the United States defeated Germany in WWII only twenty years previous. My parents took time to visit a few German restaurants to partake of their cuisine. My favorites became *fleisch* (meat), *spaetzle* (noodles), and *kartofflesalat* (potato salad). At eight, I was a wee bit young for *bier* (beer). I'd also enjoy "going through the fence." That American boy that always bought *brotchen* (bread roll) and *gummi* bears with his German marks was me. Where better to live in Germany than the home of the famous Brothers Grimm, spinners of famous fairy tales?

Saturdays, though, became my favorite day of the week. Every Saturday, without fail, the base put on a special movie doubleheader for the kids. Operated by the servicemen's wives, these movie treats took place in a recreation center. The films cost 25 cents with popcorn galore and other snacks an extra 10 cents. The showings began at about 10am and continued into the afternoon. I can still hear the clickity-clack of the 8 millimeter projector. Our guardians didn't bother to supervise us much. This resulted in throwing popcorn and screaming and laughing and carrying on like a bunch of…well…kids! Titles included *First Men in the Moon*, *Jason and the Argonauts*, and *The Wonderful World of the Brothers Grimm*. Laurel and Hardy shorts also appeared with regularity, prompting additional popcorn avionics.

Other adventures occurred during my time in Kassel. On a family visit to visit my father's brother Charles Edgar, also stationed in Germany, we stayed overnight in a rather ancient village. Uncle Ed and Aunt Frances had six children, all living in a ramshackle apartment on the top floor. One bathroom serviced two families. After walking through the village, my cousin Frank, two years my senior, pointed out a candy store. We traveled along with my cousin Bobby, two years my junior. Frank possessed the money and he purchased three *zuckers*, German lollipops. Frank gave one to me and kept the other two. Then, Frank yelled out "Run!" and we ran down the hill away from a lagging Bobby. My young cousin cried when he got home and Frank eventually gave him his lolly.

On another occasion, vacationing in the famous ski resort of Garmisch Partenkirchen, my parents and I stayed at a hotel. One afternoon, as my parents were enjoying a cocktail in the lounge, they allowed me to play miniature golf in the basement of the hotel. The elaborate course thrilled me even as I played alone. No other patrons played while I putted around. On the eighteenth hole, I smacked my ball straight up a hill. My ball landed in the cup. However, when I went to retrieve it, I could not find it. My ball was missing. Immediately, my mind conjured up negative thoughts. Am I going to owe the hotel a golf ball? What will my parents think? Will I go to jail? Frantic, I went upstairs and flagged down a maître 'd. Oh my, he only understood German. Unable to get my point across, I panicked. Finally, I was able to get someone to follow me down to the basement. My hands flailed, trying to explain my predicament. The man calmly reached behind the 18th hole. There, inside a drawer, was my golf ball. He tossed it up in the air and chuckled. Silly American kid, he probably thought.

My father's parents, Emery and Freda Hetrick visited two of their sons during my time in Germany. Neither had flown in an airplane before, and despite initial reluctance, seemed to enjoy themselves immensely. Our family trips resulted in partaking in local cuisine, visiting museums, and sightseeing numerous castles. That is, when my grandfather wasn't being lectured by my father on his clock collection. Both men being mechanically inclined, their discussions concerning clock mechanisms escaped my interest. By golly, my father seemed to speak with much authority on the topic, observing clock manufacturing and history. My grandfather seemed particularly impressed with German ingenuity and aptitude, erasing his previous misgivings. During my grandparents visit, we all went to a rather somber place; the concentration camp at Dachau. Similar to my lack of knowledge about WWII, the horror that was Dachau could not be understood by my developing mind. When I asked about it, all my father could say was, "A lot of people died here."

Although I did not appreciate them at the time, the sightseeing trips to German castles were a highlight. Three particular structures stood out; Wilhelmshöhe Palace in Kassel, and the fairytale Neuschwanstein and *Schloss* Linderhoff, both in Southwest Bavaria. The latter two were construction projects of Ludwig II of Bavaria and monuments to his hero, composer Richard Wagner. Suffice to say, all three contained fascinating stories. Neuschwanstein and Linderhoff, in particular, designed by "The Mad King" Ludwig II, whose biography is one of the strangest in human history.

Unfortunately, a terrible tragedy struck our family.

My infant sister Marianne was born on September 27, 1966 and died that same day. As far as I know, no one in the family ever interacted with the baby. These circumstances, considered a hardship by the Army, forced our family to return to the United States in early October. Marianne was buried at Arlington National Cemetery.

Being a military brat in a foreign country brought many challenges and opportunities. The constant upheaval of leaving old friends and making new ones taught me not to take too many things for granted. Simply living in a foreign country also allowed for many experiences related to another culture and its peoples. The main lessons learned were tolerance, humility, and a healthy respect for others. Thanks to my parents, and especially my father's attitude, home didn't have to be America. Home could be appreciated as anywhere one lays their head down at night. For those years, acquired through serendipity, I'll be forever grateful.

My formative years, on German soil.

A Killer Among Us

A stiff, morning wind whips through Patch Barracks. Brittle leaves swirl in circles, some lifted into the early autumn air. While mothers lovingly peer outside their apartment windows at their progeny, fathers practice soldiering about five miles away. The children shout boisterously. Little boys imitate their daddies with their toy guns and serious expressions. The girls squeal about the fortunes of their dolls.

Then, staccato bursts destroyed the calm of the kitchens.

"We interrupt this program to bring you a special bulletin. A man brandishing a knife broke out of a local prison. He is serving time for the murders of his entire family. The man is believed to be in the Stuttgart area. He is about six feet tall with a ruddy complexion. Take precautions. More details will be passed along as they become available."

Military moms listening to the radio broadcast, scurried outside to warn their children. Within minutes, the apartment complex was transformed from vibrant playground into ghost town.

With the killer still at large, a growing hysteria gripped Stuttgart. Chilling details about the case surfaced in the local papers. Though the man confessed to the horrific crime, the bodies of the slain family members were never found. For the next several days, the news stayed the same. Children were cautioned to stay indoors. Bulletins about the man consistently exposed the fears of the townsfolk.

"A man fitting the killer's description was observed rummaging through trash receptacles at the park, however, no further details are available." said one radio announcer.

"An unidentified, bedraggled, unshaven man, believed by many to be the killer, was seen running through the streets," proclaimed another broadcaster.

However, with each news flash, the mystery man appeared as elusive as ever. The police offered few clues. The apartments now resembled prisons...or sanitariums. Mothers were becoming slightly daft with their broods inside all day. Fathers, used to the rigorous discipline of their jobs, lost all control of their kids. The fighting and yelling increased incrementally.

For one precocious eight-year old and his buddies, the return to the great outdoors was a godsend. It was impossible to play army cooped up in an apartment. Soldiers march and fight and die outside. How would the tanks rumble? Where could they fire their weapons? How could a mortar possibly fit outside a tiny window? What Stuka fighters and B-17 bombers would risk taking off and landing in cramped living rooms? Finally, there were only so many corners to peek around indoors.

"Everybody knows that!" the boys whined to their mothers.

After a week went by with no resolution to the case, a few parents began to let their children venture outside. Soon, others followed suit. Slowly, Autumn was vibrant again with the gleeful noise of children. Days passed. The weather turned colder.

The war game was proceeding splendidly. This campaign was conducted on a drizzly day at the hill-top ruins of a WWII German hospital. Leading up to the site was a gravel road which emptied into a paved street. This short street led to a series of military buildings, including an MP station. Jimmy Frederick, the freckle-faced radio man, had been killed in a firefight with the enemy. However, quick-thinking Tommy Harris had seized the dead man's equipment and was frantically calling for reinforcements.

"This is K69er Alpha. Heavy Casualties. Send help!"

Just then came another screaming enemy rocket. The blast blew Platoon Leader Sgt. David twenty feet into the air. The boys were dying fast but enjoying every minute. All knew they'd be in for a tongue-lashing from their mothers when they got home. Their clothes, faces, and hands were caked with mud.

Suddenly, as Tommy was crawling through the muck, he noticed a strange formation in the wet earth. He scraped his fingernails. The earth had turned a dull white.

"Guys! I found something!" exclaimed Tommy.

Herbie Martin, Billy Knudson, and the "deceased" soldiers all moved towards Tommy. The war games were over. When they arrived to investigate with their friend, a few of them had the same,

9

sickening feeling. These were buried human remains! Could they be the family members of the killer?

Tommy blurted out, "Let's tell the military police!"

Tommy immediately began to race down the hill, the other boys following in his wake. Down the gravel road they ran, their hearts beating wildly. This would surely be big news. Tommy and his friends would inform the authorities who would then dig up the bodies. Forensic tests would be conducted and one mystery would be solved. The boys would be heroes, perhaps getting their pictures in the papers or appearing on television! Visions of fame danced in their collective heads. Five minutes later, the excited eight-year olds arrived at the station. Tommy and his group were panting heavily.

"There's a body up there. On the hill. And he did it!" shouted Tommy.

"Calm down, son," said a beefy-looking sergeant named Foster.

"Now, tell us the full story," reasoned the squarish-jawed Sergeant Jones.

Tommy caught his breath and proceeded to relay the entire tale. He told of how he and his buddies were playing on the ruins of the old hospital and how he had discovered the bodies in the squishy mud. Tommy's confession must have been convincing. After some talk among themselves, Sergeant Jones decided to organize some soldiers to visit the site. In all, about ten armed privates marched their way up the hill, commanded by Sergeant Foster. Sergeant Jones forged ahead in a jeep. The boys, meanwhile, raced up to the location to meet with their real-life counterparts.

The suspense for Tommy and his friends was nearly unbearable. These brave soldiers would find out the truth and they'd all be heroes! After a few minutes, both parties converged on the site. Nearly everyone was huffing and puffing. Sergeant Jones wasted no time.

"Detail, halt!" screamed the authoritative Sergeant Jones.

"Tommy, where is the location?" said Sergeant Jones, his voice toned down considerably.

"Right here," pointed Tommy.

"Private Stafford, begin digging right in that spot. Tell me what that stuff is," said Sergeant Jones.

"Sure thing, Sarge," answered Private Stafford.

The young private buried his shovel into the soft earth, mixing the whitish matter with the dark brown hues. After turning over the mud with his tool several times, Private Stafford announced, "It's not a body, Sarge."

By now, all the men in the detail had nudged forward to get a look. Sergeant Jones peered into the whitish-dark terra firma. Tommy and the boys looked puzzled. If it wasn't a body, what exactly was it? Sergeant Jones grew impatient.

"Detail, attention! OK, men, the excitement's over. Let's get this show on the road. Private Stafford, back in line! Forward, march!" yelled the Sergeant.

The men cocked their rifles back over their shoulders and began their regimented descent down the hill. Sergeant Jones pulled away in his jeep. The marching men remained as perplexed as the boys. However, in keeping with their orders, they trudged along. This had been the most fun they'd had in months. Keeping the peace could never be confused with the heart-stopping excitement of battle. The march continued until the one private in the formation couldn't stand it any more.

"Permission to speak, Sergeant Foster!" said one soldier.

Sergeant Foster relented.

"What was that mess back there?" questioned the private.

Without changing his cadence, the sergeant informed his men.

"Sergeant Jones used to grow them back home in Kentucky. He says they were giant mushrooms."

The marchers broke out laughing.

"Settle down, men," quipped Sergeant Foster.

Meanwhile, back at the hospital, Herbie and Billy looked at each other in disbelief. Tommy, who'd started it all, wiped away his tears. David and Jimmy knelt down and began to dig away more of the squishy mud.

"They didn't even tell us what it was!" wailed Tommy.

11

That afternoon, all of the boys returned home. They were quiet as church mice. No one, it seemed, wanted to stay up to watch television. They just curled right up into their comfortable beds after wolfing down dinner. War games were invigorating but exhausting.

When Sergeant Harris arrived home that evening, he hugged his wife Betty and then quickly found his favorite chair. Propping his feet, he tried to relax from the rigors of a week of camping out.

"There was an uproar today the last day of bivouac. Some of the guys were talking about a 'mushroom detail.' I couldn't quite make it out. Then, on the radio on the way home, I heard this story about some boys playing soldier who found a giant mushroom," said Sergeant Harris.

"Oh, it's probably nothing," sighed his wife.

"Where's Tommy? I don't hear him."

"He's in bed. He came home a muddy mess. I'm sure he was up the hill again. I gave him a bath and some dinner and he wanted to go right to bed. He was babbling something about that killer when he nodded off," said Betty.

As they say, based on a true story. Tommy Harris is my pseudonym.

Salted-in-the Shell

"But, Daaaad!" the boy whined.

"All right, We'll go to the ballgame. But, I won't enjoy it," the father cautioned his son.

Tommy Henderson was as small as his crew-cut was short, and just short of eleven years old. At his dad's insistence, Tommy had to sport the insipid haircut. Always ridiculed by his more progressive classmates, the "military" look helped to create distance between father and son. Mr. Henderson had been in the Army since he was a teenager in the 1940s, lying about his age to enlist. Mr. Henderson wore the buzz-cut along with his perfectly-creased pants and tried to project that lifestyle onto his son.

Tommy had been following the fortunes of the local major league team, the Washington Senators, since last season. Washington's entry was in the throes of another lousy campaign in 1968.

As with previous editions, the team was weighted down with baseball mediocrities. First baseman Mike Epstein sported Elvis-like muttonchops, but could never hit like The King. Shortstop Ron Hansen made an unassisted triple play and was rewarded with a one-way ticket out of town. Faster-than-lightning Ed "The Steak" Stroud, utilized his talent by popping up and racing back to the dugout. Rookie centerfielder Del Unser could have passed for the ball boy. Catcher Paul Casanova, a perpetually smiling Cuban, barely hit his weight. Backup catcher Jim French was famous for diving all over the diamond only to drop weak foul tips. In the pitching department, the Senators endured another season of undelivered promise. Even the Washington manager seemed right for the job. Jim Lemon, a fairly decent slugger in the 1950s, had survived playing on the Washington teams of that era, who also lost with extreme regularity.

The only player of note was the gigantic Frank Howard — a six-foot-seven inch behemoth known primarily for bashing tape measure home runs and weather altering swings. When Howard connected solidly, the baseball assumed radically new shapes temporarily, before settling into the empty outfield seats of

13

cavernous D.C. Stadium. Due to its circular, closed configuration, the stadium was known for trapping sound inside its concrete shell.

To satiate his baseball interest, Tommy woke up before his parents to see how the Senators fared the night before. He'd sneak out of the apartment to peek at the neighbor's *Washington Post*. Invariably, the deadline-oriented newspaper would simply print "late game" next to the results. Worse yet, the *Post* would sometimes carry a partial summary of the game until the fifth inning. Thus, Tommy would have to wait until school ended to hear the disappointing ball scores on the radio.

All through the summer of 1968, Tommy kept pestering his dad to take him to a game. Tommy had waxed eloquent about how Jimmy's dad took him to see games and how Billy's dad played catch with his son every weekend. Tommy begged his dad to buy a new baseball glove so they could renew the ancient father-son tradition. Mr. Henderson, never athletically inclined and of medium build, finally broke down and bought a glove. At first, the elder seemed uncoordinated and threw "like a girl," according to Billy, who'd sometimes joined in the games of catch. After a while, though, Tommy's dad developed a whip-like throwing motion. Tommy's dad also learned to catch the ball more often than not.

When Tommy felt his dad was ready, he annoyed him again.

"Daad, you promised!" Tommy would say as the summer wore on.

One week night, the two piled into the family station wagon to see a game between the Senators and the Chicago White Sox. When Tommy and his dad arrived at the stadium, they were greeted at the ticket booth by a smiling, gap-toothed man. Tommy was so excited he asked the man who was going to win the game tonight. A victory in Tommy's first game would vindicate all those nights hiding a transistor radio under his pillow to listen to the play-by-play of broadcaster Dan Daniels. It would also greatly satisfy the lad who spent his weekends watching his heroes succumb on television with voice lamentations provided by Warner Wolf.

"Pipe down," his dad said gruffly.

"Section 212, seat 14, dad, where's that?" said Tommy.

"Follow me," said Tommy's dad.

It wasn't that easy, though. Mr. Henderson had difficulty understanding the seating pattern and had to ask a kindly usher, who was roaming the stadium carrying a well-worn rag.

The usher pointed to a nearby concrete ramp. Beside the ramp was a concession stand selling hot dogs, peanuts, soda pop, and beer. Tommy begged his dad for a hot dog and a soda.

"All right," said Tommy's dad, aware they'd left the house before dinner.

"Can I have some peanuts, too?"

Tommy examined his food while his dad picked up a beer and paid. The peanuts seemed odd, salted-in-the shell.

"Dad, what are these, how do they get all the salt inside a peanut?"

Mr. Henderson didn't pay attention, too busy nursing his beer and peering at the ramp. Tommy's dad motioned stiffly for his son to come along.

The two walked up a steep grade into the stadium's seating section. When Tommy saw the vast expanse of green and the giant-sized dirt in the infield, he gasped. This couldn't be the right place. No man could possibly hit a baseball that far. The magnitude of the stadium far outstripped Tommy's image from the games he'd seen on television. Tommy and his dad showed their tickets to a nearby usher. The man unfolded their chairs and then wiped them clean. As they sat down, the players below were practicing. While Tommy's dad sat rigid in his seat, Tommy noticed the impossible distances that the players were throwing and batting the ball. Smiling broadly, Tommy tore into his hot dog and soda combination. It was the best food he'd ever eaten. When it came time for the peanuts, Tommy turned to his father.

"Dad, have some."

Tommy's dad grabbed a few peanuts from the bag.

"Dad, can I go down there and try to get an autograph? I see Frank Howard!"

The boy giddily raced down the long concrete steps towards field level. He spied his hero Frank Howard, who was blistering throws to young Del Unser.

"Are you gonna hit one tonight, Mr. Howard?" Tommy

15

blurted out.

The Washington slugger slowly looked up into the stands before resuming his practice tosses.

"I'll sure try, son." said the baseball star.

Tommy couldn't wait to get back to his dad to tell him the news.

"Frank Howard is going to try to hit a home run for me tonight!" Tommy gushed to his dad.

A verbal biography of Howard followed. Beside himself with glee, Tommy explained that Howard had once hit a home run with one arm in the World Series for the Dodgers!

"He's bigger than Babe Ruth and he's the top home run hitter in the American League!" Tommy raved.

"Settle down," said Tommy's dad.

Talking about the Senators' slugger Tommy's dad offered, "He's sure a muscular guy, but you know something, he's got a crewcut just like us!"

"Oh, Daad," sighed Tommy.

After the National Anthem that Tommy and his dad stood proudly for, the game began. It was over quickly. The White Sox pitcher Tommy John completely dominated the home team, winning 6-0. Frank Howard struck out twice with titanic swings against the crafty veteran John. When the Senators punched routine fly balls to the outfield, the few fans in attendance mockingly cheered. Long before the final out, the faithful had departed the park, convinced of another loss. When the game ended, the stadium echoed with the muffled sounds of exploded styrofoam cups, sounds far louder than the weak Washington bats.

"Well, I saw my first game! It's a shame that they lost," Tommy enthused.

On the walk toward the car, a still-jubilant Tommy asked.

"Can we go again, dad?"

"What, to see them lose? I thought you said that Frank Howard was going to hit a home run." said Tommy's dad, disgusted.

Tommy skipped along, realizing that there would be other games. Although this would be the only game with his father,

Tommy would see thousands more, at the ballpark, on television, and on the radio. Within a few years, the attendance-poor Senators departed Washington to relocate in Arlington, Texas.

"Frank Howard's going to hit more home runs," said a confident Tommy, "Just not tonight."

Father and son at the ballpark, at last. This time, I'm disguised as Tommy Henderson.

My Days as Willie Mays

As the sun splashed the gathering with its warm rays, I adjusted the bill of my Panthers cap. With all the strength my eleven-year old body could summon, I reared back and threw the baseball. Intended for the heart of the plate, the sphere veered slightly off course. I cringed as the ball sailed wide, right between the shoulder blades of the waiting batter. A dull thud reverberated through the ball yard. Parents and kids jumped up and screamed in the ensuing pandemonium. Two coaches raced toward the scene, joining the umpire, a young catcher, and the crumpled body of the injured boy. On the safety of the mound, my face turned as white as a sheet. It was my first pitch in the 1968 Falls Church Little League.

I could hear them all saying, "Are you OK? Does it hurt?" I prayed the boy would be alright and that all of our lives could return to normalcy. Meanwhile, a series of freakish thoughts entered my brain. Suddenly, the warm summer day turned into an inferno. I was sweating like a condemned man. The ball that had been nervously returned to me by my catcher, seemed cursed. I stared down into my spanking new glove at the baseball, hoping that the last few seconds had never happened. Sooner or later, the police would arrive, and they'd whisk me off the jail. I was convinced my fate had been sealed by a single errant pitch. Who would save me? My parents? Despite my pleadings, neither my mother nor father were in the stands to witness my debut. But, they'd sure find out when the police called them.

Perhaps my fears were a direct result of my familiarity with baseball history. In 1920, ace hurler Carl Mays of the New York Yankees fractured the skull of Cleveland shortstop Ray Chapman with a pitch. There were no batting helmets back then yet the ball ricocheted back to the infield where it was thrown to first base. The Yankee players thought Chapman had inadvertently struck the ball. Chapman dropped to his knees and was taken to a hospital. He died the next day, without regaining consciousness. So affected was Mays, that he never again duplicated his sterling pitching form. From then on, Mays was vilified in baseball circles. Would I be the

18

Little League Carl Mays?

Fortunately, for me and everyone involved, the smelling salts must have done the job. After a few interminable minutes, the boy groggily rose to his feet. With his coaches helping, he wobbled down to first base. A near chorus of "Attaboy, Jimmy!" and "Hang in there's" cascaded from the crowd. To help calm me down, the umpires allowed a few practice pitches. This time, my catcher barely needed to move. Because of my new found fear, I simply lobbed the ball over the plate. My easy-does-it forty five foot tosses prompted our manager to come to the mound.

"Don't let it bother you, son. Go back to throwing hard," said Mr. Bishop.

With each subsequent batter, I began to follow Mr. Bishop's advice. My pitch repertoire consisted of fast, faster, and fastest. Little League managers stressed that curve balls could ruin the arms of young boys. Unfortunately, my teammates behind me could have fallen asleep. There was nothing for them to do, but squint towards home plate and fake looking half-interested. My wildness continued. For every batter that I walked to first base, though, I struck out two. No one even managed a loud foul ball. Our team batting was only slightly better. The Panthers, with the slugging of our first baseman Timmy, punched an occasional ball to the infield and outfield. The Cardinals didn't realize their gloves were designed for catching. We scored several runs this way and won easily 7-1.

By the end of the game, my arm felt like it was going to fall off. Mr. Bishop, with his son Mike, congratulated me for my winning effort. To celebrate, Mr. Bishop treated the team to a late afternoon of piping-hot pizza. We gathered outside at the ballpark complex to eat our pizza and sample our favorite clubhouse drink, a suicide. This was a concoction of Coca-Cola, Seven-Up, and Dr. Pepper mixed together. I couldn't wait to get home to tell my parents about the triumph. However, my dad just shrugged when I told him and my mom didn't seem to understand why I was raising such a fuss. We won our next few games to finish with a perfect 5-0 record. When I wasn't pitching, Mr. Bishop stuck me on third base. I'm not sure if I liked playing the infield, but it was a welcome

19

break from the pressures of being on the mound. Pitchers were the focus of everyone's attention on the field. This thought set my heart beating faster but also mortified me. I was deathly afraid of making the kind of mistake that I'd made to my first batter. In time, I learned to reconcile my nervousness. However, such was my desire during a game that I could not conceive of losing. For me, every game, every pitch, was a life-and-death struggle.

During one of my games playing third base, Mike Bishop took the mound. He managed to load the bases with none out. The batter blooped a soft liner towards me near the bag. I caught the ball, and as Mr. Bishop and other teammates screamed at me, I stepped on third base, and then ran the runner down wandering off second base. Not quite aware of the moment, I'd just completed an unassisted triple play, a feat nearly unheard of in professional baseball, and even more fantastic in Little League.

After our season ended, our league organized an All-Star game comprised of the best kids. I was named the starting pitcher. Our side won the ballgame but about the only thing I remember was the temperature. Both teams labored under the intense heat, drinking plenty of water and Gatorade. Following the All-Star game, Mr. Bishop surprised me by saying that I'd been "called up" to the Hodges Home Improvement Remods.

"What?" I said.

"The Double-A season's got about a week still to play. The manager of the Remods called me to ask if you'd be interested," said Mr. Bishop.

"Wow, Mr. Bishop," I gushed. "I'd love to play more ball. When's the first game?"

"Saturday." said my now former manager.

This story documents my one and only year playing Little League baseball.

Charles E. Ricks, Teacher Extraordinaire

Charles E. Ricks loved his kids. Dozens of them. Year after year.

Truth be told, Mr. Ricks earned his living as a teacher. To be precise, he taught at Shrevewood Elementary in Falls Church, Virginia for the school year 1968-1969. That's when I, through wondrous serendipity, chanced upon his sixth-grade classroom, the unforgettable Room 215. The first day of school began in tumultuous times. The Vietnam War raged, political assassinations and riots roiled the nation in the spring and summer, and a presidential election loomed.

To say I was nervous would be an understatement. My father, an Army cook, served overseas in that war, causing family to fear for his safety. My mother struggled to hold down the fort with her three children; myself, and her two younger daughters. The school was new due to our constant moving and the teacher was a man. I knew it would be different having never been taught in elementary school by anything other than sweet young and older ladies. Despite all the trepidation and adjustments, Mr. Ricks calmed all of my nerves with his experiential and socialization styles of instruction. Indeed, we sharpened our reading skills, created better sentences, and polished our mathematical abilities. However, Mr. Ricks fervently believed that childhood learning would be better served by doing things, different things, and experiencing them all together in a classroom setting. Observations by our teacher and of each other informed our critical thinking and allowed us to bond together.

On day one of school, having introduced himself as Mr. Ricks, the socialization began. We were told to sit in our desks, as he had already designated by his planning. "Boy, girl, boy, girl," he stated, and this became our seating arrangement for the year. Our previous year's behavior of passing notes and spit-balling were strictly prohibited. Respect for self and others resonated just like Aretha Franklin's hit song. That same day, Mr. Ricks informed us of his teaching philosophy. "Learning is paramount, but we will also have fun," he said, with a beaming smile breaking across his face.

As his students, we may have sensed early on that Mr. Ricks wasn't just an average teacher. And he went about proving just that, day after day.

These memories came flooding back, over fifty years later, as I spied my "Autograph Booklet" in a box of important papers. The document was a mere five pages in length, on mimeographed standard sheet paper, compiled by Mr. Ricks himself. The cover indicated the year, grade, teacher's name, and featured the four schools each of us would matriculate to, including my own, Luther Jackson Middle School. The phrase "On to much success and happiness" also adorned the cover. Inside were class rosters of students, their addresses, and class officers, all duly noted. Mr. Ricks paid particular attention to class superlatives which included our class as having the highest PTA representation.

The Daughters of the American Revolution (DAR) recognized one of our classmates as the most outstanding sixth grader. By secret ballot, we also selected the Most Popular, Best Looking, Most Likely to Succeed, etc., and these individuals were recognized in the booklet. Also included was the statement that our class was selected to eat in the last lunch period due to our good behavior. Documenting this success was important to Mr. Ricks and he made it important to us.

As for experiential learning, it would be impossible to list them all.

As eleven-year-olds, we read the entire Shakespeare plays of Julius Caesar and Macbeth, over many weeks at a time. All students participated, even though none of us understood the full meaning of Elizabethan language. As a result, the readings took place without props, a stage, or dramatic representation. It was the words that mattered.

To buttress our literary experiences, we ventured every day across the hall to an empty classroom. When those students were eating lunch, we read silently to ourselves for 15 minutes, the idea being to learn to read for pleasure. The school provided no such materials. We read books of our own choosing, from home, which encouraged learning in that environment also. At that point, I was reading Edgar Allan Poe and Beverly Cleary, two rather polar opposites. But, this solitary reading time offered an audio accompaniment. In the front of the room was a large operative fish tank, which gurgled bubbles. Loudly. For several years afterward, I could hear these bubbles whenever I picked up a book.

Poem recitations, which were staples of an earlier teaching age, taught us memorization and public speaking skills. Mr. Ricks assigned a poem to learn on our own as homework. When our day came, we each stood up in front of the class, initially as petrified children. In time, after several iterations, we became polished orators. Incredibly, although knowing all of the text has faded with time, I still recall the poems given to me; "If" by Rudyard Kipling, "Mending Wall" by Robert Frost, and "It Couldn't Be Done" by Edgar A. Guest. Each of these pieces served as my own inspiration in later years. Mr. Ricks, in his wisdom, knew that this was the lesson of the exercise.

For art class segments, we learned stitchery, block printing, papier maché, and sewing flags. My own block print of the United States Shield garnered second place in a school competition. Mr. Ricks explained each in meticulous detail first. Most important point was in the doing, and learning these skills together. The actual artistic quality proved an afterthought.

One day, Mr. Ricks said he had an exciting announcement to make. "We are all going to be parents," he gushed. At our age, we probably all became confused. It's a good thing, I didn't relay this information to my own parents. Within a short period, an incubator arrived in the class and was set up with two bright lightbulbs, one warming each egg inside. Mr. Ricks then instructed that we were going to write a collective journal, detailing our observations. Time passed by and one day, the excitement nearly boiled over. Thanks to Mr. Ricks' boundless enthusiasm and careful whispers, we were all asked to remain perfectly quiet and still.

One baby chick began pecking at its shell. Slowly but surely, the shell became discarded and a baby chick emerged. We named it Peanuts and watched gleefully as it toddled unsteadily about the cage. The other egg, however, did not hatch. Although it did not occur to the class at the time, those eggs were us. The scientific experience of watching these chicken eggs symbolically served as a cycle of life lesson. Some of us don't make it...like my baby sister. Others carry on and thrive like myself, and the sisters she never knew.

Modern dancing, complete with Motown and rock songs were also part of Mr. Ricks' curriculum. To accomplish this, we moved all of the student desks to the edge of the classroom. The center then became a dance floor. After again herding his standing students into the "boy/girl" configuration, Mr. Ricks placed a vinyl record on the portable turntable and cranked up the volume. Honestly, I did not know what to think. Perhaps, none of the other students did either. Diana Ross and the Supremes sang "Baby, baby, baby, where did our love go?" and the dance party began. Mr. Ricks pointed to a couple of his choosing and off we went. As the class cheered us on, one by one, each couple shimmied and shook their hips to the beat. Mr. Ricks did not interfere or offer tips. When my turn came, I practically fell down, and quickly earned a deserved reputation as the worst dancer in the class. In time, however, the laughter turned to oohs and ahhs. This socialization exercise really contributed to class camaraderie. Another song that stuck in my mind during these dance parties was "American Woman" by The Guess Who. And, we didn't just dance one time, we partied several times every week during the school year, always with different partners and frequently with The Supremes.

Another lesson involved learning to enjoy food from other lands. In addition to pizza, we sampled tacos, curried chicken, and fish roe. Mr. Ricks did not use the word caviar, perhaps realizing the reputation of the word and the practice of eating as being common to the very rich. What did we know then about that? We were all suburban kids. Perhaps, Mr. Ricks wanted us to overcome fear of eating different kinds of food while recognizing other cultures.

As I turned to the last page in the booklet and looked at the autographs of my classmates, I noticed that all of them were merely signatures. Except one. My first childhood crush, the athletic Robin Kabrich wrote, "To a great outfielder, catching flies." Mr. Ricks wrote, "To the baseball fan who is a fine student to teach." Simple words, perhaps, but ones I'll cherish forever.

Incredibly, over twenty years later, in 1991, I received an unknown phone call. My first book as an author, *MISFITS!*, had just been published and I was honored to be interviewed for a story that ran in the local *Potomac News*. The caller stated his name as Charles Ricks. He inquired if I was the author of the book and if I attended Shrevewood Elementary. When I excitedly answered in the affirmative, he joked that he remembered me as the worst dancer in the sixth grade. No detective case identification could be more solid as evidence of the caller. We chatted briefly about my baseball book and he mentioned his long, educational career. Mr. Ricks then invited me to his upcoming retirement party as a principal and subsequently sent me an invitation. To my regret, I never went.

In the fifty years that have elapsed, I've recognized several truths about Charles E. Ricks. He was an amazing, positive influence whose profound impact cannot ever possibly be documented. His teaching methodology involved equal parts experiential teaching and socialization. All his students, as he frequently stated, were his favorites. He loved life and recognized the worth of each child, with his own deeply rooted love for teaching and for every human being. That unerring love he wore on his sleeve for all to see. I've always wondered what/if other students think about him. Did they recognize his impact?

In these times of adulation for sports heroes, movie stars, and political figures, we should rightfully be celebrating our real heroes, the indispensable teachers. Here's one, small tribute. Thank you, Mr. Charles E. Ricks, wherever you are.

For a certain teacher, the real heroes in this world.

High School Daze (I)

Ah, high school. Teenage angst. When the desires of independence and sexual awakening begin to take shape. When being "popular" in school often serves as an overriding principle. When the pressure of graduating with good grades dominates conversations among parents and peers. A time when kids face the upheaval of transitioning from pimply-faced pre-teens with braces to young adults with part-time jobs. We all navigate the odyssey of adolescence, in our own way. And, we're the better for it.

From 1971-1975, I embarked on that strange journey, totally unaware and unprepared for how it would unfold. Like being a military brat, it was a time of disruption

After graduating from Luther Jackson Middle School in Falls Church, Virginia, I spent part of my summer visiting my two aunts, Jeanne and Rose Marie Perri in Punxsutawney, Pennsylvania. My days were spent trying on clothes from Albert's Men and Boy's Wear, lovingly purchased by Aunt Rose Marie. She insisted on dress clothes and even neck ties. For a kid primarily used to blue jeans and t-shirts, this adjustment proved difficult. Aunt Rose Marie brandished her trusty measuring tape. I felt a bit uncomfortable when she placed that tape on the upper portion of my inseam. Nonetheless, she bought me a dozen shirt and pants ensembles and a few ties *to boot*. The long out-of-business Albert's was owned and operated by Albert Greenblatt.

My Aunt Jeanne treated me just as special, always buying me Kit-Kat candy bars and introducing me to the staff at Stewart's Drug Store, another now defunct business in town. Jeanne worked as a clerk there for many years. She introduced me to the other clerks and owner/pharmacist Al Gretz and his partner Jimmy Gigliotti, a distant relative. My aunts really doted on me. When I wasn't being feted with gifts, I palled around with my cousins who lived directly across the street.

Nights were spent on the porch listening to our beloved Pirates' baseball games on the radio. Bob Prince and Nellie King manned the microphone, with the colorful Prince constantly blurting out his exhortations for the home towners. His phrasings were as colorful and loud as his sportscoats. When Pittsburgh barely won after blowing a big lead, he'd exclaim, "We had 'em all the way." A baseball hit into the new astro-turfed Three Rivers Stadium became "a bug on the rug." High pop-ups were "home runs in an elevator shaft." Close safe/out calls on the base paths resulted in "Safe/out by a knat's eyelash." And, in one quite wincing moment for all concerned, Pirates second baseman Dave Cash once took a groundball to the crotch. Prince said, "Ooohh, right in the coconut." Aunt Jeanne didn't usually sit with us but our threesome always included Aunt Rose Marie, her boyfriend Tom Hergenrother, and myself. Sipping Coca-Cola, eating Nabisco snacks, and listening to Prince's Pirates equated to paradise. On occasion, Mr. Hergenrother treated a McIntyre's Pizza, still my favorite.

That same summer Al Gretz, (with his son, his friend, and I) drove us to Pittsburg to witness a Pirates doubleheader with the Los Angeles Dodgers. On the way, our foursome discussed our heroes, in the middle of what would become a championship season. Our excitement was at fever pitch as we stood in line at the ticket booth. We couldn't help but notice the large crowds gathering outside the stadium. Unfortunately, a man came on a loudspeaker to announce the games were sold out. Not having any tickets, Mr. Gretz assumed we could purchase them the day of the game. The walk to the car and subsequent eighty-mile trip back to Punxsutawney occurred in near silence.

During that same summer visit to my aunt's, I attended the annual carnival at the Armory Field. The carnies set up on the largest patch of grass in town. I attended with my cousin Bob with tickets purchased by aunts. In small town Punxsutawney, the carnival was a big deal. As youngsters, we rode the rides and sampled all the junk food we could stuff in our face. Bob, two years younger than me, saw or participated in nothing that could scare him. However, I wasn't so sure when I entered the tent of an old-fashioned freak show. I might not have seen Siamese Twins or pinheads. But, several items in jars filled with formaldehyde gave me pause. When I'd ask Bob what they were, he'd just shrug and say, "It's probably fake. That's not a baby's head."

My Freshmen year began at ancient Fairfax High School,

established 1930. Our class attended the rickety monstrosity until the Christmas break. The school simply smelled bad and I never adjusted to keeping books in one's locker. Next door to the school stood a shiny new McDonald's separated only by a chain link fence with a gate. Although taking lunch was forbidden except in the school cafeteria, sneaking over to Mickey D's proved to be far too much temptation for Fairfax High students. For most of the time, I followed the school's rules, but one day I joined the scofflaws. Peer pressure got me. In January 1972, the new Fairfax High School opened on Old Lee Highway to much fanfare. Our family had moved from the heart of the city to Country Hill Drive, just a short walk away from the new school. A radical new school design awaited the first class of students. Fairfax High now boasted of shiny, multi-colored lockers, open-air classrooms without doors, carpeting in much of the school, and a rubberized gymnasium floor, far different than hardwood basketball surfaces. My adjustment to this environment seemed easier, if only for the newness of the design. Fourteen-year-old freshman hormones were kicking in, but my shyness prevented me from pursuing similarly-aged co-eds. Overall, my school year experience at Fairfax helped to calm my nerves.

As a sophomore, our family moved again prompting a change of schools and more adjustments. Our family now resided in an apartment in Pinewood Plaza and then Margate Manor in the same development. Within walking distance stood W.T. Woodson High, my new environs. I met some great friends at Margate including Rusty Gibson, Mike "Killer" Keating, Peter Brichant, and Jay Cooper. We passed the time talking about girls, talking about sports, and playing wiffle ball and table hockey.

I met Reginald P. "Rusty" Gibson in the spring of 1972. He played wiffle-ball with neighborhood kids, sporting his Baltimore Orioles cap and jersey featuring Brooks Robinson's Number 5. My Pittsburgh Pirates had defeated his Baltimore Orioles in the World Series that previous fall. Our first meeting occurred as I needled Rusty about the outcome of the baseball season. His initial pushback gave way to a smile, recognizing our common love of baseball. Our future meetings revealed his obsessions. Rusty was a drummer who worshipped Brooks Robinson, the Orioles, and legendary jazz drummer Buddy Rich. He spoke about all these topics with an extreme passion. Indeed, his bedroom sported posters of the same. His name Rusty fit perfectly, as he luxuriated in his shoulder-length orange hair. Rusty hated his given name of Reginald.

When it came to my table hockey forays, Peter Brichant and I perfected the "ram it home" style. Using the levers for a left winger with the left hand and the center with a right hand, we could twirl our players around to keep the puck away from our defenders. Then, in a quick hand-eye left/right hand combination, we could zip the puck from the winger to the center and push extremely hard on the lever controlling the center. The movement startled amateurs. With proper timing, the goalie never had a chance. My friend Bob Karnes later joined in our neighborhood hockey fun.

Free-spirited but quiet twenty-year-old Jay Cooper impressed my mother, who believed he'd be an older mentor for her only son. She met him at the local swimming pool, and asked him to come meet me. Jay and I became fast friends, even being invited on a family summer trip to New York state. This, despite my dad's commentary, "That boy needs a haircut," referring to Jay.

Dad drove us to New York City first. But the combination of a sweltering day and impossible traffic drove us away. We headed to the West Point Military Academy for a couple hours, on dad's insistence, and then looped around to Cooperstown to see the National Baseball Hall of Fame. That part of the tour was my insistence, especially to see a plaque for the newly enshrined Roberto Clemente, who had perished in a plane crash a few months earlier. The group was generally cranky about the Hall, but I could have spent days looking at the exhibits and pondering the glories of baseball.

I also secured several other friends I'll now call the Camelot Kids, since they lived in a swank subdivision nearby. Among them were Louis Rainey, John Lee, and Scott Rigdon. At that time Led Zeppelin's "Stairway to Heaven" was released and it became so popular among our crew that we all memorized the lyrics and sang it lustily when it came on the radio. Our other activities included playing touch football in the cul-de-sac, where curbs were part of the field and the sidewalk was out of bounds. Skinned elbows and knees became part of our ritual and they hurt. Complaining about the pain meant you weren't a man. Some of these friends egged me on one day in gym class. Run by the legendary basketball legend Red Jenkins, I "dressed out" as per usual. We were taught basketball fundamentals before playing in a game. I was the kid who never touched the basketball. With gym class under an hour, somehow I managed to get on the court. The ball got away from some kid and I managed to corral it. About twenty-five feet from the basket, my buds yelled out "Shoot!" I tossed up my long-range non-jumper. Swish! From that moment forward, someone started calling me "threat" and the name stuck. All through that year at Woodson, I became "Het the Threat."

Sometime in my sophomore year I purchased a hand-held Super 8 movie camera and a projector. I had saved up for it by combining my allowance and various monetary birthday presents. Very quickly I discovered filming to be an expensive hobby. Not fully understanding the financial outlay or the limitations of this cheap equipment, I plunged forward. I spied a compatible roll of Super 8 film, labeled as "50m." Assuming that meant 50 minutes of time, my initial filming attempts began. I brought the camera to the local swimming pool and pointed it at people diving. I turned it on to capture cars going by and people walking, filming any movement. Then, the roll of film ran out. 50m meant fifty meters of film, about two and one-half minutes. My days of dreaming to be a film auteur fizzled. More allowance would be needed to develop the film and purchase more for future endeavors. But, sometimes when I inserted the film into the projector, I noticed its inconsistent spooling. This resulted in occasional stoppages as the film burnt on the projector and projected that burning on the viewing screen.

One early filmic success involved the concept of "butt races." By using an inexpensive device called a cable release socket, I could press a button a shoot a few frames at a time. This experimental foray led to several friends sitting on their rear ends on the Woodson high school track. They raised their hands as if steering a car. I pressed the device. The "drivers" then moved

30

slightly forward and changed their hand movements. I pressed the device again. Repeat, repeat. Car wrecks were incorporated into the action. Although this race took two hours to film, when played back it showed high schoolers careening around the track at high rates of speed. Mack Sennett's Keystone Cops would have been proud.

School academics at Woodson seemed rather mundane. However, on Sunday, April 1, 1973, a local event occurred that dramatically changed the entire school year. A weather announcement of a "tornado watch" broke the radio airwaves earlier in the day. Then, at precisely 3pm, all hell broke loose. A rare tornado ripped through Fairfax County and the local area, downing trees, damaging property, and causing mass panic. The neighborhood wasn't exactly known as Dorothy's Kansas. A visiting friend, John Lee and I were playing a table-top sports game from my apartment. We watched in horror from my third-floor apartment window, as the storm rampaged. This tornado flew right down Persimmon Drive, buffeting trash dumpsters into the air and shattering the glass of car windows. In nearby Pickett Shopping Center, patrons in the Safeway grocery store jumped into the meat displays for safety. Others stopped their cars and prayed. In that same shopping center, a parked and empty school bus rammed into a state-run liquor store, completely destroying inventory. The tornado also removed roofs off buildings nearby. My high school, W.T. Woodson, suffered massive damage, with reports of the school gym now sharing space on the highway. The carnage lasted no more than ten minutes and by some miracle, no one was killed. My high school building did not re-open for that school year. Instead, we were all bussed to Oakton High School. Oakton students attended from 7am to noon, while Woodson students started at 12:30 and ended at 5:30pm. This logistical nightmare probably cost school administrators and teachers some long hours. Because Woodson suffered such damage, many students might have been relieved. Test taking all but ended with exams being so waterlogged as to be unrecoverable.

I could have been asking out girls, but instead chose to stay on the sidelines with my "peeps."

High School Daze (II)

In the summer of 1973, my father decided to uproot our family from northern Virginia to his hometown of Punxsutawney, Pennsylvania. He'd retired from the Army after a 20+ year career only a year earlier. After some careful planning, he continued his current career as a carpenter. His father Emery, mother Freda, and other family members were thrilled about the decision. My mother did not mind. My two young sisters, age 8 and 4, offered no resistance. I, however, beginning my junior year of high school, was totally against the move. And I said so repeatedly, unnerving my parents. Unlike previous apartment living arrangements, we now occupied a house on 127 Beyer Avenue. The three-bedroom, yellow-painted house was near the top of a steep hill. The property sported a two-car garage also, but no cars ever parked there during our stay. Instead, my dad converted it into a workshop for his numerous wood projects. Our green, gas-guzzling station wagon found its way into a gravel driveway. After some quick explorations and talking with the neighbor kids, I learned of a shortcut to high school through the woods. Every day I made this trek, sometimes braving the elements. Otherwise, my walking journey could have been more than twenty minutes. With the shortcut, it became less than ten. The shortcut also offered a much quicker route to my grandparent's house on 22 Lewis Street, when I visited them.

On the first day of school in my Junior year at Punxsutawney Area Senior High School, I encountered a bully. The incidents occurred in homeroom, the first class of every day. Students sat sorted alphabetically. In my row, Calvin Hetrick, myself, and Robert Hetrick comprised one section. Despite our common last names, neither were related to me. Homeroom in this school amounted to little more than reciting the Pledge of Allegiance and taking attendance. Most of the hour could be spent studying. In the teacher's desk seat, a woman devoured her reading assignments daily, head down, paying little attention to the class. For reasons unknown, the guy behind me named Robert Hetrick decided to bully me. Without a sound, he snuck his hand up behind my head and flicked my right ear with his fingers. Startled, I spun

32

my head around. He pretended to be looking elsewhere. Classmates behind me, attuned to the moment, chuckled. The teacher went right on reading. Fifteen minutes or so passed and the bully did it again. This time, when I turned around, he had turned his head also, acting like he was talking to his buddies. The ridicule laughter continued anew. The next day, he did it again and again, spacing his torture out and making it impossible to understand when the next flick would come. I confronted him with "Do you have a problem?" but not in a loud tone. He responded, "No, do you?" The teacher at the head of the room, noticed nothing. Day three and four came and went with more of his taunting. Robert Hetrick, a "tough kid from Rossiter," was much taller and stronger than I so I dare not confront him physically. On day five, I decided enough was enough. I made up my mind to take bold action immediately after his next finger flick on my ear. He did it again and I jumped out of my seat demonstrably, headed toward the teacher's desk, and began a loud tirade. I screamed at the teacher, explaining the situation and naming the perpetrator. My classmates sat dumbfounded and silent as I railed at the injustice. The teacher walked back to Robert's seat and forced him to leave the classroom. The three of us ended up in the principal's office. I, with my explanation, and he, with his lame excuse. The principal made Robert apologize to me and promise to never engage in such behavior again. Robert Hetrick soon found himself suspended from school for a few days. When he returned, his disruptive urges disappeared. He never bothered me again.

As a kid from the suburbs of northern Virginia, my adjustment to small-town life included much puzzlement. First and foremost was the idea that everybody in town knew everyone else. One could mention any name in Ruth and Harry's restaurant and instantly the response would be, "Oh yeah, (person) is …" If you don't think that keeps tongues wagging, you've never lived in a small town. In a late October 1973 class, it became eerily apparent I was one of the few male students in the school. Did they all contract mononucleosis, or what? The females in my classrooms may have been snickering about my presence. While I pondered this phenomenon, I asked a teacher. She explained that students may take three days off from school for hunting season. My ignorance in the matter made me completely unaware of this Pennsylvania practice. The teacher then asked if I wanted to take some time off. My reply was that I was not a hunter and had never shot at an animal in my life. "That's OK, you can still relax for a few days." Again, I disagreed and went right on learning.

In January 1974, I encountered another oddity, this one specific to the town. A school assembly featured two speakers, Charlie Erhardt and Sam Light. Erhardt manned the mic at the local radio station WPME for decades. Sam Light was an American original, appearing in top-hat and tails. Both men spoke of the upcoming glories of Groundhog Day on February 2nd, Punxsutawney's pride and joy and no small percentage of the town's commerce. In effect, each speech served as a pep rally for an oversized rodent.[1]

One of Punxsutawney high schooler's main pursuits on Friday and Saturday nights was "cruisin'". This involved little more than a car and some beer. A six-pack would suffice for solo drivers. A case of beer might be needed for cars with multiple passengers. Simply put, the sport featured riding up and down the town's main streets, Mahoning and Findley, at a high rate of speed, honking horns, and vomiting out the window, if necessary. For reasons unknown, athletes frequently had their cheerleader girlfriends tag along for increased fun. I am proud to report that I never participated in such nonsense, preferring instead to visit with my friends or relatives on Pine Street. The cheerleaders, in their short skirts and blouses, remained tempting, however.

My long-time friend Bob Karnes and his parents invited me to Sarasota, Florida each summer between 1973-1975. In many ways, these two-week vacations manifested themselves as silliness on steroids. Bob and I cut-up at every turn, doubtless driving his parents quite mad with our hi-jinks. In each year, our travel from northern Virginia to Florida began in his step-father John Hans' small Toyota. Mr. Hans drove halfway down and we'd stop in a Holiday Inn, before resuming the final leg the next day.

---

[1] Detailed information on this annual event occurs in *Groundhog Day, 2020*, in this volume.

Bob, ever the prankster, decided on a specific act of torture in 1973. The travel days were challenging, four souls inside a tiny car for eight hours at a time, heat blazing outside, air conditioning full blast. Bob's deviance involved him drinking copious amounts of prune juice as we headed south on interstate I-95. Needless to say, prune juice produces some rather unsavory effects on the human body, which was Bob's plan all along. He freely invited us to share in the drink. We all declined. When Marilyn Hans, Bob's mother said, "John, roll down the window!" we all knew our suffering had just begun. After that episode, Bob's parents forbade him to drink prune juice in the automobile. Thankfully, John Hans played along with our antics, singing songs in his mock-Popeye voice. "Oh, let someone, believe in your head!" Mr. Hans sang in full throat. We all laughed, never quite knowing what he meant. That first year, we stayed in a Spanish-style hacienda apartment, owned by Bob's grandparents. For the next two years, we vacationed in a house on the outskirts of town.

Over the next three summers, the antics created by Bob and I in Florida have allowed us, years later, numerous and sustained belly laughs. Frequently, they start out as "Do you remember...?" and devolve into us laughing so hard we begin crying. In restaurants, despite Bob's perfectly mannered parents, we assumed ridiculously overblown British accents. We visited two Sarasota landmarks, the Ringling Circus Museum and Cars of Yesteryear. The latter building's cars were interesting, but hardly a match for old-timey arcade games, which consumed Bob and I for hours. While those activities provided fun, they could not compete with our epic pranks and mis-steps. Wandering through a jungle zoo, containing alligators, birds, and other Florida fauna, Bob and I planned our next caper. A parrot perched atop a tree spouting out nonsensical phrasings. Bob's parents had moved forward, away from us and unaware of our developing plot. We noticed an elderly couple trailing behind us on the winding path. Thinking quickly, Bob and I got the parrot's attention and then stated, "You're very old and you stink!" We slinked slightly forward awaiting the elderly couple to arrive at the parrot's location. When the old couple arrived, the bird spouted out his sarcastic greeting. The couple's indignant reaction may have resulted in them questioning each other's judgment to visit that zoo.

Another prank involved asking pretty waitresses in restaurants for their autograph. We'd ask, but without malicious intent. One particular waitress named "Rita" broke into an odd song-and-dance when confronted with our unusual customer behavior. With comedic mannerisms, Rita prattled on about families ordering food. "I wanna hamburger, you wanna hamburger…", she said, delighting all of us at the table. Clearly, Rita was in the wrong profession at the wrong time. She didn't belong as a waitress in 1970s Florida, she belonged in vaudeville, or the circus. As the years creeped along, Bob and I oft-repeated Rita's routine, that is, if we could get past the guffaws first.

In 1974, I brought my father's old Army survival raft with us to Florida. Although it took forever, Bob and I took turns blowing up this monstrosity, khaki in color, and made of a coarse, tough rubber. Once the raft was in seafaring shape, Bob and I paused to catch our breath on the beach. Our next maneuver would be to paddle the thing out into the water with the two of us hanging the upper half of our bodies on the device. The plan seemed to be successful. We basked in the sun's rays and the Gulf's blue waters for a few hours. Bob's parents relaxed on the beach, sipping piña coladas under umbrellas. Our pleasures satisfied, we returned to the house. At first we didn't notice, but when we took our respective showers, we both became aware of the redness in our chests. Our backs and legs were sunburned, but our chests throbbed with stinging pain. Apparently, the surface of the raft scratched and rubbed our skin raw. The idyll of the day had dissolved into placing wet towels on our bodies to alleviate the heat. For the next several days, Bob and I did not leave the house.

If that year's beachcombing excursions were curtailed, the next year's didn't happen at all. That summer, the Hollywood film *Jaws* raged across theatres. In the first few days of that vacation, Bob and I attended a screening, while his parents picked us up later. The movie petrified our young sensibilities. In the movie's plot, a great white shark runs rampant, devouring beachgoers. Bob and I decided on staying behind while his parents retained their sand and surf activities. Our fears may have been well-founded as Sarasota is a hotspot for shark activity and also the site of a world-famous scientific team studying these beasts. Another near animal encounter occurred as we returned back to the house one evening. As we were nearing the house, a loud thud startled us. We'd likely hit something in the road. "What was that?" Bob's mother asked. "Don't worry," John said, and he kept driving. Shaken by the incident, John said to Bob and I in a stern voice, "Now, when we get out of the car, you two are not permitted to look." With the car parked, Bob's parents headed directly into the house. Naturally, disobeying Bob and I sneaked up to the front bumper of the car. Blood, matted hair, and skin clung to the car's exterior. We'd hit, and likely killed, a stray dog.

Although I did not partake in cruisin', I spent hours on end at my two aunt's house. Although these spinsters were the only occupants, two other individuals frequently stopped by; my uncle Dr. Ernest P. Gigliotti and my aunt Rose Marie's boyfriend Tom Hergenrother. On Friday nights, while other high schoolers wooed their girlfriends, I'd visit my two aunts.

Besides my parents and grandparents, Jeanne and Rose Marie were my closest adult friends. We got along famously. Mild-mannered Jeanne secured my first job at Stewart's Drug Store in the fall of 1973. She'd been a clerk at the business for decades. My duties included stocking shelves, sweeping and mopping floors, and helping to unload the supplies truck. I got along well with owner Al Gretz and his pharmacist partner Jimmy Gigliotti. At this job, my duties earned me $1.65 an hour. I saved for weeks to pay for my first calculator, a fifty-dollar Texas Instruments device, which I used for baseball statistics. Once, when stocking feminine products, Jeanne came over to ask me what I was doing. I said, "You know, putting up those lady things." The tease complete, Jeanne and the other ladies working in the store chuckled at my naiveté. No matter, Jeanne's kindness towards me could never be compromised, especially for someone thirty years her junior.

Far more talkative and outgoing, Rose Marie sometimes spoke and sang in Italian. Like her sister, she kept their house in meticulous order, always clean, always dust free. So much so that visitors, including family, needed to enter through the rear door. This was despite the fact that just past the front door, the plastic carpet runner extended straight through to the kitchen. Indeed, the old Addams family jingle may have applied, "Their house is a museum, when people come to see 'em..." But, if Rose Marie seemingly harbored a dust rag in her hand, she put it down when she walked "up street." This woman did not need a car. She had her two churning feet and she walked as if her legs were on fire. Like something out of a silent movie comedy. I believed it impossible not to like Rose Marie and her quirky mannerisms.

Besides listening to Pirates' games on the radio, we indulged Tom Hergenrother's fantasies; Penn State and Notre Dame college football. Mr. Hergenrother always found time to comment on his beloved Nittany Lions. "That boy from Aliquippa, he's gonna be a beast." "Spring practice is coming up. I can't wait." Or, "We look to finish top five this year." With both football teams being remarkably successful, they always managed to appear in bowl games or play for the National Championship. Watching either of these teams in a bowl game with Tom Hergenrother was a special treat. A salesman with Nabisco, Mr. Hergenrother showered the Perri sisters with product. Chocolate chip cookies, crackers, and other munchies became game time staples. We slurped down Coca-Colas, always fizzing on ice and always poured from large bottles.

Then, there was the irrepressible Uncle Ernie. A bone specialist, Ernest Gigliotti became a legend in town with his kindly heart and expert bedside manner. A wing at the local hospital is named after him. He'd show up at the Perri house for a few minutes, just long enough to grab the local paper. In a flash, he'd be out the door, off attending to his patients. Dr. Gigliotti was the closet thing to a perpetual motion machine I'd ever seen. Soft spoken but garrulous, he lived and breathed his profession. Both my parents, addicted smokers, would not dare light up around him, or they'd face his wrath. With the exception of one occasion, I never spent more than ten minutes with him. In a rare meeting with him as a kid, he drove me outside town in his small car. Dr. Gigliotti explained to me on the ride that his vehicle did not use gasoline. Instead, it received magical energy from a plane that had crashed nearby.

Dumbfounded by this magic energy source, I queried if anyone else knew about this. "No," he said. "It's a secret between you and me." At the time, I swallowed his canard whole.

Fortunately, I met and hung out with several friends. My "peeps" were comprised of Tom Henry, Ed Zatsick, John Caliguire, and myself. On several occasions, my cousin Bobby joined in. We all shared interests in various sports, but little else. In effect, our gang's similarities and differences propelled our friendships forward, in the group and amongst each other. Common activities included attending high school football and basketball games, playing pickup football and basketball, talking sports trivia, and bowling.

A budding guitarist, Tom Henry ran track and participated in the school's cross-country team. A fun-loving braggart by nature, Henry often challenged me to athletic competitions. A couple of times, we ran the cross-country course which cut through woods behind the school. I held my own, believing that the sport wasn't so much a race as it was good exercise. All finishers were winners. Tom Henry's track experience involved running hurdles. After being egged on with epithets that I was "soft" or "weak," he challenged me to race him in the 100-meter hurdles on the school track, located inside the football stadium. I begged off, but finally relented. In those days, the field was open to anyone daring to use it. After a lesson from my competitor in how to clear hurdles (running in stride vs. jumping over them), we assumed our positions. Off we went. Likely showing off, Tom tripped on the first hurdle and never recovered. I beat him easily despite having never run hurdles before. Was he mad! Nonetheless, our friendship endured, and Henry's braggadocio began to wane. No more did he talk about bowling 300 games, being a better guitarist than Eric Clapton, or hitting a baseball 400 feet. I knew Tom Henry had never done any of those things.

Excitable Ed "Zeke" Zatsick loved baseball, basketball, and football, in that order. Unlike the rest of us, he always participated in school skits and plays. In the annual Variety Show, Ed appeared as mustached and dastardly Snidely Whiplash, attempting to foil the hero and abscond off with the girls. He was a natural, an entertainer with flair, and he loved every minute on the stage. Ed had another passion, though. Sports trivia, especially baseball. Along with myself, he memorized baseball statistics and other sports records. Over foot-long hot dogs served in the school cafeteria, Ed and I competed head-to-head in an obscure competition. In time, other students joined in to try to stump us with their questions. Baseball questions might be "Who holds the record for the most career home runs?" or "What pitcher won the most games?" We'd have to not only answer with a name but the exact number as well. Ironically, the answer to the first question changed during my high school years from Babe Ruth 714 to Henry Aaron 755. Those questions are simple examples. Other questions were far more obscure, such as what is the most lopsided score in college football history? Answer: Georgia Tech 222, Cumberland 0 in 1916. That's not a typo. While sports trivia may seem a tad dry, Ed and I always shared belly laughs, poking fun at our teachers, history, politics, pop culture, the town we lived in, and ourselves. With Ed, no topic was off limits.

John Caliguire, quiet and studious and a cousin of Tom Henry, arrived from New Mexico during my senior year. He lived at a house resembling the Addams Family mansion at 200 Pine Street, right next to the bowling alley. He followed and enjoyed sports like the rest of us, but John's true passion was chess. He enjoyed the game so much that he conducted chess-by-mail games with numerous people around the country. The idea was to exchange postcards with each individual move. In his room, John had at any given time, numerous chess boards documenting each play-by-mail game. Although I did not partake in chess and never learned the game, I found the practice fascinating, understanding that games might last up to two years. Patience being a virtue, John Caliguire captured this slogan in spades. John also displayed an odd personal habit; when making a point, he'd repeat, "Huh, huh, huh?" to try to get you to agree with him.

My cousin Bobby Hetrick, two years my junior, cannot be understood except in his feats of athletic prowess. Tall and sinewy, Bobby possessed muscles and skills all of the rest of us could only dream about. On the day Elvis died, August 16, 1977, Bobby and I were enjoying a friendly game of neighborhood baseball. He strode in to bat while I manned left field. I knew of his strength and backed up considerably. It didn't matter. Bobby smacked the ball so hard and far, it flew high over my head, and promptly headed into another county. I began to chase the ball down, but soon realized my futility. All the participants simply stopped and looked at him in wonder. In sprinting, no one could catch Bobby. He ran like the wind with his boundless energy. When it came to bowling, Bobby accomplished the impossible. He rolled the ball down the lane so hard and fast, the pins frequently soared up into the air. On at least two occasions, I witnessed Bob score a strike without hitting the head pin. The power of his ball lifted several pins upward. When gravity took over, the airborne pins crashed down upon the others leaving none standing. Unlike Tom Henry, Bobby didn't need to brag about his talent. He simply did it, and then walked away with a grin.

In my junior year, a new football coach arrived on the scene to guide the Punxsutawney Chucks. His name was Jack Cassebaum, a man with an unusual past at other schools he coached. As motivation, he'd have his starting players carry around a football at all times. On one occasion, Cassebaum parachuted out of an airplane to juice up his troops. Except, that story is apocryphal, as he never employed such a tactic.[2] Nonetheless, Coach Cassebaum fired up his charges in a season filled with heartbreak. Injuries devastated the squad early on, forcing Punxsutawney to resort to underclassmen to win games. Close losses occurred in the first three contests by a combined 13 points. Blowout losses followed with the Chucks being outsized and outmanned at every turn. Cassebaum did not give up, though. Prior to its big rival game with the Dubois Beavers, a bonfire lit up the night sky in a community pep rally at Armory Field. In front of a frenzied crowd with his players all dressed in their football jerseys, Cassebaum walked up to the microphone. "We went 0-9 just to psych out Dubois," Cassebaum yelled. "And we're going to beat them tomorrow!" The crowd's roars broke the night sky. The next day, a rare Saturday game

---

[2] John Walk. "Former Football Coach Jack Cassebaum Dies at 75." *Lancaster Online*, September 2, 2015.

commenced. The game took place on a crisp November morning in Punxsutawney's field. Powerhouse Dubois sported two of the area's best in running back brothers Matt and Paul Suhey. Both would later star at Penn State with Matt Suhey making it all the way to the NFL, as a blocking back for some guy named Walter Payton. It started out promisingly for the red and white clad home towners. Dubois received the opening kickoff, and fumbled it into the endzone for a safety. In the first few seconds, Punxsutawney led 2-0. But, as they say, the cart not only fell off this horse, but the horse ran away, never to return to the farmer again. The final ended 51-2, in favor of the visitors. I watched from the stands, extremely disheartened by the result. For the entire season, Punxsutawney finished with ten losses and only 58 total points scored. The opposition tallied 254 points.[3] The season may have been an abject failure, but Cassebaum and his boys soldiered on. A week after its conclusion, another pep rally took place in the school gymnasium. In front of a delirious crowd and his players, including those injured, Cassebaum again stepped up to the microphone. "Next year, we'll win at least five games,…or I'll quit." And, he meant it. Cassebaum's act of courage propelled the 1974 team to a 6-4 record.

For thirty-seven seasons at Punxsutawney (13) and Knoch High School (24) in Saxonburg, PA, Lester Shoop coached high school basketball. He garnered 500 wins, retiring in 2005.[4] This incredible record is due to his perseverance and intense practices. Players run and run and run, and then run some more. The training built toughness and stamina. Although Shoop's Punxsutawney hoopsters did not win any championships, they remained competitive. Attending their games allowed me to mimic Shoop's intensity, cheering on my heroes and classmates. Every possession became a life-and-death struggle. Coach Shoop's name seemed a perfect fit for basketball, too.

That same school year, my two aunts Jeanne and Rose Marie introduced me to a neighbor friend on Pine Street. Both women knew of my interest in writing, hence the meeting. Their neighbor

---

[3] *The Mirror*, Punsutawney Area High School yearbook, 1974.
[4] Bill Beckner, Jr. *TribLive*. November 27, 2005.

stated that she had been a teacher at the high school. She offered me a special opportunity. In her career, she'd come across a Swiss family living in Lucerne who had a kid my age. She proposed that Edgar Stutz and I become pen pals. I eagerly agreed. For the better part of the next decade, Edgar Stutz and I became frequent writing correspondents. I explained my love of baseball and rock music. He countered with his soccer and skiing experiences and his growing fandom of reggae superstar Bob Marley. We exchanged cassette tapes of our speaking, songs of our musical favorites, and photographs. Edgar spoke and wrote very good English. He composed his missives with beautiful fountain pen handwriting on vellum paper making his letters works of art. While he learned about American culture, I learned nuances about Switzerland's mountainous landscape, their multi-lingual culture, and their history. Because of Edgar, I've longed to travel to Switzerland. Perhaps, someday, I will.

The late Jack LaMarca, whom the Punxsutawney Area High football field is named after, taught gym class during my time at the school. Although I enjoyed gym and cross-country running in particular, one sport left me humbled, yet strangely uplifted by the experience. That sport was wrestling. Mr. LaMarca taught us the basics; its initial beginning moves, the points system, takedowns, how to dominate opponents, offensive wrestling, escaping, sportsmanship, and so on. After studying these lessons in great detail, we'd embark on matches against our classmates. Because of my size, only one opponent suited my weight class. That boy was Frank Harl III, whom I wrestled on at least three occasions. Actually, he wrestled. I served as sacrificial lamb. In every match, Frank made mincemeat of me, pinning me to the mat. Mostly, within seconds of the opening whistle. My classmates howled, berating me constantly. The kidding was largely good natured. I just did not grasp wrestling. A deeply devout Christian, Frank ended every match with a handshake, as per wrestling's code of honor. But, mild-mannered Frank added something else, something unforgettable. After he whipped my ass, as he reached out to shake my hand, he'd come closer, shoulder to shoulder. Frank whispered, "I'm sorry." With those words, whatever humiliation I felt for

43

losing, magically disappeared. Ironically, more than forty years later, in a local restaurant, I spied a short, stocky man sitting next to me at the counter. I inquired of him, "Can I ask you a question?" "Sure," he replied. "What's on your mind?" I stammered that I had known a Frank Harl back in the mid-seventies and that we went to high school together. "Are you Frank Harl?" I asked. He answered that he was not, but Frank and he were buddies who had wrestled together at the University of Iowa. I could not quite believe his answer, and inquired again about legendary wrestler Dan Gable. The man responded by detailing wrestling's stranglehold at the University of Iowa and their rival Iowa State. "You get crowds of twenty thousand at these events. It's bigger than basketball. And yeah, Dan Gable is a real hero in Iowa."

In the summer of 1974, my friend Bob Karnes visited me in Punxsutawney on an extended visit. By a miracle of scheduling, he'd stay at our house for a few weeks before his parents would pick him up. We'd then drive off to visit John Hans' relatives in Pennsylvania before turning south for the very long drive to Sarasota. As usual, Bob's visit took on madcap airs. It involved "rat hunts" in dark, abandoned alleys; sneaking into empty "haunted houses;" and meeting my cousins, aunts, and friends. As to his meeting my grandparents, they offered their typical response, "That boy needs to cut his hair." It could be said of Bob's adolescent years that he hadn't a serious bone in his body. We also spent large parts of time engaged in walking around town and filming with my Super 8 movie camera. One such feature was the unfinished, low-budget horror film "The Hand." The movie starred Tom Henry, his brother Rick, and a mysterious, murderous hand, which appeared behind corners and in the bleachers of the high school football field. Anything for laughs.

By the summer, my camera had became far more than a prop for my adolescent exploits. Four separate films followed, each with their own storyline. "A Fire in Tiny Town" involved a toy town and construction paper "fire" documenting the activities of the town's residents and the fireman heroes to mitigate the damage. Once again, the cable release socket allowed for the animated magic. Unaware of the Hollywood film of the same name, "Good Day for a Hanging" starred my younger cousin Ricky "Bubba" as a murderous outlaw. When captured, the bad man was placed in a cardboard jail, from which he easily escaped. When re-captured, the outlaw paid with his life with western-style justice. The third film featured a mysterious scene, but not really a plot that followed through. My mother, good sport that she was, was stabbed in the heart by an unknown assailant as she reposed on the couch. Spoiler alert: we used red food dye rather than ketchup. When dad came home, we told him that mom had been murdered. Later, we all watched the video to prove it. The final film of the bunch became the longest story I ever created, running time six minutes. "A Game of Cards" told the story of high school hoodlums Ed Zatsick and Don Kachmar. Involved in a cutthroat game of poker, the two could not escape their fate when robbed and killed. The intricacies of the card game, the men's argument, and the shocking double-murder surprise at the end allowed to no small degree of filming satisfaction. Obviously, I'd watched far too many violent movies and it showed up like gangbusters.

My father had taken advantage of the sizable attic space in our house and paneled off half of the area to create another room. This became my new room, an upgrade from the previous tiny space located at the top of our staircase. Unfortunately, due to a lack of central heating and air conditioning, the room posed severe limitations. To compensate in winter, he purchased a space heater, but at the time space heater technology could not be considered safe. In summer, a fan became a necessity to ward off the intense heat. The night before the first day of my senior year, I was awakened by strange screeching and flopping sounds. Not knowing the source, I raced down the attic stairs, woke up my parents, and complained about the strangeness taking place in the room. While my dad investigated, I retreated to my old room. Fortunately, a bed still remained there. Concerned about the hullaballoo, I awaited father's analysis. When he returned a few minutes later, flashlight in hand, he explained the noises. A bat was in the belfry. I tried hard to get a good night's sleep as my father promised he'd take care of the problem in the morning. Solved! By the time I returned home from school and my father from work, he relayed the story of the bat's demise. My grandfather shot it between the eyes as it slept.

As a senior at PAHS, I had the distinct pleasure to be taught by one Terrence Aloysius Fye, or Terry Fye, in English class. His class occurred just after gym class. English class was about reading, writing, and analyzing literature. The previous year, I'd been treated to the vibrant Mrs. Paxton, with whom we dived headlong into Dickens' *A Tale of Two Cities*. But, Mr. Fye emphasized writing in a journal, constantly. The more output, the better. The topic? Anything you wanted to write about. Every Friday, Mr. Fye would dutifully collect each student's journal. By Monday, each journal would be returned to the students, with his pithy, but thoughtful remarks. While writing in a journal may have sharpened student's skills in this discipline, its real purpose was hidden. Years later, I realized that the exercise offered the opportunity for a voyage of self-discovery.

Miss Hoover taught Journalism class. I believed this would give me more opportunity to write, and thus I picked this course as an elective. The initial classes started with the teacher learning a bit about each student. She then requested volunteers and/or assigned each of us to a long-term project. Among them were school newspaper beat reporters, feature article writers, and artists. My classmate Bob Gretz chose to cover our school basketball team. With my interest concerning sports, I would handle the football team. Compared to actual journalistic outfits, our stories were spartan and basic. After all, we were just learning the intricacies concerning interviewing, writing copy, and mastering the storytelling elements of who, what, when, where, why, and how. I attended the first home game and penned up a short piece about its highlights and big plays. Unlike an actual journalist, I did not embed with the team. There were no locker room quotes. This was high school! The second game of the season occurred on the road in some far-flung western Pennsylvania locale. Due to a lack of funds and time, I could not make the bus trip with the team. My reportage of the game suffered. I was forced to cobble together a piece based on the information in the Punxsutawney *Spirit* newspaper. Basically, I switched some words around. Due to a deadline, my story ran in the school newspaper, without attribution. A two- or three-week lag time occurred between games and school news articles. Unfortunately, in a subsequent class, Miss Hoover summoned myself and Bob Gretz to a private conversation. She asked me point blank, "Did you attend the game?" When I stated my situation of non-attendance and using the *Spirit* as my source, Miss Hoover tore into me like a hot knife through butter. She raised her voice and frothed something about plagiarism and the fact that I could not do that again. Bob Gretz, who had nothing to do with my transgression, may have been there to hear Miss Hoover's warning. To ensure there'd be no repeat performance of my *faux pas*, Miss Hoover "fired" me from covering the team's road games. Another classmate substituted in my stead. For the rest of the season, I brought a notebook to home games, obtained a team roster, and acted every bit the cub reporter. All except for a silly hat and a pencil behind my ear. Going forward, I fully incorporated the journalistic lessons into my prose.

With graduation fast approaching, the school held an awards assembly for the seniors. Recognition awards were passed out for clubs like Art Club, Spanish Club, and Future Business Leaders of America. I sat next to friend Tom Henry, who offered a few choice congratulations for the Betty Crocker Homemaker Award. When the winner was announced, Tom blurted out, in a voice loud enough for many to hear, "stand up and show your cookies."

May 23, 1975 finally arrived. Graduation night took place on a sweltering hot Friday evening in the school auditorium. Not an empty seat whatsoever. Our caps and gowns were secure, bright red for boys, white for girls. We'd been practicing for weeks. Everyone knew the routine. All that remained was execution. With our sweat drenching in those long gowns, we hugged, shared stories, and lamented that our time together would soon fade to black. My walk across the stage to receive my diploma was pro forma. My biggest fear was tripping. But I made it, shaking hands with administrators and teachers, and hearing the polite cheers from the audience. High school, the smiles and the sorrows, the learning and the laughter, was over. And life's newest challenges awaited.

The end or the beginning?

Confessions of a Fast-Food Worker

In northern Virginia, circa mid-1970s-1980s, Roy Rogers Family Restaurants served as an alternative to McDonald's and Burger King. Many fast-food aficionados preferred Roy's over all others. The reasons numbered many, but unlike most, Roy Rogers boasted of roast beef, fried chicken, Double R Bar Burgers, and a "Fixin's Bar," where individuals could ladle on lettuce, tomato, onions, mayonnaise, ketchup, and mustard on their sandwiches to one's heart's content. Then there was the barbeque sauce; sticky, syrupy sweet goodness with just a hint of pepper. The theme was different too, offering cowgirl servers dressed in appropriate modest blouses and skirts and counterpart cowboy cooks, dressed in jeans, western shirts, and ten-gallon hats. Silly? Yes. Effective? Very. Due to dime novels, books, and film for one hundred years, cowboy culture was never far from the American mindset. Roy Rogers' marketing plan took full advantage of that fact.

Like square-jawed Gary Cooper in *High Noon*, I strode into Roy's with my six-shooter, eager to make an impression with my first full-time job. OK, maybe that's a slight exaggeration. In actuality, I had graduated from high school two years earlier. A fairer description of myself would be a pimply-faced, nervous wreck. But, Roy's needed to hire young people over eighteen years of age, to comply with the law of operating the Hobart electric meat slicer.

Those early days comprised of long training sessions. Manager Ed Fanning taught proper techniques like placing the roast in the circular-bladed slicer, adding au jus flavoring, cutting the meat into mouth-watering slices, and then carefully placing it on a large bread bun. Imagine one of those mechanical claw machines from the carnival. Your fingers needed to mimic those claws in order to drop the meat onto the bun. Safety in the care and cleaning of the machine was paramount. One false move and you could easily lose a finger, or your entire hand. The Hobart machine was unforgiving with its fast-rotating circular blade and guard device. As the days progressed, I learned how to cook the slab of roast beef, prepare chicken for the portable pressure cooker, grill hamburgers, and drop French fries into boiling grease.

A typical day (7am-3pm) working at Roy's involved four individuals in the morning; the manager, myself, Carol and Lori, whose last names I've forgotten. The manager stayed mostly in his office, working on financial figures and making phone calls. Carol prepared the hamburger, feeding a machine with cold ground beef in one end and grabbing perfectly stamped patties from the other end. Lori served as main hostess, preparing the store by cleaning the tables, stocking the Fixin's Bar, and getting the cashier drawers ready for business. As for me, I unloaded the thrice-weekly truck filled with food and supplies. Down the ramp they came, boxes heavy and light. Yours truly sorted them all and placed them in the respective places in the freezer, giant walk-in refrigerator, and on rear-of-the restaurant shelving for napkins, straws, and carry-out bags. Emptying the truck utilized only myself and the driver tossing items down the ramp. The job comprised about an hour's time of strenuous exercise. Once this task was completed, I prepped/sliced ham and onions in the Hobart. Careful cleaning of the machine followed, guard off, employing chain mail gloves and liberal amounts of water. At ten o'clock, several other employees arrived such as two female cashiers and the cook, in charge of the chicken and roast beef cooking operations. The griller and French fryer also showed; they being a burger flipper who fried ten at a time and a kid who dropped frozen potatoes into a bath of boiling hot grease.

With the staff in place, the manager would gather us all for a brief pep talk offering words of encouragement. At 10:30 in the morning, Roy's opened. I was required to take an early lunch break. Frequently, I opted for a Double R Bar Burger, a large hamburger with a slice of cheese on the bottom bun and thinly sliced ham on top. With fixins, this was a meal in itself.

At 11am, the customers began to trickle in. By 11:30, the lunch rush emerged in full swing. Carol departed for the day. Lori worked the lunch room with her intoxicating smile, and all the other employees took up their positions. Manning the Hobart, I sliced up roast beef sandwiches, always fresh and made to order. This Roy Rogers Family Restaurant offered up a cacophony of sounds with the hustle and bustle of a small community. The pungent aromas of roast beef, hamburgers, and chicken all melded together in the busy milieu. By the time 3pm rolled around, the day staffers welcomed in the transitioning evening shifters.

Every once in a while, I'd be asked to leave the slicer behind and become the cook. This job required extreme timing to prep and cook the chicken and roast beef to keep everything fresh. Food didn't sit around under heat lamps in this joint. To prepare a "run" of chicken, the cook emptied and then washed a plastic bag containing about four chickens; breast, thighs, legs, and wings. The wash took place in cold water in the kitchen sink area. Once rinsed, the pieces would be placed in a pan of eggs and then batter-dipped in Roy's special recipe breading flour. The pressure fryer would be opened and the chicken would be dunked into a metal tray, one at a time, in the boiling hot oil. One must not touch the grease or their day and employment would likely end with a trip to a hospital. The fryer would then be closed with a ship-style navigation wheel for about twelve minutes. When a bell rang, the wheel would be reverse turned. Piping hot, crispy chicken resulted.

Cooking roast beef involved an entirely different process. First, a slab of pre-cut, uncooked beef received a hand-patted round of seasoning salt and placed on an aluminum cooking tray. The beef was then weighed on a scale. A precise chart containing cooking times must then be followed. Now came the unusual method of cooking beef inside out. Six separate heat induction pins were skewered into the beef, three on each side. Once in the oven, cooking the roast took about fifteen minutes. The cook then coordinated with the roast beef slicer man to insert the beef into the Hobart. As previously stated, timing proved critical.

Believe it or not, working an eight-hour fast-food shift could never be confused with a walk in the park. By the time the day ended, exhaustion set in. Legs were sore from standing for hours on end. Arms became tired by constant movement. Sometimes, minds numbed due to excessive stimulation. In my situation, I could easily walk back to my family's apartment, but I chose to drive, exercising my teenage freedom. Invariably, my mother greeted me with a proverbial, "Oh my God, why don't you take a shower?" My two younger sisters also mentioned my intolerable smell, and not in a nice way. So it went, weekday after weekday for a couple of years. Through it all, I felt I'd earned every penny. I made some great friends and met my first girlfriend at a Sunday All-Hands meeting. Roy's fast-food warriors often would tell jokes about the managers and our experiences. For the guys, one of our favorites involved being able to stand our greasy jeans up against the wall. Fortunately, living at home and being frugal allowed me to save up enough money to buy a new car.

Working at Roy's full-time allowed for many hi-jinks and madcap situations, some pleasant, others not so much. The managers, including the affable Ed Fanning and Marty Bear, taught us to fear our General Manager, a guy named Funkhouser. He stopped by every three weeks to terrorize the managers, and they in turn terrorized us. I'm glad to say Mr. Funkhouser never bothered me. Even then I knew that it would be his underlings that he would yell at, and not the restaurant workers. What did Funkhouser care about a bunch of teenagers?

After one such food prep morning, I spied a tiny piece of ham on the unguarded, un-revolving slicer. We were about to open the restaurant. Having already removed my chain mail gloves protection, I swiped at the ham with a paper towel. Oops! In an instant, the blade turned a crimson red. I had sliced my finger. Manager Marty Bear acted fast. He wrapped up my finger with a hand towel and ordered Lori to drive me to the emergency room. Several stitches and much embarrassment later, I returned with a splint on my finger and a large bandage. At this point, I was flipping everybody the bird. Incredibly, the manager made me place a standard plastic glove on my hand and get back to work. There I was, running the slicer, like nothing had happened. Had any Health Inspector been on the premises, I am convinced that Roy's would have been ordered to cease operation.

People come and go and toiling at Roy Rogers offered no exception. One such individual was an ex-con co-worker named Ray. This person existed to frighten others. He'd brag about killing others, doing drugs, and his time spent in the pen. Ray made extremely nasty comments about my girlfriend, who worked there as a cashier. Many employees complained about Ray, but apparently the manager wanted to give him a chance. Thankfully, he departed after a few months, probably mixed up in some of the very things he'd bragged about.

Roy Rogers' managers constantly talked about meeting budget, sometimes threatening cutbacks to staff if we didn't meet quotas. I never thought this fear-mongering productive. As a small measure to assert our independence as workers, we decided to push back. I'll admit it. I was the prime instigator. We didn't intend to hurt anyone, but we wanted to make our statement get the manager's attention. One late evening, we created a home-made sign to hang in the men's bathroom stall. The sign read, "Due to budget cuts, this restaurant is experiencing shortages. The Management requests that you use both sides of the toilet paper. - Roy." Needless to say, the normally mild-mannered Marty Bear blew his stack. He yelled and screamed at us the next day, vowing to fire the employees responsible. Bear ranted and raved. I stepped forward and offered a sheepish apology. We staffers looked at each other and grinned ever so slightly. And just like that, Marty Bear chuckled like a cartoon version of his namesake. We all broke into guffaws and laughed like hyenas.

The summer time heat contributed to another moment, and a most embarrassing one at that. The restaurant contained two grease traps built into the floor of the kitchen. Once a month, two "grease monkeys" would enter through our rear door armed with a giant hose. They'd open the traps and suck the excess grease from the traps into their parked truck outside. No words can possibly describe the noxious odor which emanated from these two individuals and the grease traps they serviced. I thought that this surely must be the worst job in America. How could these individuals be married, or have girlfriends, or kids? Think, my daily shower times ten. In addition to the traps, the chicken fryers contained a large metal pan below that also collected excess grease. Originally, the captured grease would be largely liquified and quite hot. After many runs of chicken, these pans would fill up. However, only when sufficiently cooled could these pans be emptied into a 55-gallon drum outside the restaurant's rear. And, when cooled the liquified grease started to coagulate into something more solid. A frothy, smelly mess that would gag a rat. Unfortunately for me, one of these pans needed an emergency emptying in the middle of the lunch rush, due to volume. The chosen sacrificial lamb was me. A full pan probably weighed several dozen pounds. Careful not to spill this precious cargo, I transported it to the rear door. Then, I placed it down so that my hands would be free to remove the lid off the 55-gallon drum. The stench of the hot day mixing with this frothy brew overpowered me. I stepped back to lift the pan and dump it into the drum. Unfortunately, I lurched ever so slightly due to unsteady footing. The grease from the drum and the pan splashed back up into my face. Hot and lukewarm grease. I had officially entered grease monkey-dom. Ray should have been the one carrying that grease.

Sadly, the manager requested to speak to us one early morning. Ed Fanning relayed the news that the Roy Rogers Family Restaurant next to Landmark Mall, Alexandria had suffered casualties the night before. This restaurant was located about ten miles away, on Route 236. A man hid in the bathroom until closing and attempted to rob the restaurant. He shot the manager and three other employees to death, after ordering them into the freezer. One female employee survived by playing dead. After the man left, she stayed in the freezer until next morning when the next day manager arrived. To her horror, her husband was one of the victims. By odd coincidence, over a dozen years later while working for the MITRE Corporation, I met two men very involved with the incident. Both worked at Roy Rogers as managers at the time. One discovered the bodies.

The one-and-only Roy Rogers himself scheduled a trip to our namesake restaurant. The real Roy Rogers (born Leonard Slye) was an American icon, a singing, modern cash-cowboy star of his own television show, numerous films, and purveyor of more western merchandise that could fit in his saddle. Toy guns, hats, figurines of his likeness and famous horse Trigger, figurines of wife Dale Evans. And on and on. There was even a Roy Rogers Museum. Long past his prime, in his seventies, Roy still thrilled newer generations with his band, the Sons of the Pioneers. This group performed cowboy ballads when "western" remained a part of

Country & Western music. By golly, I watched Roy Rogers' reruns as a "buckaroo" on television. Yer darn tootin'. As it turned out, the fact that Roy Rogers would play a concert at Roy Rogers Family Restaurant did not appeal to my teenage sensibilities. I was *somebody* now, with a new girlfriend and a new Dodge Omni automobile. Given the choice between seeing a washed-up cowboy and my girlfriend, well, you can guess the choice I made. Besides, both of us thought his appearance would be a circus. Boy, were we right. We were returning from a trip to the beach in her car, when the newsflash broke over the radio. "Roy Rogers, cowboy icon, was performing with his band in Fairfax today, when a young boy stepped from the audience and slammed a pie right in his face." The incident caused a hullabaloo, prompting some angry words into the microphone that shocked his long-time fans. On-site police quickly shoved the perpetrator into the side door, where the morning delivery truck parked. Needless to say, the concert ended then and there.

Sometime in 1978, I resigned. My days of cooking and slicing up roast beef sandwiches ended gracefully. Per custom, I gave my two-week notice, leaving behind numerous friends and memories. Overall, my first full-time job taught me responsibility, focus, and the importance of working as a teammate. These building blocks served me well into my future career. Hardees eventually purchased the Roy Rogers Family Restaurant chain and re-branded these stores into Hardees. However, public clamor kept a handful of Roy's stores still open in northern Virginia and Maryland. And the roast beef sandwiches taste as juicy as ever.

From 1976 to 1979, I worked at Roy Rogers in the Pickett Shopping Center in Fairfax, Virginia.

I Could Not Tell the Difference

For a period of about one year beginning in 1978, I worked for a commercial cleaning company, located in Vienna, Virginia. The job entailed accessing office buildings late at night to pull trash, mop floors, vacuum carpets, change lightbulbs, dust surfaces, etc. Owned by operated by Ken Carpenter and his partner "Tikey," the company provided its workers with a variety of cleaning products and a buffer, whose operation required strength and finesse. Transportation logistics fell on the workers. Nothing about the job seemed particularly difficult, except the late hours. Each job must be completed before 5am the following day.

My partner in this enterprise was one David Beauregard, who sported the van needed to haul around our equipment. The work took between four and six hours per night, with considerable amounts of driving between locations. Despite Dave's company, working for this cleaning service remained a lonely pursuit. During our training session with Ken Carpenter, he emphasized that failure would not be an option. The buildings scheduled must be cleaned or his employees would be fired and his company's reputation would suffer. The locations of Carpenter's contracted buildings included office buildings in and around Northern Virginia. We cleaned two rather unusual spaces, a telephone company building and the concourse of the Pentagon.

The telephone company job involved occasionally mopping of the floor. However, we also had to change burned out long tube fluorescent lightbulbs located high on the ceiling. To reach the bulbs, one had to climb ladders located on the circuit floor for just that purpose. The circuit floor contained tall racks with miles of wires wrapped in every direction. The light bulbs were part of banks of lights lighting the racks. In our training walkthrough, Ken Carpenter told us to be careful changing these bulbs as one did not want to break them. An accident here meant a loud pop and some nasty white chemical finding its way into your eyes. Although I changed all the bulbs successfully, the fear of losing my eyesight loomed large.

Cleaning the Pentagon concourse also offered challenges.

One whole section of the building is dedicated to stores and services like a bookstore, barbershop, a bank, and an insurance company. No problem, except I was genuinely concerned armed soldiers would burst into our work and haul us away. In hindsight, it seemed ridiculous, but working in the dead of night never suited me. This particular affliction played a big part in cleaning a medical facility in Vienna.

One evening Dave Beauregard called me to explain that he could not work that particular evening. He'd make the supplies available if I came to his house to pick them up. No worries, except working completely alone. Dave also handed off the keys to that evening's lone job, the aforementioned six-story medical facility. Dave and I had cleaned this building dozens of times, taking about two hours for two people. The thought of working by myself for four hours created a mild panic. To compensate, I called my friend Bob Karnes. I explained my predicament and asked if he could accompany me to the work site that evening. At first, he said that he couldn't due to the late hours. I then turned on some charm, telling Bob I'd treat him to his favorite restaurant located directly across the street. The Amphora served food twenty-four hours a day. Bob relented and asked if he could bring along a friend. Enter Hank Lowman. After I explained the ropes to these gentlemen, we started in earnest after midnight. I'd save mopping and vacuuming for another night. Hank began at the top floor, pulling trash and working his way down. Bob and I started in the basement and would work our way up to meet Hank. When finished, we'd meet in the middle and head over to The Amphora for early morning chow. That was the plan.

The basement contained two rooms; one was a doctor's office and the other a room to conduct immunizations. I fumbled with the ring of multiple keys, turning on the light to the doctor's office. It took but a minute to grab the trash cans, replace plastic liners if necessary, and dump the detritus into our larger rolling trash cart. All went smoothly in that first basement office. The immunization space was a far different story. As I again searched for the proper key, Bob stood behind me, unable to see my field of vision into the room. Before I could switch on the light, I spied the figure of a woman, head down in a chair. "Run!" I screamed to Bob at the top of my lungs. I bashed the nearby elevator buttons and we headed to the first floor. "Bob, go get Hank! And meet me back in this office!" Surely, by now, the ghost of this woman must be searching for me. With my heart pounding through my chest and my brain racing in full-on terror, I plopped down in an office chair. A thousand ants crawled in my pants. A phone sat on a desk with the phone number to the main switchboard for after-hours emergencies. Bob and Hank soon joined me. I dialed the emergency number.

A lady answered in a pleasant voice, but I prattled on about the dead body in the basement. "M'am," I stammered. "Maybe she was left behind in the room, and had a fatal reaction to her dose!"

"Calm down," the lady said. "We can send over an officer."

In what seemed like hours, both Bob and Hank tried to talk some sense into me. "Tell us what happened," they queried.

"She's there and she's probably dead." My imagination raced out of control. It's likely that I'd seen way too many horror movies. Now, I was starring in one.

"Let's just wait for the officer," Bob said.

Within a few minutes, two uniformed Fairfax County officers arrived at the front door. I let them in and explained the whole situation. "Let's have a look in the basement," one of them said. Bob, Hank, the two officers, and I headed for the basement immunization clinic. I didn't have to open the door, but I switched on the light. There in the chair sat the woman, just as I spied her earlier. The ghost had not chased me down. One of the officers dared to step over to the woman. He lifted her head and then communicated with the other officer. "It's Thursday, right?"

The other officer nodded in the affirmative. "That's Annie," he said. "She comes in every Wednesday."

"Annie?" I puzzled.

"Resusci Annie, they use her to teach CPR. She's a dummy."

I could not believe it. I had freaked out over an inanimate object. I sheepishly walked over to Annie. I noted her life-size and life-like features, her mouth, and a chest that could fully simulate a human chest breathing. Annie was made of rubber.

"Annie's a dummy, officers, and so am I." I could not tell the difference between a human corpse and a training prop.

The next day I called my boss to explain the weirdness of the previous night. He could not stop laughing. "Yeah, I was in the building earlier that evening. I saw Annie on the floor and propped her up into the chair. I left her there for you."

Working past midnight sometimes causes problems, especially when ghosts are involved.

How I Spent My 21ˢᵗ Birthday…in Prison

On September 22, 1978, I didn't exactly celebrate my birthday. Instead, my day unfolded *inside* the Virginia State Penitentiary in Richmond. No country club lockup this, the prison facility ended construction in 1804 and began hosting executions of men in 1908. Several years later, I spied a curious newspaper article concerning its demolition in 1991.

My prison experience did not involve incarceration. Thanks to solid parenting, I'd never been arrested, did not do drugs, or steal cars. In fact, I'd never even received so much as a parking ticket.

Rather, the tour was by invitation. At the time, I attended George Mason University part-time. Asked by fellow student and friend Steve Riddle to join the staff of the university's literary magazine, *Phoebe*, I eagerly accepted the challenge. Our staff received dozens of submitted poems, short stories, and artwork. As a group, we decided on content for inclusion in the magazine. Staffer Steve Riddle knew *Phoebe*'s editor, Patty Summers, quite well. Enter George Mosby, Jr. In previous editions, talented Mosby, Jr.'s poems had been selected for *Phoebe*. One of them concerned baseball legend Willie Mays. In a meeting to decide on content for the upcoming magazine, Patty read aloud an amazing letter. The letter was an invitation to a Creative Workshop for all *Phoebe* staffers. The author of the missive was Mosby, Jr., postmarked Virginia State Penitentiary. The poet resided as an inmate at the facility. Needless to say, the staffers looked at one another, mouths agape. We didn't speak for a few moments pondering the letter's meaning. When someone finally broke the ice, our discussion centered on the difficulty posed by the letter. Apparently, the prison system approved the idea. Other questions swirled in the room. Would we go? What was the level of risk? To her credit, Patty Summers phoned the prison to ensure the legitimacy of the letter and assess risk. Over the next few weeks, Summers and Mosby, Jr. worked out the details. We'd share poetry readings with the inmates. Inmate artwork would hang on the walls for all to enjoy.

We departed Fairfax in a van for the drive to Richmond.

Seven participated; Patty Summers, Steve Riddle, Linda Garden[5], Jo Miller, Lynn Fogarty, Bob Karnes, and myself. Other staffers declined the invite. Our not-so-motley crew included poet Bob Karnes, who was not a student at George Mason, but rather a friend of mine who expressed interest in the event. It didn't take much cajoling to Ms. Summers, who may have been thinking about the adage safety-in-numbers. Our drive south was frightening. Admittedly, all we talked about were the possible dangers awaiting us. Fear of the unknown, with an emphasis on fear.

Our arrival in Richmond proved our point. We waited an inordinate time to be processed. Armed guards questioned our presence, then searched each one of us with a hand-held metal detector. Ms. Summers brought staffer's poetry in a manilla envelope and the guards requested an examination of the writings. When satisfied, the guards walked us to a visitor waiting room. Inside prison walls, we noticed the starkness of the place; imposing hallways, green bars, cement floors. This is what loss of freedom looked like. After an hour waiting, we were again walked through the facility, traversing a courtyard filled with lush green grass. Along the route, we noticed numerous warning signs about the conduct of visitors. Inmates could not receive anything whatsoever from visitors. It wasn't only the sights, it was the sounds. The heavy clash of metal on metal constantly reverberated within the walls. Our guard escorts informed us that they'd be willing to remove any of us from the facility if we felt threatened. Not exactly the most reassuring statement. Also noted was the guards never referencing inmates or prisoners, but rather as "residents."

As we entered the next visitor room, I could not help but think of time spent with my father watching old black-and-white prison movies. Burt Lancaster starred in *The Birdman of Alcatraz*. Susan Hayward played the ill-fated Barbara Graham in *I Want to Live!* My fascination with these genre films continued into adulthood. Now, here I was, within prison walls. I didn't have to wonder what it was like anymore. I now knew. Oppressive, anxiety-

---

[5] Linda Garden's story about her prison experience was published in *Phoebe*, 1979.

filled with heavily-armed guards watching your every move. Despite all this, each member of our group was welcomed with cordial handshakes. George Mosby, Jr. introduced himself as did several others. No doubt they were the prison organizers of the event. We all sat down at a couple of circular tables in the room. The guards stood silently nearby, ringing the small room. There were seven of us, all white, and about forty of them, all black. Some popular music played softly over speakers. "Would you all like a can of coke?" About half of us accepted. Before the reading started however, came several admissions of guilt. Mr. Mosby, Jr. stated that he stabbed his wife to death in the stomach. Others revealed the reasons for their current predicament, including rape. Upon these admissions, I felt my whole body shake. Only the poetic readings could calm me down. But, I wasn't the only one needing calming.

One of the first readers was Bob Karnes. Behind a lectern, Bob said, "You see this hand. If you listen to this poem, yours will be shaking, too." Given prisoner experiences, it's doubtful any of them would be nervous listening to an outsider's poetry. More likely, Bob was projecting his own petrifying fears. As we read one by one, light applause occurred. Our poetic topics just did not concern our listeners. In nearly every case, the prisoner readings involved railing about "the system" and "the man." As they read their "Social Justice" poetry, all professed their innocence and being trapped in the world of incarceration. George Mosby, Jr.'s reading offered real poetry, penetrating insights and observations on the human condition. My impression was that the inmates really didn't understand Mosby, Jr.'s intellectual forays. Steve Riddle did not read, but spent a fair amount of time questioning our attendance. I read a mediocre poem with muted reaction. The guards continued their scowls. When I finished, all I could think of was the irony of "a captive audience."

The relative ho-hum of the event contributed to the overall malaise of our group. What on earth were we doing here? Was this a good idea? After the last reading, however, we all discovered the reason for our visit: entertainment.

The final reader introduced himself as "Sir Dog" and began a soliloquy for about five minutes before he started reading his poems. The energy and mood in the room brightened dramatically for this reader. Catcalls rang out from the men. At times, it became difficult to hear the speaker over the raucous din. In prison, all inmates acquire a nickname. No exceptions. Sir Dog rambled on about coming to Richmond from another prison. Much to his chagrin, he heard about an inmate who also called himself "Dog." To distinguish the two men, an informal truce was declared. The original "Dog" in Richmond became "Dog Essence" and the moniker "Sir Dog" was born. He read three poems, notably "Love, Shitty Love" and a highly sexual suggestive piece about licking. The licking story rambled on with obvious connotations about intimacies between a man and a woman. It used phrases like sugary sweetness and descriptions of a male tongue fully enjoying his explorations. Sir Dog offered a most spirited reading. The prisoners hooted and hollered. I couldn't speak for our group, but Sir Dog delivered with all the timing of an expert comedian. To conclude his licking poem, he reached behind his back and pulled out a large lollipop. His poem was about candy all along! Even the taciturn guards smiled at this one.

As we prepared to depart the scene, after about ninety minutes, I requested Sir Dog join us at our table. We decided on a friendship based on writing to each other. Our letters, over about two years, were censored per prison policy. However, I did learn that he was serving time for multiple drug offenses. Sir Dog lived in a world I could scarcely imagine. I've often wondered whatever happened to all of the inmates we met. Without doubt, some talented men wasted away behind prison walls. Their paintings and drawings, like their poems, revealed their inner struggles.

Piling back into the van for the return trip, Ms. Summers offered a question, "Well gang, what did you think?" As we headed back to the secure world we inhabited; family, shopping malls, cars, we couldn't shut up. Each one of us talked at length about our just concluded event. Inside the van, our fear and anxiety dissipated like the inexorable daily drop of the sun. Dusk fell over southern Virginia as we shot up I-95. It's likely that all of us reflected to ourselves that simply viewing our sun equated to freedom.

Don't Look Down!

The four of us, Robert Karnes, Steven Riddle, Gaston Naranjo, and myself, all in our early twenties, met at Lake Accotink Park in Fairfax, Virginia. Despite the date of December 18, 1979, crisp temperatures awaited, unseasonably mild with no precipitation. The following day I would be headed off to San Antonio, Texas. In a sense then, the gathering served as a final hurrah of friends, before my impending date with the United States Air Force. Our plan was to rent two paddle boats and meander across the waters for an afternoon of relaxation. No alcohol or drugs were part of our day, or any day.

Idyllic Lake Accotink Park, surrounded by dense forest and hiking trails, contained a small food stand; a squeaky, old carousel; mini golf; and areas to fish. Giddy children's laughter wafted nearby. A tall, active Southern Railway wooden train trestle perched on the left side of the lake. Rising forty feet in the air, the trestle stood as a proud monument to an earlier America.

Indeed, on an historic note, the original wooden bridge crossing trestle dated from 1851 and served as a supply line for the Union Army during the Civil War. Efforts were made by the Confederacy to burn the structure, but it was quickly rebuilt.

Despite our vast personality differences, no one in the group pursued toxic, self-defeating behaviors like guzzling spirits, smoking cigarettes or dope, racing around in fast cars, or crashing skulls in bar fights. A few of us had girlfriends, but no real serious affectations. Some might describe us as a boring, naive group. After all, who goes paddle boating at that age?

And then came the dare.

For reasons unknown, perhaps relating to the group's own lack of searching out exciting pastimes or my impending basic training assignment, I decided to challenge the group to commit to a short journey. No small feat, we all trudged up a steep incline to one side of where the trestle started. The idea was then to walk, or run, to the other side. No one knew if or when a train would barrel straight for us. There was no room to dodge the train, except to jump straight off the trestle and likely into oblivion. Should any locomotive strike us in mid-walk, we'd surely be splattered to a bloody pulp before being sent to our immediate doom.

I crossed first, about one hundred yards worth, legs trembling, but carefully making sure not to slip and get caught between the beams. Once the journey started, there could be no turning back. A voice inside my head warned, "Don't look down!" Peril awaited every footstep compounded by the fact that we'd be able to sense the rumble of the train and hear its piercing cry long before we could see it. My heart pounded like a jackhammer, with fear driving me onward and only one thought in mind, to escape to the other side and safely off the train track. My other friends ambled behind. Each of us crossed the trek slowly but with extreme focus and purpose. Somehow, despite our self-induced danger, we all managed to make it across. Our moment of temporary madness subsided.

Once across the trestle, we worked our way down through steep woods onto flat land. Congratulatory handshakes and back slaps followed, each of us perhaps believing we'd cheated death and became men that day. About fifteen years later, two other friends of mine excitedly described a fishing adventure from which they returned that morning. The pair fished in the riverbed just below that same trestle we'd crossed years earlier. How could fishing in a riverbank be described as "exciting"? As they waited for their bites, they explained, they heard a loud pounding noise above them. A train rushed past above blowing its shrill horn. Then they heard a dull, sickening thud, looked up, and watched in horror as a figure tumbled down the steep hill in front of their view. They put down their poles and raced to the scene. What remained of a man lay sprawled amongst broken branches. Apparently, he had decided to walk the trestle, ignoring the "DANGER! Stay off Train Trestle for Your Own Safety" signage.

Sometimes, in youth, we know not what we do.

USAF Basic Military Training

Surviving United States Air Force Basic Training depends on understanding two simple principles. First, the entire six-week course is a mind game, meant to mold thinking to obeying orders of superiors without thinking of consequences or any other consideration. Second, adherence of the idea of an "Air Force Way" supersedes all other notions of doing and being. Once these concepts take firm grip on one's mindset, basic training becomes an inexorable passing of time until completion. In fact, these concepts form the basis, in large degree, to all militaries throughout the world.

In September 1979, I decided to join the United States Military. My father, grandfather, and several uncles had all served, most on my father's side of the family. All volunteered for the United States Army. However, my uncle on my mother's side, Frank Perri, had achieved the rank of Colonel in the Air Force, and was currently stationed in San Antonio, Texas. Without anyone in the family knowing, on my day off, I drove a short distance to the Fairfax Circle shopping center in Virginia, and walked into the military recruiting office. All branches were represented; Army, Navy, Air Force, Marines, Coast Guard. Each service had their own room. As each recruiter barked at me to enter their area, I quickly entered the Air Force office. My uncle Frank Perri had been my deciding factor. My interview lasted about an hour with my recruiter promising service, education, and travel. I opted for a "deferred enlistment", where I could "get my affairs in order" with family, job, girlfriend, car, etc. I'd report to basic training in San Antonio on December 19th. My parents and sisters offered only positive reactions. Initially, however, to determine job suitability, I'd have to take the Armed Services Vocational Aptitude Battery (ASVAB) test.

Two weeks after enlisting, I took the ASVAB. Mostly a general knowledge exam about material learned in school, the test proved quite easy for me. I finished the exam in three of the four hours required. What I remember most, however, was the administrator of the test beginning the session with this odd statement. "You'd be surprised at how many fail this instruction, and thus will be immediately disqualified." Test attendees were offered a pencil and a sheet of blank paper with the instruction to print our name and date in the upper right-hand corner of the paper. After spending about fifteen seconds on this task, I awaited further instructions. The administrator then walked around the classroom and grabbed three attendees' sheets, ordering those whose papers he removed to stand up. He then said to those standing, "Please leave the room. Thank you for your time." Looks like Uncle Sam had figured that failure to follow that simple instruction removed them from United States military consideration.

The next few weeks raced by. I offered goodbyes to my family and friends, quit my job at the cleaning service, and sold my new car to a priest. Our family enjoyed picnics and cookouts, prior to my departure. There were final stops in favorite places, including local restaurants. My father's words, upon hearing of my enlistment, echoed though my head every day. "Listen and do what they say. Look straight ahead and show no emotion." He remained a most trusted source, having served over twenty years, including two tours of Vietnam and as aide-de-camp to two generals. Finally, a call came from my recruiter on the results of the ASVAB. He stated that due to my extremely high score on the test, I could qualify for "intelligence" work. Honestly, at the time, I did not know what that meant. When he mentioned this unit's elite status, my ears really perked up. My duty station would likely be overseas in England, Germany, Spain, Italy, Korea, or Japan. Words could not possibly describe my excitement at these prospects.

The Air Force beckoned.

My late afternoon flight to San Antonio's Lackland Air Force Base, the only basic training site in the USAF, proceeded smoothly. That is, for one as nervous as myself. My seating partner and many on the flight also headed to Texas, and we swapped brief tales about our lives. When the plane landed, we were whisked away by bus in the middle of the night. After about ten minutes, in the darkness of the vehicle, an unknown man started talking in a loud voice to the group. His words seemed threatening and intimidating. Apparently, he would be our Training Instructor (TI), which we quickly discovered. Before too long, the bus stopped and the screamer identified himself as Sergeant Hughes. "Off of the bus! Get off and grab your bags." We tumbled off the bus onto a blacktop and retrieved our single piece of luggage from underneath the big vehicle. A dim lightbulb flickered above. "Line up! About ten per line. Hurry up!" With growing alacrity, the group followed his commands. "Pick 'em up!" The sergeant wanted us to lift our luggage off the ground from our first formation. "Put 'em down!" Thus, the sergeant implored us repeatedly to lift up our bags and then place them back down. Over and over he bellowed. "I wanna hear one noise! Pick 'em up! Put 'em down!" After at least five minutes of this exercise, our group became better and better at the task. Thud! With Sgt. Hughes finally satisfied, he ordered us to march, as it were, towards some buildings. We carried our luggage though the pitch-black night. Air Force Basic Training, and my particularly rocky adventure with it, was underway.

Upon arrival at one building, we clomped to an upstairs dormitory. The large room was divided into two bays with a center separating wall. The TI's small office was housed straight ahead from the door. Restroom facilities with about six toilets or "head", six sinks with mirrors, and showers for a dozen men, stood off to the right after entering the dormitory door. No stalls or doors separated the toilet units from each other; they just formed a straight line in the room. Each bay contained twenty-five beds, all equidistant, all neatly made with military blankets on top. "Gentlemen, pick your bunks!" With that, we each chose our beds. Each bunk had an accompanying locker for clothes and personal items. "You're all gonna need some sleep. Put your bag under your bed. Strip down to your skivvies! No talking! Lights out in five minutes!" None of us seemed to know what to expect, but I imagine this is where the phrase "Nervous in the service" was born. In five minutes, the room became as dark as outside.

In what seemed like a few minutes, light flooded the room. A trumpet blared over the loudspeakers in the dormitory, loud enough to wake the dead. This was reveille, an obnoxious get-out-of-bed reminder that we'd all hear for the next six weeks. Sgt. Hughes burst near the front of each bay, gesticulating like a madman. "Get your moldy asses out of bed! Get up! Get up!" It was five thirty in the morning. Our rest probably lasted no more than three hours. Bleary-eyed at first, our activities over the next forty-eight hours could easily be described as a whirlwind. In a regimented way that began and continued through to graduation, we showered and shaved, put on our clothes, and listened intently as Sgt. Hughes taught us the ins and outs of dormitory life. Everything from hanging clothes properly, to making our beds, cleaning the area, and being assigned our personal keys on a chain. These keys must hang on our necks 24/7 for the entire basic training course. We did everything as a team, or a "flight" as our unit was called in Air Force parlance. We also learned about the dreaded "341" form, one of which must be kept in the shirt pocket at all times. This tiny piece of paper served as a dual Excellence/Discrepancy Report, which could be requested by the training instructor at any time. "Gimme a 341" meant that the trainee must reach into their pocket and hand over the form, which almost always meant a screw-up in some way. The form would be filled out on the spot by the instructor, in front of the rest of the flight, causing extreme embarrassment to the unfortunate targeted. Ostensibly, the 341 then found its way into the hands of the training instructor's superior, who would decide on appropriate punishment.

After being taught some rudimentary skills that morning, we marched to a barbershop, where several men awaited with electric clippers. The barbers sheared us all like sheep, about six at a time, with each haircut lasting probably less than ten seconds. We went into that room with our individuality, we exited without it, all of us looking the same. Clothing issue followed, with fatigues, hats, boots, chosen for us based on a previous weigh-in and height check. No trainee could refuse the pre-ordained sizing, unless they were egregiously incorrect. Another day, in our new uniforms, involved medical tests like eye exams, immunizations, and the infamous rectal exam. Our flight trainees were told to line up in a straight line, drop our pants and underwear, and then bend over. A doctor, whose job I did not envy, then walked down the line looking into everyone's rear end. With rubber gloves, he prodded inside each of us for God knows what. People don't normally think of themselves as cattle, except for these first few days of basic training. Misery loves company.

The next day, shortly after reveille, showering with our newly minted haircuts, and shaving, Sgt. Hughes verbally attacked our flight. As our entire group stood at attention, in bare feet and underwear, he raged, "Whose is this?" Our Training Instructor held up a safety razor in his hand. He continued, "Who left this in the head? Your mother is not here to clean up after you!" Not one of us standing there barefooted and trembling could even contemplate what would happen next. He yelled again, this time with renewed vengeance, "Step forward if you own this razor!" With that, Sgt. Hughes cocked back his arm and snapped the razor forward, as if throwing his best underhand pitch. The metallic object skittered around one room, bounced off a back wall, and continued into the next room. No one dare move a muscle, but this careening sharp missile could easily cut some unfortunate's foot. "Step forward!" Like all the others, the insides of my brain spun around like a top. "Check your personal items locker!" he demanded. The entire flight turned around and began to examine their lockers. I bent down, key still around my neck as was required, and checked mine. No safety razor was noted inside. My heart skipped. Upon command, we rose again and moved into formation. I stepped forward, owning up to my mistake. "Finally." For the next five minutes, Sgt. Hughes administered a vicious, unmerciful, tongue-lashing. Indeed, I heard some mild chuckling from my teammates. At that moment, I remembered my father's words to "look straight ahead and show no emotion." The advice served me well. However, for the next several weeks, I became the sergeant's personal verbal punching bag. He teased me constantly, until he figured that he could not break me.

For the next several days afterward, we settled into a routine. Reveille woke us up out of our socks. Showering and shaving came next. We put on our clothes and headed down the stairs for morning roll call. Sgt. Hughes emphasized daily the precise week and day of training. Then came breakfast and daily military classroom training for about 90 minutes. Physical Training

(PT) and marching practice, or "drill" occurred next, each day building upon skills from the previous day. We returned to the chow hall for lunch and then later back to the drill pad for more marching. We spent an inordinate amount of time in drill, routinely logging in several hours per day. After this, more classroom instruction followed until the chow hall beckoned one final time for dinner. Dormitory instruction occurred in-between our activities, especially in the first days of basic training when we learned to iron our underwear into a perfect 6 x 6 inches. Sgt. Hughes also taught us the fine art of polishing boots; wetting a cotton ball and rubbing it on a small portion of the boot, using that same cotton ball to dip into black shoe polish, rubbing that same wet spot. Repeat over and over until a "spit shine" brightened the entire boot. Every night of every day.

From 6:30pm until 9:00pm lights out, trainees were allowed personal time. During these nightly hours, shining boots encompassed about two hours. Trainees usually spent the last half-hour preparing clothes and/or writing letters home. The latter became highly encouraged by the Training Instructor as a connection to one's own family. I frequently spoke with my "next door neighbor" but made a careful effort to not acquire friends in this environment. As soon as basic ended, we'd be off to our tech school assignments. The routines associated with basic training occurred on weekdays. On weekends, training didn't stop. The TI wasn't around, but selected individuals led the flight through Saturdays and Sundays. Weekend duty was lighter, with no classroom training, but plenty of time exercising and on the drill pad.

Concerning the drill pad, the process of learning to march in formation in a group of fifty men, is difficult to describe. The exercise depends on precise timing. We drilled to a cadence set by the TI, or his assistant. When successful, only one sound can be heard upon the placement of the left foot and then the right foot. Legs moved to the cadence with the body upright. The slightest variation on the sound, even to fractions of a second can be noticed by the TI. "Your left, your left, your left, right, left!" We learned to march and halt, column left, column right, column half-left, column

70

half-right. Training each of these movements took time, patience, and much yelling by the instructor. After about fifteen minutes of marching, the marcher's mind entered into a kind of trance, listening intently for the commands, but performing them nearly without thinking.

Sgt. Hughes spiced up things by carrying around a hand-sized metal spittoon for his chewing tobacco. He also taught the flight other marching-related activities. Routinely, we'd leave the drill pad and march around the base with the guidon, or flag bearer, proudly carrying Old Glory. Two "road guards" were also employed holding portable stop signs on opposite sides of the road, facing traffic. Sgt. Hughes yelled "Road Guards out!" These trainees, at the front of the formation, would spring to life and run out into the road. The road guards assumed an authority position by buckling their knees and holding their signs.

I was one of those road guards, having been volunteered for the position. On one early occasion, upon the command, I raced out into the street and managed to point myself in the opposite direction. Sgt. Hughes exploded by stating in a voice the entire base could hear, "That car's gonna run right up your ass, son and kill our trainees! Turn around!" Whoops. Live and learn.

On another occasion, Sgt. Hughes caught our "house mouse" marching out-of-step one day. The "house mouse" was usually the shortest man in the formation, as we marched with the tallest to the shortest down the line. He called "Flight Halt!" and came striding back to the man. After a terrible screaming fit, we started up again. Sgt. Hughes then paused the formation again and came back, this time yelling at me. "You thought it was House Mouse, but it was YOU! I made a mistake." I began to believe that Sgt. Hughes could hear a hummingbird from a mile away.

From Monday through Friday for about three hours per day, we were lectured in USAF and military standards. The instructor specialized in the task. We learned the technical details of managing the dormitory, uniforms, drill, rank and respect for authority, Air Force history, personal hygiene, reporting structure, human relations, and a whole host of other topics. Emphasized in the course was that paying attention to the processes, rules, and

71

regulation would be hugely beneficial to the trainees. Although the course was no-nonsense, on rare occasion the instructor took time to add a few funny personal anecdotes. Most of them involved this or that trainee, like ourselves, who did "dumb things."

In addition to the daily military classroom work, marching or "drill" occurred so frequently that it became second nature. After weeks of training, Sgt. Hughes decided his flight was ready for the Ten Miler. We prepped for the event by being informed about a week in advance that this march would define our physical regimen up to this point. This Ten Mile hike included backpacks with cans of "Meal, Combat, Individual Rations (MCI), which we were to consume in the great outdoors. Sgt. Hughes led us in calisthenics first such as jumping jacks, pushups, and stretching exercises. Then, the march began. We strode off the drill pad and then up and down the sidewalks on the base. Sometimes, Sgt. Hughes mixed in his spittoon metallic-sound right into the cadence. At first, the march was pleasant, as the flight viewed parts of the facility not yet seen. The chapel, the recreation center, static plane displays. A few minutes in, the flight entered our trance-like phase, which continued for the rest of the march. "Left, right, left," Sgt. Hughes barked, and we obeyed like lapdogs to his command. Even though it was January 1980, the mild Texas sky offered up a comfortable fifty-degree day, perfect for drill. In an instant, however, all that changed. Without warning, the lightness of the day switched to night, if only for a few seconds. A gigantic flock of birds, possibly blackbirds or crows, flitted across the sky, obliterating the light of the sun. The flock flew by in massive numbers and then, as soon as they had come, they were gone. This remarkable phenomenon cannot be forgotten. Luckily, the rest of the march continued without incident. That evening, however, in personal time, we rubbed our bare feet for blisters as much as we spit shined our boots.

About half-way through the training, I experienced an emergency health situation. The upcoming training day was more important than most. Our flight would be inspected, outdoors in formation, by a female officer. After hearing about this upcoming event for a few days previous, our flight probably felt collectively a bit nervous. Sgt. Hughes kept reminding us of the inspection's gravity, as this would also be a major referendum on his leadership. After morning breakfast, we headed back to the dorms to "square ourselves away" to prepare for the inspection. Despite the fact that we had already showered and shaved to begin our day, our TI reminded us to shave again, "as smooth as a baby's bottom." The flight clomped upstairs to the dorm. Collectively, we grabbed our razors from our personal items locker and headed for the "head." We hurried. After a few minutes, we were all back at our personal items lockers to return our items. My personal items locker was situated on the bottom, near the floor. Reaching down with my own head, because I was not allowed to remove the locker key from around my neck, I struggled with re-opening the locker. My safety razor was inches away, as I had placed it on the floor to open the locker. In the flash of an instant I lost my balance. My left wrist tumbled right into the safety razor. Blood pooled on the floor. Seeing this, my next-door bunk mate yelled for Sgt. Hughes, who quickly bandaged up my wrist. Within minutes, an ambulance whisked me and that same bunk mate away to Wilford Hall Medical Center. I remember being very talkative on the trip, explaining to my fellow trainee and an EMT that I'd let the flight down, embarrassed myself, and may be in jeopardy of continuing basic training. My fellow passengers supported me, however, but treatment and reckoning awaited. My emergency room doctor quickly fixed my wrist with stitches but the inevitable question arose. "Son, did you try to hurt yourself?" I repeated, "No, it was an accident," and explained in detail the events that led me to the hospital. Shame and humiliation filled my voice. Needless to say, I missed the inspection, but recovered sufficiently to re-join the flight later in the day. With a bandaged left wrist, I didn't exactly inspire confidence, believing that many of my teammates probably viewed me with suspicion.

Another lesson involved guard duty. As usual, Sgt. Hughes explained this frequent military duty. By his schedule, over several weeks, we were each individually ordered awake by the previous guard to stand at the dormitory door. For two hours. Lacking sleep. Only authorized individuals could enter our space. "Sir, may I see your badge or military identification to enter?" These words must be memorized and recited by the trainee. By design, during each shift, someone would come to the door. Following the trainees' spiel, that someone would place their ID up against the glass portal of the door. On occasion, the badge could identify the holder as Mickey Mouse, or other such trickery. For guards that incorrectly allowed access to unauthorized individuals, a very public flight shaming would follow. And, Sgt. Hughes relished the opportunity to spit you out just like his tobacco juice. Only worse.

Monotony has never been so fully defined as basic trainees in a chow hall. Eating "three square" every day in the chow hall nourished us, but hardly provided any social opportunities. After the training instructors informed us of the importance to eat, and eat heartily for our energy, we all followed suit. The time to do so, though, was extremely limited. We'd grab a tray and wait in line like zombies to receive our food and then devour it silently.

One weekend, probably due to boredom more than anything else, we devised a plan. After drill, the flight was allowed to mingle with each other for about fifteen minutes. We could talk among ourselves, make phone calls, or just rest. Several of us devised a decided to "prank" our "sister flight," located on the first floor. During our parallel training, our instructors goaded us into competing with each other. We'd learn about their training triumphs and failures and they ours. On this particular weekend day, our rivals performed "kitchen police" (KP) duties in the chow hall. On pre-ordained signal, all our flight rose to place our trays and plates in the kitchen, overwhelming our brethren. The House, one of our weekend leaders, didn't like the maneuver and chided us. He told Sgt. Hughes and that next Monday, our TI exploded. He ranted for a few minutes about our unprofessionalism, but when it was all over, he let out a hearty laugh. Sgt. Hughes seemingly knew what would happen next. Sure enough, when it was time for our KP duty, our rivals returned the favor.

After a long buildup by Sgt. Hughes and a visit to the site, our flight was excited to run the Confidence Course the next day. We'd run, climb, balance, rappel, sweat like pigs, and get filthy dirty. The Confidence Course was Air Force-speak for an Obstacle

Course, filled with all manner of barriers and physical booby-traps. That night, as we shined our boots and prepped our clothes, local weather turned nasty. A huge thunderstorm rolled in that swamped the Course, and remarkably cancelled the event. I breathed a sigh of relief. Somehow, I knew I'd end up face down in a mud puddle.

Nearing the end of the program, our flight trained at the rifle range over two days. The first day involved classroom learning of the rifle and its various components. The instructor literally broke the gun up into several pieces and re-assembled it. He named each piece and emphasized the importance of the cleaning of the weapon. The instructor repeated the breakdown and re-build several times. Each trainee received a rifle at their table and needed to re-assemble it. The trick occurred when the instructor turned out the lights. Thus, we re-assembled the weapon in the dark. After this lesson, we marched a short distance to the range. The instructor then taught us various body position techniques. aiming, and safety precautions concerning the weapon such as never pointing the gun barrel as anywhere but at the target. This "dry fire" exercise did not utilize bullets. We'd get our chance the next day for that.

On day two, "wet fire" commenced. Believe it or not, at the age of twenty-two, I'd never fired a weapon other than a BB Gun or a bow-and-arrow as a kid, with my father. Throughout my life, I've been a firm anti-gun advocate. Despite many objections, I'd long ago decided that owning and using a gun did not define me or elevate me to becoming a man. With that attitude, the poor quality of my rifle range score was not surprising. In all likelihood, I scored the lowest in the flight based on 100 shots. Fortunately, my failures that day did not disqualify me from basic training. The United States Air Force is hardly known for their marksmanship ability. We leave that to the Army and Marines, who battle mainly on the ground.

Finally, the last week of basic arrived, and with it, the coveted wearing of the "blues" uniform. No more fatigues. No more boots. Just an honest to goodness light blue shirt, dark blue pants, and "cover" for our heads. Sgt. Hughes informed us daily of the week and day of training. Now, we were here. The week included, for those interested, a night-time "liberty" trip to the

Chapparal, a recreation center, wherein trainees could dance with a young lady, similarly going through basic training. Needless to say, our flight featured dozens of pent-up guys eager for this opportunity. In addition, we could also view the Riverwalk, a San Antonio landmark and later attend a San Antonio Spurs basketball game. I opted for neither, concentrating totally on finishing the course without any more faux pas.

In week six, the most demonstrable feeling persisted as one of pride. Like high school seniors at prom, our flight earned our way as the new big kids on the block. We assembled in the morning with pride. Instead of the daily dread of reveille, we welcomed its blare with an invigorated energy. We ate with pride. We drilled with pride, marching around all smiles. Only one last hurdle remained, and that was parade. As time moved to our final day, Friday, Sgt. Hughes' voice, previously a foghorn of screaming and yelling, became our voice of inspiration. He constantly reminded us that week of our accomplishments, and our every milestone. By golly, we might have collectively thought our hearts would burst out of our chests. Under this backdrop, "Pass in Review" commenced. Our parents, by invitation, could attend this final parade on our final day.

On a large parade ground, looking and feeling our best, our flight marched with other flights. We strode by the "brass" and other dignitaries, following Sgt. Hughes' penultimate order, "eyes right" as we passed the parade stands. When, after passing about two more yards, Sgt. Hughes bellowed his final order, "Flight Halt!" Basic training was over. Much handshaking and hugs followed.

For all those who have served their country.

Epitaph

During my Air Force basic training in 1979/1980, one of our classroom assignments was to compose a short epitaph. These final tombstone thoughts were to encapsulate the life of someone very near and dear to ourselves. We were to write an epitaph of our own lives. In addition, we would write the yearly dates of our birth and death. Uncle Sam, in his imminent wisdom, allotted us fifteen minutes for this task.

The assignment made most of us feel a bit uneasy. Was this going to become an "official" military document that would follow us to our graves? Literally. Our country was not at war, but the Iran Hostage Crisis was entering a third month. Were these simple epitaphs part of an upcoming United States plan to invade the middle east country? Or perhaps, did the Air Force just want us to think a bit about our lives and our place in the society and country we were serving? Either scenario was entirely plausible.

I thought for awhile, jotting down some empty words. I had determined that I would live for eighty years— a decade more than the Biblical three score and ten. My stone would then read "Joseph T. Hetrick 1957-2037." The words came much harder, though. I just couldn't think of anything that would fit. Finally, I decided on some word play. After much scribblings, they poured onto the page.

> He was the product of a troubled age,
> He took the trouble to productively age.

Last week, I saw these words rummaging through papers in my attic. They probably don't mean much of anything. However, I thought that I'd try to analyze them after all these years. Certainly, the first line would fit into about any year of the 20th century, the most violent, vicious, tumultuous era in the history of mankind. The business about being a "product" is somehow apt in this age of commercialization. The latter sentence does fit my personality. I believe, first and foremost, in a life of productivity. I can't sit still for even a few minutes, preferring to read or write or have my hands busy doing something. I am a compulsive organizer and straightener. When I'm cold and in the grave, I'd like to have something to leave behind for my family or fellow human beings. It's my artistic mentality, to have something survive beyond myself.

Perhaps, as I grow older, I'll reassess my life and write a new epitaph. For now, though, I'm sticking with this one.

An early musing about mortality.

Technical School

Following basic training, the Air Force paid for a round-trip flight home to visit family and friends. This brief, one-week stay in February 1980 was heaven-sent. My family treated me to home cooking and my friends laughed heartily at my crew-cut. When I returned to Texas, I bused over 200 miles northwest from San Antonio to San Angelo. USAF Technical School took place at Goodfellow AFB from Feb-Sep 1980. Quoting a fellow airman when we were serving our first duty assignment overseas, "It was hot, but it was home." In fact, one day during my tenure there, the temperature reached one hundred seventeen degrees (117) Fahrenheit.

As per usual, the first few days required some serious re-adjustment. I shared a room with another tech school student. The adaptation occurred easily enough, however, I noted several nuances concerning the base. Goodfellow AFB was quite small, so much so that one could walk from one end of the base to the other in about thirty minutes. There was no movie theatre. Films were shown, but only on rare occasions. The base contained a formerly used airfield, but currently inactive as a runway. We lived in an apartment-style three story dormitory, located in a quadrant of buildings. The center of the "quad" featured benches, sidewalks, and an open field of grass. Happily, for all Air Force personnel concerned, we were considered "elite" and thus were not required to be in formation. Marching and inspections also became concepts in our past. The USAF considered the intel school to be stressful enough. Most remarkable though, was the beautiful Texas sky. With no discernable hills or mountains, the sky seemingly started just off the earth's surface and went on forever. This light-blue majesty of nature defined our base landscape.

Due to the sensitive nature of our studies, I will refrain from commenting on the school curriculum itself. However, this missive will focus on "the further adventures of…"

These adventures started on a Monday morning. About fifteen of us met in a Quonset hut classroom. Because our classes had not yet begun, we were all forced into a duty known as "casual."

That first day dissolved in the most boring and wretched eight hours imaginable. We all sat there with an instructor telling us that he'd let us know if any assignments came up. He sat at the head of the classroom in a teacher's desk with a telephone, while we sat in school desks. Lunch and the end of this experience could not come fast enough. The second day arrived with dread, all of us possibly knowing that another day of this would drive us mad. After an hour in, a lieutenant (LT) appeared. We jumped out of our seats to salute him. He calmly then asked for eight volunteers. Despite the old military saw, "Do not volunteer for anything", I decided to end the madness. My hand shot up, without knowing exactly for what I was volunteering. Anything, however, would be better than wasting a day away in that Quonset hut. One other person reluctantly raised their hand before the LT picked six others. The LT and the eight of us walked out of "casual" and into our unknown assignment.

We followed the LT's lead and went to a nearby blacktop. He walked over to a parked car nearby and pulled out an American flag. The lecture lesson and demonstration began on proper folding of Old Glory. The fold required four people who completed the precise task by folding the flag into a pyramid with the blue stars field on top. A white glove hand was then placed on top of the flag. We then trained in a small marching formation, still unaware of where all this was heading. The LT spoke, "Gentlemen, we are all going as a funeral detail." The LT explained that an Air Force veteran had died and the family had requested a military burial, paid for by Uncle Sam. An Air Force insignia van pulled up. We all piled in, heading for the church. We arrived in a poor section of the city.

A dust storm kicked up as we walked inside a modest Baptist church. In the front of the building was the deceased in his casket, dressed in his Air Force blues. Nearby stood a choir of women. The family seated themselves in the first pews. As the service began, the minister delivered a powerful, touching eulogy for the fallen man. Emotions ran high. People wailed in anguish. Every person in the church were African American. Our funeral detail, to a man, were white. The contrast could not have been more stark. Once the singing began, the mood in the church shifted gears. Tears reigned down among the congregants, but no longer tears of sadness. The members swayed in their pews, the choir dominated the proceeding, and that special joy of gratitude for one man's life took center stage. This astonishing singing exhibition lasted about twenty minutes. Nobody could ever ask for a better send-off into the next world. I, as a twenty two-year old, had never witnessed anything like this. What followed was largely pro-forma. After the casket was closed, we draped it with the American flag. The crowd gathered outside in the swirling dust that was this San Angelo day. I participated in the flag folding, which we presented to the widow of the deceased. Our assignment complete, we re-entered the van and drove back to Goodfellow.

After classes began, tech school settled into a routine. Early morning wakeup, breakfast, classes, chow, return to classes, back to the dorm, chow, sleep. I made several friends, most notably John Tickner and James Swinney. John came from Syracuse, New York and we'd frequently talk about the white-hot basketball rivalry between Syracuse and Georgetown University, of whom I was a fan. John also adored Bruce Springsteen, a man who spoke to him, sang about the struggles of blue-collar workers, and whose concerts he'd frequently attended. Unfortunately, John was a chain smoker and heavy drinker, who enjoyed a good time at bars. Nonetheless, John and I participated in deep conversations about religion, politics, music, sports, and the meaning of life. For those times, I will be forever grateful. Another friend was Jim Swinney, a hell-raiser who eventually washed out of tech school due to being accused of cheating. Mostly John's friend, Jim always accompanied John to Friday and Saturday night drinking excursions at the club. The only time I'd be caught dead in the club was eating at the small restaurant. A steak dinner with salad, baked potato, vegetable and drink cost exactly four dollars in 1980. To pass the time, on weekends, some buddies and I rode a bus to San Angelo Mall, to dine on Chick-fil-A and Orange Julius.

Terror and astonishment broke up some of the routine. In late April, walking to school on a foggy morning, radio reports delivered the news of a failed United States military rescue of hostages being held in Iran. Eight brave U.S. Marines died in the aborted raid. That same day, rumors circulated among the student body that because of our expertise, we'd be going to war, if the situation escalated. This frightened many students, but emboldened others. I was in the former category.

A few weeks later, I stood in front of the base commander answering his question, "Did you try to harm yourself, airman?" I'd been summoned to respond to the incident from basic training. "No sir," I said. The officer repeated the question several times, rephrasing it slightly. I stood firm. After this maddening grilling, to both our satisfaction, the officer dismissed me. I saluted, executed an about face, and exited the room.

In August, word filtered among the students that some kid had not missed a single question during tech school exams. This astounded just about everyone, who probably believed this school to be a most rigorous academic experience. According to the Air Force, Goodfellow training was rated among the most difficult of all tech schools.

A brief overnight trip to Mexico offered another weekend diversion. John, his girlfriend Pauline, and I drove to Del Rio, Texas first. The town hosted Laughlin Air Force Base, in close proximity to the border. Despite the weather being extremely windy, John wanted to get in a round of golf. He played against Pauline while I tagged along. My previous golfing experiences had taught me that I may have been the worst golfer in the world. After a late breakfast, we rode over the border into Ciudad Acuña. Once there, we discovered a straight, unpaved road in the middle of town. Dust storms kicked up routinely, forcing one to turn their heads away from the swirls of dirt. John quickly headed for a bar. Pauline opted to wander the main street. I decided to stroll alone. We were to re-meet at a pre-determined time and place about two hours later. This would be plenty of time for John to knock a few back; for Pauline to shop for nice, colorful dresses; and myself to stumble about, astounded by the whole scene.

After a few minutes, I managed to find myself off-the-beaten path, but not before being accosted by packs of boys wanting to shine my shoes. "Gringo! Gringo!", they shouted. I did not speak Spanish, and pointed to my tennis shoes. It wasn't long before I spied more children wandering about shoeless with dirty faces and rags for clothes. They hollered in their native tongue, and played as most children do, without worry or care. Undoubtably, they lived in the various shacks nearby. The poverty in this part of town saddened me for these occupants. I was grateful for my own lot. As I choked up, I returned to the main street, unable to look further at the degradation. Unlike the children I met, my money burned a hole in my pocket. Determined to have a souvenir of my stay, I purchased a cheap vest. Later, after some haggling, I bought a soapstone Aztec Warrior chess set for my friend Steve Riddle, back in Fairfax, Virginia. The final price was thirty dollars. The two hours having elapsed, our group met back together on main street. John asked if we wanted Mexican food before heading back. I declined, as did Pauline. We'd seen enough of Mexico.

On our return north, border patrol stopped us for an exceedingly long time to search the car. They asked us to get out of the vehicle as they checked inside and out, including the trunk. I was especially worried about John, whose breath smelled of cheap Mexican beer. Luckily though, we survived this event and they waved us through. My trepidation continued as John drove erratically through the Texas countryside. Upon arrival back at Goodfellow, my unease calmed considerably.

As the weather heated up in west Texas that summer, my best friends conspired to play cupid. The mark was me, without a girlfriend at tech school. By choice. I believed that military romances, especially at this transient stage, were self-defeating. Nonetheless, they plowed forward with their insidious plan. My best buddy John Tickner, and his girlfriend Pauline set me up. I won't use their persuasive language other than to say that it was full of vulgarities. After much disagreement for over a week, I finally relented. This first blind date would also be my last. We would travel off-base to the Western Skies steakhouse and dine as two couples, John and Pauline, and my date and myself. The Saturday night arrived, and with it, my first meeting with a girl whose name I've long forgotten. When I saw her, I was most confused. Short and stocky, my Army-gal date sported more muscles than I did. She walked around haughtily, like a female body builder. Femininity was not one of her attributes. But I was committed and determined to make the best of it. We all hopped in John's car and drove about five miles to our venue. We all made small talk during the ride, and try as I might, I probably failed to hide my nervousness. This gal could crush me with her bare hands! She quickly revealed when I asked about her hobbies that indeed, she frequently lifted weights at the gym.

As they say, everything is big in Texas, and the Western Skies steakhouse experience proved no exception. Everyone but Pauline ordered a steak. The meat actually took up the whole plate, a thick cut of sizzling beef, whose aroma could make carnivores out of the staunchest vegans. Sides of broccoli, baked potatoes, and French fries were also served. Earlier, a mouth-watering salad appetizer started us off. The only thing missing was an on-site cardiologist. As we gorged on our meals, we kept the conversation light with mundane topics. Thankfully, the meal finally ended which meant the date would be coming to a close. We zipped back to the base. John and Pauline departed. My date and I lingered outside in the still steamy air. I know she expected a kiss goodnight, but I disappointed her. She even asked me into her girls-only Army quarters. I made several excuses and then walked back to my dorm room. I felt nothing for her, no sparks flew, and our blind date dissolved into memory. Over the next few days, I received numerous phone calls from her, asking me if I wanted to get together again. Each time I refused, content to let the whole thing go. Finally, after about five of these calls, I summoned enough courage to tell her, "Thanks, we had a good time, but I am just not interested." I could hear her whimpering and then she hung up the phone. I never saw her again.

Learning of one's initial duty assignment became the most anticipated event of the entire technical school experience. Like everyone else, I shared this sense of excitement, knowing that I would most likely travel overseas. Being an Army brat whose father was stationed in Germany and Italy, this offered much appeal to me. Finally, after being told by our instructors that we'd be informed by "official orders" within a week, the day arrived. Honestly, sleeping at night during this week became more challenging. Each of our class members was handed an envelope containing the prized information, signed no less, by a Colonel in the Air Force. I carefully opened the enveloped and discovered that I would be heading to San Vito, Italy, located geographically on the heel of the boot. Goodness, this was an Adriatic beach town. Unbelievable. I could not wait to tell the news to my mother, whose parents were born in the old country. In the subsequent phone call, my mother screamed to my father, "Joe, he's going to Italy in September!" My father went on the line and was speechless in English. Thinking quickly, he uttered in very poor Italian, *Va bene*, or "all good." My mother took the receiver again and exclaimed, "Wait until your aunts hear about this!" Two of my mother's six sisters lived together in Punxsutawney, Pennsylvania. These two, Jeanne and Rose Marie Perri, were two of my best friends. The next day, they both called me, ecstatic to hear the news. Said Jeanne, "You're going to meet a nice Italian girl and get married," she said, as a matter of fact. Rose Marie gushed that I needed to immediately learn Italian. "Go get a book and study. By the time you get there, you'll know it." These same women frequently greeted me with the Italian custom of pinching my cheek. I hated it. Now, I felt like they were pinching me on the phone. The nature of these women's vicarious joy cannot be overstated. Nor can their subsequent disappointment.

About two weeks later, I was approached by an airman unknown to me. "I heard you got Italy," he said. "I got Japan, but I don't want to go to Asia. We can swap, if you'd like." Confused, I asked him what he meant. He stated that if I agreed, and since our assignment dates were the same, we could meet with the base commander and request a trade. "You can think it over a few days," he said. Indeed, I thought about the issue long and hard. I knew I'd be risking the ire of my mother's side of the family. However, the wonder of what promised to be a completely new experience won the day. Japan sounded romantic and exotic and thus my choice. We reported to the base commander after making an appointment. Meeting an officer, knowing he'd judge on military bearing and salutes was nerve wracking, but five minutes and three signatures later, it was all over. In September, I'd be off to the Land of the Rising Sun. As feared, my reversal upset my mother, but crushed my aunts. They acted shell shocked for the next phone call, but quickly forgave me. Every one of my family said the decision was my choice. That made me feel better, at least.

The upcoming graduation nearly overwhelmed all participants, as the summer stretched into fall. Still intact was the now verified story of the kid who never missed a question in the entire course. Also intact were unsuccessful efforts by my friends, especially John Tickner, to get me drunk. My refusals to imbibe alcohol always thwarted their tries. However, the final test occurred on a September Thursday. A feeling of massive relief among my classmates naturally turned to commentary of a celebration being in order. "OK, I'll go to the club," I said. As the evening proved, this decision was ill advised.

Our entire class attended the event at the club and sat together at a few tables. Everyone felt good, the stress of tech school in our rear view. The next day would involve my Air Force classmates cleaning our classroom. Following about three hours of work dusting and mopping floors, we'd receive our diplomas in a semi-formal ceremony. At least, that was the plan. For now, though, the party was on! "Lighten up, Tommy!," admonished Athena, now married to buddy John Tickner. Everyone in our group ordered beer and drank with reckless abandon. Except me, who had also not eaten dinner in all the excitement. With Diana Ross' latest disco smash "Upside Down" cranked at maximum volume, Athena grabbed my hand and shuffled me to the dance floor. My inexperience at dancing forced Athena to chuckle. She wasn't the only one. Stumbling and bumbling I went. When I finally returned to my seat, the exhortations of my classmates intensified. "What'll it be, Tommy? It's on us." Try as I might, my refusals melted away. Relenting, I ordered a small carafe of white wine, served with a very thin-stemmed glass. I took a sip, then another, and soon the wine had disappeared.

From the wings of the club, a live band set up shop, tuning their instruments. When they began playing, I silently cursed to myself. They played C&W music. Ugh! Then again, we were in Texas. With John egging me on, another carafe appeared, with a new wine glass. Unlike the first bottle, I downed this one in a jiffy. By now, my mood escalated to near mania. I slammed the glass on the table with such force it shattered. Two glasses now destroyed, another carafe followed. That glass also succumbed. My friends shielded me as long as they could. Emboldened by the alcohol, I jumped from my seat onto the long table and shouted for the band to play some Black Sabbath, a heavy metal British band. Seeing this, the club bouncer appeared and summarily deposited me out the front door. Two friends escorted me, but I was busy committing more ridiculous maneuvers. I leaped new piping like an Olympian, part of the foundation for a new building. When I arrived at the quad, I vomited after barely making it to a bench. My friends took me to my dorm room, woke up my roommate, threw me into a shower, dried me off, and then tossed me into my bed naked. My first official assignment placed me in a funeral detail. This event could have been my own funeral. The next day, our classroom cleaning went on as expected. Our instructor walked in, told us about the materials, and walked away. For my part, I simply sat outside the classroom door, trying to stop my head from exploding. Three hours later, the instructor returned and the graduation ceremony began. To this day, I don't know quite how, but I managed to remain upright long enough to receive my diploma. My cumulative grades for the entire course earned me high honors, enough for second in the entire class. Goodfellow Air Force Base receded into a blur.

The further adventures of...

Misawa Air Force Base, Japan

The extremely long travel from Goodfellow Air Force Base in San Angelo, Texas to Misawa, Japan commenced on a crisp late September day in 1980. Initially, I flew alone, having no one to share the journey. Fortunately, once at Travis Air Force Base in San Francisco, I spied Athena Tickner also making the same trip. We could choose our seats on the plane and Athena and I sat together. From Travis we proceeded north to Anchorage, Alaska for a short stopover. From there, we re-boarded for the long haul southeast along the Kamchatka Peninsula and then the Kuril Islands. We landed next at Yokota Air Force Base in Tokyo, Japan for another brief layover. This time, we boarded another flight north to Misawa Air Force Base in Honshu. Athena's company definitely relieved the boredom of the marathon travel day. She regaled me with stories of her family back in Boston; her Greek father and Japanese mother producing the attractive girl sharing this new adventure. In many respects, Athena was coming home, having been raised in Japan. I countered with the Army experiences of my father, grandfather, and uncles.

Despite the mind-numbing distance of the flight, Athena and I prevailed. When we could see the Japanese mainland on the glidepath to landing, both our excitement levels reached fever pitch. When we finally touched down in Misawa safely, I let out a sign of relief enough to blow out a hundred candles. In those first, heady days as we settled in but before work schedules were determined, Athena introduced me to Japanese food and drink. We changed our dollars to yen coins and bills and tootled around the small downtown.

After a first meal of noodles, walking back to the main gate, I noticed a rather peculiar odor. Hoping it wasn't either one of us producing unwelcome flatulence, Athena noticed my sour face. "That's the sewer system you're smelling." Indeed, parallel to the sidewalk, was an open-air ditch, wherein brackish water flowed.

The initial in-brief for new arrivals offered mundane commentary about high standards in the Air Force, military bearing, professionalism, and keeping one's "nose clean." Nothing unusual compared to what we'd heard before at basic training and tech school. However, several comments about our geographic region and our hosts stood out. Before there was a Misawa Air Force Base (MAFB), the Japanese used the Pacific Ocean contours to practice bombing runs. The sea and land closely resembled Pearl Harbor, Hawaii. Pilots mock strafed the area, in advance of the attack in December 1941. The briefing sergeant also related to be forewarned that marijuana grew wild just behind our barracks. Cultivating the crop would be immediate grounds for dismissal from the service and a dishonorable discharge. The last briefing comment involved a Japanese word: *tomodachi*, which means friend. Japanese people were described as being very polite and friendly fostering and demanding respect. Although I did not realize it at the time, the word *tomodachi* describes virtually every new encounter with a Japanese person. This was part of their standard greeting and they were referring to Americans. I would later process this kindness as utterly remarkable, considering the United States obliterated Tokyo by air raids and dropped the only two Atomic Bombs ever in wartime.

Within the first several days, pre-work schedule, I decided to "go native." Having some extra yen bills in my wallet, I boarded a shuttle bus for the main gate. I walked into numerous stores in the downtown area, before ending at a liquor store. As stated previously, I was not much of a drinker, but decided to purchase a bottle of the mysterious rice wine called *sake*. Among bad decisions, this one ranks high on my list. The *sake* bottle I bought was rather large, its label filled with even-more mysterious Japanese writing. The middle-aged male clerk rang up the sale, placed the bottle in a bag, and bid goodbye. When I arrived at my single-man dorm room, I pulled out an eight-ounce glass and poured the liquid in, filling the glass to near full. Then, I took a quick sip. The *sake* tasted bitter and salty. The next time I lifted the glass, I took a gulp, like a hot shot downing a beer to impress friends. Alternately, I paced the small room, laid on the bed, sat at my desk, and took large swigs of drink. I poured glass after glass, and impressing no one, drank them all up. I'm not sure how much *sake* went down my gullet, but after about an hour, I crashed on the bed. My subsequent sleep lasted about twelve hours, far longer than usual. When I awoke, I felt as if a freight train roared through my head. Only the fact that the next day did not include work, saved me. As the pounding continued, I struggled to sit up in bed. Standing up was out of the question. I decided to wait it out. Lunch time came and went, without my participation. By dinner, however, I wobbled around the room and somehow made it to the chow hall. "What happened to you?" some of my buddies asked. "You don't want to know," I replied. A few days later, I caught up with Athena in the dorm. After I told her my story, she asked to see the bottle. Nearly empty, she picked up the bottle and was able to understand some of the writing. "Oh my God, Tommy," she exclaimed. "This is cooking *sake*, you could have died!" Friends always tell the truth.

Living conditions on MAFB seemed tolerable. In effect, the facility was separated into two entities; Security Hill and the Main Base. A distance of about eight miles, with a golf course in between, was the difference between the two. Security Hill, a.k.a. The Hill, was where we lived and worked. Six two-story barracks-style buildings comprised the living quarters for unmarried Air Force personnel. The buildings were about thirty years old, having been built during the Korean War era. Men and women lived in separate barracks. A cafeteria (chow hall), recreation center, supplies building, and gym rounded out the rest of the Hill. All work took place in the Ops Center, powered by the "Elephant Cage." For the uninitiated, I'll leave them guessing as to its purpose.

The single-man rooms themselves were small and plain with a bed, a desk, and an armoire. Each floor contained twelve individual rooms, two bathrooms, and a communal relaxation area called a day room. Of personal concern was the fact that my room was located next to the day room. Only a thin wall separated me from the new technology called videos. Someone had purchased a machine and decided to run *Animal House* and *Debbie Does Dallas* loudly on continuous loop for days at a time. My privacy and sleep patterns paid the price. For months afterward, I felt as if I could recite lines from both of these films.

The chow hall featured cooks and custodial workers, all Japanese. Per United States agreement with the host country, all service positions on base were staffed by Japanese citizens. Noticeable was the fact that these individuals always seemed ready to please. One such example was a portly, colorful cook who called himself John Wayne. This John Wayne frequently joined us at our meals, not to eat, but to engage with friendly banter. In hackneyed English, he'd offer his thoughts on any subject. John Wayne, despite his girth, careened about in a small motorcycle. Unfortunately, his lust for life did not extend to one of our own. One particular girl, petite in stature, sat by herself in the chow hall. She'd gobble down a plateful of food and then return for seconds, where she'd repeat the gastronomic feat. The other service members would gasp, probably not knowing that she suffered with bulimia/anorexia. This was confirmed by Athena, her roommate. Athena related horrifying episodes that upon the young lady's return from the chow hall, she'd vomit up her meals. The girl became very sick afterwards and was hospitalized. Within a year, the world learned of this disease as American music icon Karen Carpenter died, raising awareness of its ravages.

Area wise, the Main Base was fairly expansive. MAFB served two masters: the United States military personnel of Army, Navy, Air Force, and Marines all performing their unique missions and a contingent of Japanese Air Self Defense Forces (JASDF). Except for aviation personnel, the American and Japanese forces did not have much interaction. Three entrance/exit gates enclosed the facility from Misawa proper. A shuttle bus trip from the Hill to the main base took about twenty minutes. The gorgeous golf course featured a rather large water hazard called the Pacific Ocean. Otherwise, the usual assortment of military facilities defined the main base; the flight line, movie theatre, barber shop, commissary (grocery), base exchange (department store, or BX), credit union, dry cleaners, gymnasium, pool, recreation center. As I would later discover, the Air Force pays particular attention to budgeting for recreational facilities, as opposed to other service branches.

Although I can't speak for other military positions, security work on the Hill offered extreme challenges. Suffice to say that the rotating shift schedule played havoc with the body's natural rhythms, or internal clock. Human beings are accustomed to sunlight and darkness. Unnatural disruptions to that balance can cause physical and psychological stress. Changes in sleeping and eating patterns became routine, but difficult. How I even survived this work schedule, I'll never know. On the Hill there were five working shifts. The daytime workers, known as Day Ladies, completed a standard Monday-Friday 9-5 job. No worries. However, the bulk of us worked as a group of four separate flights; Able, Baker, Charlie, and Dawg. The mission was 24/7. At any given time, three of the flights would be working. One would be on break. There were no weekends or holidays off. The work schedule, one rotation, began with four Swing shifts from 3-11pm. After this, four Mid shifts of 11pm-7am began. Finally, four Day shifts of 7am-3pm ended the rotation. Thus, twelve straight days on, three days off. Much of the time off needed to be spent to recover from the previous rotation. A small saving grace was the camaraderie of each flight. We competed with each other, had our own colors, and proudly wore exotic, hand-sewn jackets. Able green. Baker blue. Charlie red, and Dawg black. I was fortunate enough to serve with the Charlies, proudly displaying the large dragon on my jacket. What became of the garment is unknown to me, however, I'd pay a considerable sum to wear it again.

Letters home provided a welcome connection to home in the good, old U S of A. I wrote dozens of detailed missives about military life and my adventures in the Japanese countryside.[6] Every week I'd venture to my post office box on main base. Thrilled to receive mail, the letters were my Holy Grail, eagerly awaited, eagerly discovered. The core participants in this excitement were my mother and father[7], aunts Jeanne and Rose Marie, grandpa Emery and Freda[8], and friends Steve Riddle and Bob Karnes. Each offered their perspectives on life. These pieces of mostly hand-written commentary, cannot be underestimated as a sustaining force for my being halfway around the globe.

I'd be remiss about my time in Misawa without mentioning

---

[6] Many of those letters appear next, intact, as they were written at the time.

[7] Their biographies appear at the end of this book.

[8] Their biographies appear at the end of this book.

some of my buddies. Six-foot-seven-inch Barry Furnival fancied himself a videographer, filming anything and everyone with his new VHS machine. Afterward, our gang of buddies would watch Barry's results in the dayroom over cigarettes and beer. Wise-cracking, fast talking Ricky Kline seemingly took nothing serious outside the workplace, eliciting laughter from all. Jim Smith, another fun-loving prankster, hailed from California. Calling himself "Moondoggie" and then later "Moonpuppy," Smith spoke of surfing and his former beach-bum lifestyle. Tony Schloss presented himself as mad at the world, but deep down inside, he also enjoyed a good laugh. The shy and naïve Michigander Kevin Hodge couldn't stop asking the question, "Is Japan modern?" But, perhaps my favorite of the bunch was Andrea Holmquist. Andrea and I paled around on and off base, jogging, playing racquetball, and eating Japanese food off-base. In fact, Andrea and I spent so much time together that many people thought we were a couple.

Walt Foster, who I knew on the Hill, could not wait to leave the Air Force. His military commitment having ended, Walt invited friends and staged a small night time bonfire. The conflagration took place on the grounds behind the barracks. Using lighter fluid as accelerant, Walt joyfully burned his boots in defiance of his enlistment. We onlookers gawked as we sat on the second-floor landing steps.

Constant practical joking helped to alleviate the horrors of shift work. We delighted in giving each other nicknames, and then noting which ones would stick. One fellow airman received a check from the United States Government for exactly one cent. Your tax dollars at work. This story circulated around the base like wildfire. For military members, sympathy played no part. Only uproarious laughter.

On another occasion, early in the tour, Athena, John Tickner, and myself attended a safety briefing. The presenter, a sergeant whose name I've long forgotten, presented film and demonstrations of CPR, first aid, and rendering assistance in emergencies. As the briefing was concluding, he said, "Push the button, pull the chain, out comes the chocolate choo-choo train." We looked at each other with puzzled expressions. Was the sergeant trying to see if we were awake or was he auditioning for Johnny Carson?

One unusual incident occurred during my time at MAFB. As mentioned previously, Misawa operated as a dual base with American and Japanese forces. The base headquarters was a cul-de-sac, with Americans on one side and Japanese the other. In the middle of a small grass patch flew the flags of both nations. Nearby this part of the base was the base clinic. After working a midnight 11pm to 7am shift, I was scheduled for some routine medical procedure following the end of the work night. I dutifully boarded a bus from Security Hill to the main base, a distance of about eight miles. After the early morning exam concluded, I waited for the next shuttle bus to take me home. Then, two big, black automobiles slowly ambled by. The first car sported a small Japanese flag on the left hood of the vehicle. Weary from the long day, but trying to be respectful, I saluted the Japanese base commander, as was my option. The car pulled into the Japanese headquarters and the driver exited the car with the Japanese base commander. Next, ambling slowly along was a similarly outfitted automobile, with the Stars and Stripes proudly displayed. This car passed *without* my salute. This one undoubtably transported the American base commander, an Air Force Colonel. After moving past me about twenty yards, the car stopped. Slowly, but deliberately, out stepped the Misawa Air Base American base commander. He walked towards me; I instantly saluted. Gulp. The officer then put me on the spot. "Did you know you just saluted the Japanese, but not me?" I tried my best not to melt in the man's presence. "No disrespect intended, sir," I stated nervously. "What's going on?" questioned the officer. "Sir, I guess I'm a little tired. Just worked an all-nighter on the hill, then had a medical procedure. I'm waiting for a bus to take me back to the dorm." My entire military career flashed before my eyes. I awaited my fate, held completely in the officer's hands. Surprisingly, the colonel busted out laughing. He placed one arm on my shoulder. "Carry on, son. Get some sleep OK?" And with that, the officer strode back to his car.

Mid-way through my two and one-half year tour in Japan, a huge change occurred. All of the unmarried personnel living in the

94

barracks on the Hill transferred to a brand new six-story building on main base. The Ops Center remained intact. A special shuttle bus transported those without vehicles to our employment. The new facility featured two-man rooms, one "head" in the center serving bookended rooms for four people. A large dayroom on each floor, containing couches and a television, allowed for communal relaxation from the rigors of work. In addition, two telephones were shared between about fifty people per floor. The adjustment to having a roommate went smoothly, save for our suite-mates playing Journey records at all hours of the night. Soft-spoken Thad Manning, from rural North Carolina, and I shared living quarters using only separate *futons* for beds. Like the Japanese, the beds folded up, making more area in each room. Two armoires, two chairs, and a vanity comprised the rest of the room furnishings. Looking back, my pairing with Thad was perfect. We both shared interest in exploring our host country and learning their language and customs. Making Japanese friends was as easy as saying *konnichi wa* (hello), which we practiced first on base service workers. These simple kindnesses never failed to elicit smiles from the natives.

Besides Thad Manning, the best part about our new location was the chow hall, located about a hundred yards away. This cafeteria served a wide variety of food and I certainly took advantage. I discovered that eating a salad with every meal and regular exercise kept my weight steady. For carnivores such as myself, the monthly steamship round roast beef provided an unforgettable dining experience. Tempted by the aroma, the flavor of juicy steamship round made me believe I died and went to heaven. OK, I occasionally cheated. Late at night, after the dinner hour, the chow hall served greasy hamburgers and fries, for those requiring a fast-food fix. Meal time became highlights of every day on base. Fewer things in life are more satisfying than sharing a hearty meal with your buddies, far away from home.

In the January winter of 1981, I learned about a Japanese store just off South Gate that sold a newfangled technology, personal computers. After reading about them, and operating a mission-centric machine at work, I decided to take the plunge. The outlay for keyboard, monitor, printer, a cassette tape drive for storage, and a cartridge port, totaled $600+, an enormous sum for a low-ranking airman. Nonetheless, I used savings money to purchase a Commodore VIC-1001. Compared to today, this computer seems quaint. The VIC-1001 model was a specialized version of the VIC-20, sold in America. The QWERTY keyboard featured the traditional English alphabet and an entire set of Japanese characters called *Katakana*. In time, after significant self-learning, I could produce text in the Japanese language. The bulky monitor offered Cathode Ray Tube (CRT) technology. This black background monitor displayed only green phosphorescent letters and numbers, no graphics. Commodore's dox-matrix printer, in operation, could only be described as noisy. However, the cassette drive was quite problematical. Imagine the loudest shriek of a cat outside your window. Times ten. This sound occurred while saving data. The cassette drive saved files in a linear fashion only, unlike storing in sectors as with hard drives. Even more remarkable was the memory chip inside a Commodore VIC-1001. The system maxed out at 5K total, enough for about five type-written pages.

In addition to the computer purchase, I also added in a cartridge of Pac-Man, a wildly popular arcade game invented by the Japanese. Normally, one would have to place coins in these glass table-top units for one game. Now, I could play Pac-Man to my heart's content. Indeed, Thad and I spent hour after hour learning new patterns to try to defeat the "ghosts" intent on gobbling up Pac-Man. After I told a few buddies, word filtered around that I owned a computer. After much cajoling, I hooked up the unit in the dayroom overnight for a few days. Lines formed to play the game creating a cacophony of boisterous joy. The resulting Pac-Mandemonium earned me quite a reputation. Even other service members from the Army and Marines, who probably had no business in our building, came to partake in the merriment.

For about a year between 1981-1982, I became the editor of the informal magazine *Charlie's Midnight Express*. The publication, featured a hodgepodge of poetry, short fiction, comic strips, recipes, acrostics, editorials, humor, quizzes, and horoscopes. In addition, information about Japan, its people, language, and culture appeared. All submissions were welcome, thus my position resembled a compiler far more than an editor. Distribution of the rag took place on midnight shifts, when the challenge of staying awake usurped job activities. In fact, this practice came to be known as "bleeding." Overall, the best part of the magazine were the covers, a combination of surreal pop-art and science fiction speculation.

In the summer of 1982, my group Charlie Flight played for the Base Softball Championship, opposing the Naval Security Group (NSG). Softball proved a very popular recreation on base, with about eight teams competing. Depending on the participants, the sport drew raucous crowds comprised of servicemen, wives, and their children. After a round robin tournament, the final seven game series commenced. However, the games hardly resembled a bunch of paunchy guys playing ball on a weekend. These highly-competitive games were for bragging rights as champions for the year's play. The exciting series of night time action went back and forth with both teams trading victories. Softball had largely evolved into a game of musclemen pounding balls over the fence. In between, however, sterling glove play afield helped to spice up the action. What was unusual about the event occurred as a result of three people, myself, Barry Furnival, and Ricky Kline. Barry brought his video camera and filmed all seven games from our "press booth" perch. As the most knowledgeable baseball fan of the group, I offered play-by-play. Ricky, with virtually no understanding of the sport, provided color commentary. Needless to say, silliness reigned. I described the action on the field, using the names of all the Charlie Flight players. The NSG players were merely referred to as "Navy" or "Navy players." We even filmed mock commercials for beer and Dudley Balls. The comedic Ricky served as pitchman. The video could never be described as stellar production. As the night darkened, so did our camerawork. Deep into the game, without lights for the camera, players appeared as mere shadows. In game seven, however, Charlie Flight triumphed, eking out a narrow victory. The story doesn't end there. As the series moved forward, the players noticed our filming activities. Barry spoke with several participants. Soon, copies of the videotapes floated around the base. Ball playing rivals set up beer parties to screen the games. I never attended any of these events, but oh, to be a fly on the wall.

By the time I departed Misawa, I observed and noted anecdotes about the disturbing behavior of American servicemen stationed in overseas assignments. Although a majority of soldiers, airmen, and marines make the most of their tours, a stubborn core frequently bad mouth the host country and the natives. These same individuals also *never* explore off-base, unless to one of the numerous drinking establishments just outside the gate. These bars cater exclusively to Americans. I tested this phenomenon by asking several of the "old-timers" who'd served on multiple overseas missions. To a man, they reaffirmed my observation. One lamented, "they don't know what they're missing. This is a chance they probably won't have again." The men related that it occurs all over, wherever US servicemen are stationed, in Germany, in Korea, in Italy. To test the theory, I conducted a sociological experiment. I ventured into an alley just past the main gate. As the patrons were knocking back cold ones and bragging about their sexual exploits, they also gruffly hurled racist terms about the Japanese. The Japanese workers inside, all women, merely smiled, content for profits. Incredibly, these hostesses even handed out magic markers prior to Americans entering the bathroom. When I feigned a bathroom visit, I couldn't believe every square inch of explicit graffiti on the doors and walls. Unprecedented news broke on base one day that an *entire* naval unit had been removed from Misawa and sent home for rowdy, barroom behavior.

Quite unlike the military bad actors discussed above, I must have done something right in Misawa, Japan. My unit awarded me the Air Force Commendation Medal and the Good Conduct Medal on my way out the door. Much to my dismay, my Japan tour ended in March 1983.[9] In the last week overseas, I stayed at the Sanno Hotel in Tokyo. At under ten dollars a night! The subsequent duty station at Ft. Meade, Maryland proved an anti-climactic end to my

---

[9] Details of my activities in Japan and the Philippines occur on subsequent pages.

four-year enlistment. I enjoyed the work and the fortuitous summer of Ripken and Murray of the Baltimore Orioles. My two civilian bosses liked my work ethic enough to offer a job doing precisely the same thing once my military enlistment ended. I could not have been more excited to live in Maryland in my own apartment. My salary would increase dramatically. Next spring, I could attend games of my beloved Baltimore Orioles. After packing up and ending my military career, I drove home to Fairfax, Virginia for a few days. The paperwork was all signed and I'd start my new/old employment just after Christmas. Independence beckoned, until it didn't. While at home, a letter arrived addressed to me. The formal letter referenced a congressional bill initiated by Senators Phil Gramm and Warren Rudman (Gramm-Rudman Balanced Budget Act) and offered regret to my position being eliminated. The letter crushed my spirit for several months afterward. My military career was over. At 26, I was now unemployed and living at home.

Serving overseas.

The following stories detail my experiences in Japan and the Philippines.

A Day in Misawa
6-10 December 1980

I awake to the sound of planes roaring overhead. It is 9am. My drowsy body drags itself into the cold shower. I am truly awake now, ready to enjoy the pleasures of Japan. I call on a friend and we hop on a bus and head into town. The ride is long, but the scenery never boring. Today the mountains are in full glory. It is a clear, blustery fall day. As always, the sight of the shimmering Pacific is near. The waves roll and die and then surface in the subtle actions that only nature can provide.

It is lunchtime. The journey of the bus ride ends, but our trip is just beginning. We depart saying *domo* to the driver. It is an informal thanks. My friend and I take a short walk into the city of Misawa proper. In an instant we are transformed into *gaijin*. This means foreigner in Japanese. Unlike the English term, there is little negative connotation.

The streets are full of bustling Japanese. Some are old ladies with babies on their backs. Some are school kids dressed in uniform. Some are businessmen dressed in suits. Always, there is little eye-contact between the Japanese and the Americans. A friendly greeting from us can bring two reactions. One is negative. I feel as if the Japanese are sometimes intimidated by Americans. The other reaction is very positive and pleasant. They return the greeting and flash the warmest of smiles. Sometimes, they will even say hello.

We continue our walk until we come across our favorite restaurant. We have no name for it. We only know that it is Chinese by the color of the banner hanging outside the entrance. We seek the comforts of the intimate place. Once we enter, we are greeted by a lady in her sixties. She will serve us *bariyaki*, the only Japanese dish in the house. This is a dish of raw beef and onions and eggs. We are to cook our own on the hotplates provided on the table. This we do. This friendly lady also brings us rice and fish and soup and tea. All are culinary delights. We eat and thank her and pay in yen. The meal is very delicious, inexpensive, and filling.

The journey continues. We sometimes stop in stores and

look at the various things for sale. When we buy, we are careful not to count our change. This is impolite and it is like telling the shopkeeper that you don't trust him. They do not make mistakes when it comes to money.

We walk further, exiting the business district and entering the housing area. Misawans are generally farmers. They have been an agricultural community for centuries. All around us we can see rice paddies and vegetation. Occasionally a temple is to be seen or a Christian establishment. The dwellings are almost all made of wood. They seem very old and well-worn. These are hard workers. We pass old ladies in the streets that are bent over like hunchbacks, probably from years of work in the fields. Sometimes they push carts with vegetables stacked in them. In this area of town, it is rare to see men in suits. These are the workers. They wear rags and their faces are etched with the years of their struggles.

The train station lies ahead. We stare at the wonder of the Japanese transportation system. They are so efficient, these people. All of the travel is planned, precisely. It has to be. There are so many people coming and going in the station. We take a look inside to see the schedule of the rides. We cannot tell exactly where the train runs to. We cannot read Japanese. But still, there is the romance of the trains, carrying millions to far away destinations. The trains are very crowded this day. Most probably, we guess, this is normal. We walk out of the station. As we do, we get a few stares from the populace. Someday, we will ride these machines. Someday, we will go far away from Misawa. Someday...

We are almost at Komaki's. It is a relaxation/resort for the people of Misawa and the travelers from the south that come to spend some time and rest here. I have already seen this place. I am here to show my friend. But, I will keep coming back just for the sheer beauty of this remarkable estate. We enter and pay a lady 500 *yen*. This entitles us to stay all day and see the floor show and try the mysteries of the hot bath. The first thing we see upon entrance is a thousand trees and a small waterfall. It is dark inside and there are fish swimming in a mini-lake setting.

The entire complex is amazing. There are doors everywhere. Each room is full of distinctly Japanese things. One room is a museum full of wooden relics from the not-so-distant past, another contains an exhibit of phallic symbology. There are hotel rooms and restaurants and gift shops and bowling alleys. There is even a game room. But, above all, there is the temple/shrine and the imperial gardens. They stretch all around Komaki's. One gets the impression that there was a very rich Japanese man who saw his country over-run by Westernization and wanted to preserve part of Japan he missed. He spent a fortune building this resort.

Both of us are amazed by the place. It is something out of a dream. But, the dream is to savored for another time. It is time we headed back to the base. The walk is long. We see the sun dipping behind the mountains. Darkness is falling over Misawa.

Within an hour, I am safe in my room. I place my head on my pillow and start the dream. It is of feudal Japan and ladies in *kimonos...*

First impressions of Japan.

Winter in Misawa
7-8 Jan 1981

"Without going out of your door, you can know the ways of the world."

-LAO TSU

There is an immense joy in contemplation...Yesterday, while on a journey from my place of work to home, I saw a flock of snow geese. What a sight! White birds traversing the white sky, while below them on the ground lay a sheet of white. And, we are those birds, traveling to other destinations for survival. We are the wings that fly in near-silent splendor. It was a moving sight. Always in nature, if one observes, there are parallels to man and to ourselves, the observers. These birds come from the "big bear" to the West, the USSR. If they could only see and understand the Snow Goose, would there be troubles in Poland and Afghanistan?

Misawa is a lovely place this time of year. It is snowing a great deal outside this very moment. I look out my window. The flakes drift for miles until they reach the ground and melt in the ensuing summers. We can only see the last moments of a snowflake's journey to earth. But, these are the moments of dreams. Winter and cold are so romantic and seeing it all happen in Japan makes it special. I can't even describe the pleasures. Mountains rise on three sides of us and covered by the precipitation. It almost makes me long for a winter walk with a lady and then a warm cup of green tea.

A bit about tea. I am slowly beginning to love this mystic beverage. Due in part to my reading on the subject coupled with reading by Lao Tsu and Chuang Tsu and that I am in a country of immense beauty. Tea is the peaceful drink, used in spiritual contemplation for centuries. Now I am beginning to get caught up in the frenzy and mystery. What better than a cup of tea and staring at the majestic mountains of Japan?

Quick takes of a Misawa winter.

Road Trip to Hachinohe
14 March 1981

I took a trip to that town of delights called Hachinohe and had some marvelous times in Misawa. Last week two friends and I took a drive to Hachinohe. On the way we stopped the car and walked along the snowy beach. That was a marvelous natural experience. The waves were crashing on the shore to rhythmic wave swells. Awesome! Then, we got the car stuck in the snow and after trying for some time to remove it, we called on some Japanese for help. They obliged. What made it all so interesting was a group of children that were standing nearby across the street. They were laughing out loud. Our misfortunes were certainly funny. We were pushed out in the area of the road that lay in the middle of the intersection, then the car stalled...again. A few minutes later our temperamental car started again and we waved goodbye to the Japanese children and proceeded on our merry way...There is something very unique about car travel in Japan. Those narrow roads and those teeny, tiny cars! And, if that wasn't scary enough, we travel on the left side of the road. There are no highways locally as we know them. It all looks like backwoods roads. Of course, there is no mistake that we are in Japan. Our journey is punctuated by views of rice fields, religious Shinto shrines, wooden building architecture and *kanji* writing that exists everywhere. Along the way we come to a giant industrial complex, complete with billowing smokestacks and other such technological advances. One of these days I am going to get out my camera and start snapping. There is so much to see locally. To be here is love. Put yourself in the perspective of the Taoists. Experience green tea, sake, the beach, a tree, a drive in the country. It is peace. It is the everchange.

Soon, we are at our destination. Hachinohe is a vibrant community, full of the suburban/city hustle and bustle. These people have intense looks. At every turn is the most beautiful girl that you have ever seen. This is Japan. We eat and wander the stores. I fall in love again and again. I have never fallen out of love with her. Sometimes, I can't spend enough time with her. But, this is only the beginning. I will continue with my story. Even my writing is full of twists and turns and of seemingly unrelated events. But, like Japan, I am always straying from structure. I am really saying that it is almost impossible for me to plan anything here. Just go, journey, experience!

My next adventure involves a restaurant. The name of the place is New Miyaki's. Two young ladies, and a gentleman and I had the most sensational meal to date. I had chicken with cashews, shrimp foo young, rice, spring rolls, boneless fried chicken, and other delights. Even raw fish! All this food was served by the daintiest, cutest little hostess my eyes have ever beheld. She was indeed a huggable. I was bold enough to suggest to my date that she be traded for the young hostess. My date didn't take that too kindly, but she thought I was kidding. I wasn't!

The third and most current of my Nippon adventures took place in a bar, of all places. Two male friends and I became bold and brazen and ventured to Ohzu's. We all sat around and tried to make conversation with the hostesses. That was a lot of fun! A good time was had by all. After one smooth yet potent Kirin Beer, anyone can understand any Japanese. I pointed out to Komiko (one of the hostesses) that we were foreigners. She disagreed. She said we were all friends. We had our names written in *katakana* and they played some good, old-fashioned rock and roll on the stereo. As we sipped and talked and laughed, we listened to CCR and Linda Ronstadt. Marvelous! Expensive but worthwhile. So, it is twice that I have been to this marvelous and friendly little bar. Though I won't make a habit of it, it was an experience to be savored.

An early road trip yields some laughs.

Cherry Blossom Festival in Hirosaki
2-4 May 1981

It is the time of the year here to be totally involved in the beauty that is Northern Honshu. It is Japanese spring. We are just now beginning to awaken from the long winter's slumber, a lethargy that was indeed too long. Now, the flowers bloom and birds sing the praises of the renewal of spring. The Japanese are very much involved in nature and they celebrate according to the seasons. To the northeast of Misawa is the town of Hirosaki, renowned for the annual Cherry Blossom Festival. This is a two-week celebration of spring and the arrival of the short-lived Cherry Blossoms. They bloom for only a short period of time as I'm sure you are aware. These blossoms are the same ones that were given to the United States as a gift and lie in the Nation's Capital.

We saw the famous cherry blossoms and Hirosaki castle, a structure of marvelous beauty, and sat around in this giant park and took in all the scenery. We went to a Japanese haunted house, ate *yakisoba*, drank Sapporo beer, took photos of everything that moved or didn't and generally were awed by the gala event. There were, of course, Japanese people there by the score. Whenever Japanese are involved it is at least a score as there are so many of them! And all shapes and sizes, from the mamma-san holding the little baby to the totally gorgeous ladies to the hunchbacked field workers. And, there are the tipsy. The Japanese consider this occasion to be a time of extreme celebration. They will celebrate, believe me! The men could be seen in *"sake* circles." This is when a group of men sit around and drink rice wine until they die or pass out, whichever comes first. Sometimes, Americans are hauled into these feared circles and when this happens, it is the story of a lifetime. I was too wary for that and I stayed away from such behavior. They can be fatal and I'd prefer to hear the stories second-hand. A few of us did get involved with some Japanese gentleman sitting around and getting wasted on beer and eating crab meat. We drank some of their beer and ate some crab, too. Neither member of our little party spoke Japanese. Strangely enough, neither of them spoke English. It made for an interesting conversation. We did find out though that one of the Japanese gentleman had seven kids. He kept making gesticulations with his body in a quite furious manner. I'd say that he was quite proud of the fact that he fathered seven children. A good actor, he was. Yes, he detailed the entire conception and birth process in about 5 seconds. These Japanese don't mess around. There were a lot of laughs. I'd have to say that this was the highlight of the day. We all got their addresses and they got ours. That wasn't so good because they were all written in *kanji* and ours in English. We are searching for an interpreter and we think that we may write to these gentlemen. It was something I'll never forget.

Cherry blossoms and sake circles.

The $10.00 Car
June 1981

On Misawa Air Base, Japan, the car was legend.

It was little more than a box on wheels, with a rusting exterior where gold paint once thrived. The space inside measured far less than the area of a phone booth. With the windows closed, drivers and passengers fought to breathe the same air. After years of wear and tear, this Daihatsu's upholstery, once a shiny plastic, had been reduced to about a dozen rolls of masking tape. At top, full-throttle speed, the two-cylinder bucket of bolts barely broke 35 KPH, or about twenty-two miles per hour. Going down a steep hill. A few strong soldiers could probably push it faster than that. Some lawnmowers race at higher speeds. And yet, with gasoline and tender loving care, the car seemingly ran on and on.

Because of the relatively short military tours in Japan, this same Daihatsu automobile was constantly being traded among airmen and sergeants in Misawa. The car seemed to have been made in the late 1950s, when the words "Made in Japan" ensured a far inferior product than today. Over time, the price dropped from several thousand to several hundred dollars, then for a fistful of dollars and, finally to its current value, ten dollars. As a novelty, a friend of mine bought it in 1981. When our gang piled in for a road trip, we were more interested in the legend than its transportation viability or creature comforts. We'd heard the unverifiable stories about how everyone on the base knew about the famous Daihatsu, especially the old timers on their third and fourth go-arounds in Misawa who'd seen the car re-cycled to multiple owners. We'd heard about the young airman who'd driven it off the ravine (and lived to tell about it), about young couples who tried to make love in its cramped interior, but instead twisted themselves into pretzels. We laughed at the jokes about the rickshaw full of chickens that caused the puttering box-mobile to swerve nearly off the road one time, frightening its owner to death. He had caused the almost-accident himself, driving on the right-hand side of the road. Like the British, the Japanese drive on the left side.

Our actual road trip probably added to the legend of the car.

We drove several hundred yards up hill at a snail's pace until we informed our driver/owner that we should also travel in the direction of traffic. Lest of course, we wanted to end up like our rickshaw friend. On the way back down hill, the four of us stuck our hands out the window and flapped along like we were flying. After some time, we heard some pops and zings from the engine. Old Daihatsu was out of gas. The owner commented that the fill-up cost more than the car. We limped into a station. Japanese car insurance, mandatory for all vehicles, cost the owner about $300, making the venture considerably more expensive. Upon the resumption of the trip, we jalopied around the base exchange, the airport, the theatre, and the hospital. Several soldiers walking along recognized us, er the car, and waved.

By now, the car has probably got a million miles to its name. New generations of soldiers could be enjoying its quaint and reliable ways. Or maybe not. Perhaps, the gold Daihatsu has been ground into scrap metal and made into a new Japanese car. Somewhere, it could still be putting around. Maybe, it's parked in your driveway!

Musings about the car that would not die.

The Towada Hot Bath Experience
20 Jul 1981

I am a bit deflated. The much ballyhooed trip to Towada is over and I am back in my dorm ready to go back to work in this awful place. It was quite a day of excitement and now it is over. I shall attempt to describe my odyssey...

It all started when Barry Furnival and I picked up our three female companions; Terry Mayfield, a recently married Black girl who was at one time my job trainer and a very sharp Airman (selected as Airman of the Year for the 6920th); Cindy Gutierrez, a very pretty Spanish gal who is the sweetest, purest girl I have ever known; and last but not least, Miss Annie Holmquist, a girl whom I adore but have realized by now that we can be only friends. The hour long drive would begin...

We took the road to Towada-shi (the ONLY road to Towada city). It was definitely a drive through the country as is most of Japan. There were rice paddies everywhere and the occasional statue of a policeman by the road. The statues warn passing cars of children crossing. Sometimes, there are wooden dummies dressed up like old ladies instead of policeman. At any rate, they serve as reminders to slow cars down. We passed a horse farm and some very fancy Japanese houses near Towada. The Japanese have a way of having beautiful interiors in their homes, yet the exteriors are sometimes old and rotting wood. These homes, however, were well cared for on the outside. A few cows and old ladies bending in the fields later, we came to Towada town. Towada is a quaint little city, small, and unlike its neighbor to the east, Hachinohe, which beams with bright lights. From the beginning I was impressed. This was not my first visit to the town so I had some idea of how to get around. The girls soon parted and were off in the direction of the clothing stores. Meanwhile, Barry and I explored department stores and record shops. We did come across a very interesting liquor store and Mr. Furnival made a purchase. I stayed dry. Both of us had our cameras; I had a cheap Kodak while Barry had the traditional SLR. He kept wanting to take photos of the young ladies that walked the streets. (that was not meant as a derogatory comment.) Mr. Furnival had a zoom lens that enabled him to shoot closeups of the pretty women from far away. So much for that...

Soon, it was time to meet back at the car and continue onward to the hotel. Before we did however, we discovered that the girls were absent and had failed to reach their rendezvous with us at the appointed hour. So, we walked down the street a tad and went into a restaurant for a beer. The time was 3:35, five minutes after the time the girls were supposed to show. We decided to drink the beer and get back to the car ASAP.

It was to be a four minute Kirin, a moment that I will never forget. As we walked (the word is more like swayed) out of the restaurant we saw the girls coming out of a French restaurant near where the car was parked. They had showed as we found out later but said we weren't there. We all laughed and continued on our merry way. Barry was the official driver. I have yet to brave the Japanese streets; the drivers are somewhat maniacal.

In about twenty minutes, we were in Towada National Park, one of the most famous resorts in all Nippon. The park surrounds a huge lake and the scenery is breathtaking. Driving in and around the lake must be quite an experience. I may never try it for I fear for my life. Anyway, at last we came to the *ryokan*, a hotel nestled safely in the woods, the lower level of the hotel on the ground while the upper level sat on a steep hillside. From that moment on, my love affair with the Japanese idea of relaxation, began.

As the five of us entered the hotel, we were speechless. In the car we hadn't said anything because we were watching the beautiful road scenery. Now, here we were, five souls, the ideas of Western Man planted firmly in our little brains, about to embark on Eastern thought. Before the trip had ended, I was thinking like a Japanese...

At the door, we were greeted by a kindly, old Japanese woman who directed us to take off our shoes and don the traditional slippers reserved for walking in the hotel. A young gentleman took our bags and brought them to our room. From the first few seconds that we were inside this ancient, 70-year old wooden structure, we were greeted verbally by about 5-6 people. One of them was a totally gorgeous Japanese woman of about 25 years and prettier than

111

the word. We put on our slippers and made the long walk up steep stairs to our room. The walk lasted about five minutes for all of our slippers kept slipping and falling off and those stairs were the very definition of steep. At last, we were showed to our rooms. The girls were to sleep in the room opposite ours. This was no sleep-in affair.

The rooms displayed a picture of simplicity and understatement. The floors were covered with bamboo *tatami* mats and a small table sat in the middle of the non-clutter. On opposite ends of the table were two chairs that sat on the floor and had no legs! These chairs were later to become an obsession. I must get one of them as they are the most comfortable seating implement I have ever tried. On the walls hung one picture; a vase with flowers and a Japanese scroll bamboo painting. There was also a balcony with a table and small chairs, perfect for reading or having tea. I fell in love with the decor. There was no stereo or radio, but there was a television set that was not watched despite Barry's pleas to the contrary. I admired the setting and the non-materialistic things. Soon after, Barry and I and the girls put on our *yukata* and *kimono* and turned Japanese. It was a loose fitting gown, and one could easily become attached to the softness of the material. At this stage, only ten minutes had elapsed since we had entered the hotel and already I was swooning along to the music of Japan. None was playing but I was falling for this whole attitude. I wanted more.

The girls came into the room and after a brief chat, we headed back down the killer stairs to the hot bath. On the way, Barry and I stopped in the co-ed bathroom with no incident. We hurried down the stairs and soon arrived at the baths. There were three of them; one female, one male, and one both. The deal was to remain pure and we chose separate baths. We did and we enjoyed. The baths are the traditional form of Japanese bathing. One must take a towel to the room and strip naked and then soap himself up and cleanse the body and then enter a very hot, steaming tub of water. The tub was about 10 by 15 feet. There was one native in the bath as Barry and I made our first-time approach into the water. One foot, two feet, ow! the male parts and then we were fully in-- up to our necks. One dare not dip his head underneath the water and come out alive. For a moment my body tingled and then became quickly used to the sensation of heat. One movement though and the burn would start. We tried to remain as still as possible. Following the bath, Barry, fully nude, jumped up and craned his neck to see over the wall where the girls were bathing. An odd visual, indeed! We also talked in English to the Japanese gentleman. He was from Sendai, a city halfway between Misawa and Tokyo and was visiting the *ryokan* as part of his vacation. The conversation was very friendly as is the case with almost all Japanese-English communication. They are so eager to talk and always so polite and friendly. It was time to leave the baths, wash and re-enter. One cannot stay long in the baths lest he wants to become a quivering mass of melted flesh. A few more minutes and we were on our way. The gentleman had noticed that we were wearing our robes wrong and he changed them and tied them properly with the rope in the back and tied in a bow rather than the way we were wearing them. We laughed and left. Dinner was soon to be served. It was to be the most gargantuan meal that five ever attempted to devour.

Barry and I and the girls made the long trek back up the stairs to or respective rooms. We were greeted by Joe-*san*, a man who must have thought he was staying in the room with us. He appeared at every turn. He was such a kind gentleman, though. He told us that he was once in a Dixieland Jazz band in the forties and played C&W music in the late sixties to entertain the troops on Misawa Air Base. Joe-*san* was a servant that worked in the hotel. He appeared very happy to see us. We all got the impression that he handled the Americans who came to the hotel because he spoke a little English. Joe-*san* told us that he was a bass player in his bands and he was getting so much of a kick telling us of his adventures with the G.I.s. After a while, he even brought us a tape of his band from Tokyo. It was Dixieland Jazz all right and he beamed. He enjoyed our company and despite the fact that we all had a hard time understanding him, we enjoyed his.

We all gathered in the same room, the girls decked out in their *kimono* and we, our *yukata*. It was the marriage of Western and Eastern man. We must have looked pretty silly in those robes but...enter the food. The same old lady that greeted us at the door

113

brought in our food along with Joe-*san*. She carried tray after tray into the room and each time she had to brave those stairs for the kitchen was located on the bottom floor. It took about thirty minutes to get all the food up to our room. We started off with *tempura* (shrimp batter-dipped in flour that is served with eggplant, green peppers, mushrooms and other such vegetable delights). There was also fish served with the meal, as a matter of fact it was squid, and all of it was coated with the flour and batter-dipped. That was only the beginning...Two trays were then carried in filled to the brim with vegetables and beef and even plant-like flowers. We were to cook it all in a hotplate that was in the room. Cook it all, we didn't. We could only eat one tray of the stuff. We ate and we ate and we ate and then we all rolled over and we died...The combination of the hot bath and the food had made us all very tired. I saw God in that food. It was certainly one of the most delicious meals that I had ever eaten. We were all stuffed. The girls went back to their room and Barry and I stayed in ours and listened to some mellow electronic music. He had brought along his tape deck. Barry and I discussed the foibles of the day and raved on and on about the pleasures of relaxation—Japanese style. It was night and we slept like babies...on *futon*. These are the beds that are nothing more than soft mats and thick blankets. They are stored in closets after use. Again, the simplicity of the Japanese home.

It was morning--early morning--5:45am. I rose and so did the girls but Barry stayed in his comfortable mat. He didn't want to run with us. The girls and I got into our jogging clothes and off we went. I had told them that I wasn't a runner and then proceeded to blow by them on the 2-mile cross country course that circled the hotel. It was a grueling run. Halfway up- and I mean up- and then straight down. It had rained the night before and I had feared for my life as I barreled down the trail in the dirt that was disguised as mud. I nearly killed myself as I went down that hill like a jet. Somehow, I survived and then the girls marveled at my temporary athletic skills. Terry told me that I was indeed a runner, despite my early misgivings. My problem has always been motivation. We came back to the hotel and another hot bath and then breakfast of eggs and toast. Once again, Joe-*san* was there to lend words of conversation. We all had a good time and we laughed at his stories. I am yet unsure of their validity.

It was time to leave. I hated to go and right then sadness started to set in. I didn't want to leave that place and my feelings were certainly shared by other members of the party. Joe-*san* was kind enough to take pictures of all of us, the girls posing with umbrellas in a mock-Japanese poster stance. Ann drove back and this time we stopped in Towada and had lunch. I had *yakisoba*, a meal of noodles, cabbage, pork, and vegetables, simply scrumptious. The rest of the gang had *tempura* and *miso* soup. Barry stuck with his Kirin. On the way back we all talked about the day and how we all wanted to go back someday. It was a short drive home...

Adventures in a Japanese hot bath resort.

Aomori Nebuta Festival
28 July-7 Aug 1981

I could have danced all night.

I have returned from the 1981 Nebuta Festival and I'm calling the last two days the best of my life. It may be difficult (to explain) since I'm sitting back here in my room still influenced by a combination of post-Nebuta euphoria and post-Nebuta letdown.

The Aomori Nebuta Festival marks the anniversary of the defeat of the Ainu people; finally driven off the island of Honshu. In legend, a very small group of villagers/army defeated the much superior in size foe by deceiving them with huge papier-maché warriors. When the enemy saw these structures, they believed it was the Aomori Army. The Ainu fled. It is the Nebuta Festival which celebrates this historic occasion. To celebrate, people come from surrounding counties (prefectures) to the city dressed in *kimono* and *yukata*. All ages apply. Any one can be in the celebration as I shall explain later. Besides the thousands that come from all over Japan, thousands from the city of Aomori itself take part in the parade. The events consist of thousands of people dancing down the street while huge drums play a steady beat and flutes whistle endlessly. The entire parade happens at night. Besides the wildly dancing thousands (many under the influence of *sake*), there are very colorful, twenty-five foot high floats of warriors pulled down the streets. These are awesome structures, painstakingly put together in what must have been hours of work. The procession is endless. In all, it lasts two full hours, which means a lot of Japanese can go by in that time. The entire city was there, lining the streets and clapping, in general, going berserk. Before I could say *wakarimasen* (I don't understand), I, along with several of my American mates, were pulled into the street to dance and chant with the Japanese. The dance evolved into a huge circle, everyone holding hands and turning to the left. This was accomplished by hopping about on one foot at a time. The second night I went, I practically broke my ankle in the first dance. But, I could feel no pain. I was really getting excited about this Nebuta madness. We Americans were celebrities, too, drawing wild and enthusiastic applause. I cannot ever remember so much fun. But, that was only the beginning.

The first night of Nebuta, a group of guys (5 in all) had two hours to kill before our bus went back. We somehow wound up at Snack Chariot, a cozy little bar near the main street. I broke down and had a Kirin beer, talking all the while to the Mama and a certain Mrs. Taito. She was lovely but quite married and when I asked her to dance she said she was tired and sat down. Later, I was informed that it would have been very embarrassing for her to dance with me considering her marital status. My intentions were good. So, we sipped and talked and I did dance once with another girl who was not so good looking. (what the hell?) Soon, we had to leave but not before we got some SX-70 instamatic pictures of the group. We also informed the *mamasan* that we would be back the next night. They kept a picture of us and hung in right in front for all to see.

The next night we did return before and after the parade. I got a wild idea. Since so many of the Japanese were wearing headbands, we all decided to get them and wear them too. This would really make us look like we were really enjoying the proceedings. We had to know how to tie them to avoid embarrassment so we went back to the bar and asked the *mamasan* to help us. She did, flashing her warm smile. She was the only one of the waitresses dressed in a *kimono* and it sure made her look classy. After the parade was over, we returned to our cozy little bar. I met three more girls and danced to my heart's content. In many of the bars, there are microphones with a reverb hooked up to a stereo. The Japanese love to sing and make everyone feel like a star. So I danced to the Beatles classic "Yesterday" sang by one of Charlie Flight's most inhibited people. Not any more. We all had such a good time.

This girl I was dancing with was a real sweetheart; pretty and very polite. We talked and danced and had such a wonderful evening. But, I was not through. This small little bar could only accommodate about 12 people but we made room for three more patrons who were entirely dressed in parade gear (two girls and one guy). I was bold enough to go over to their table, introduce myself, and ask to sit down. They obliged and when I asked if they had danced in the parade (I knew they did) they misunderstood and got up from their seats and started dancing right there in that crowded little bar! More smiles. A wonderful conversation ensued in both English and my aborted Japanese. I did have a dictionary handy and I used it! By this time I was so excited that I was ready to jump right through the ceiling! And all too soon, it was time to leave...

The other night I was in Aomori talking to three lovely ladies and one gentleman in a club. One of the girls, a certain Natsuko, stole my heart. A wonderful conversation ensued. Out of curiosity, I asked the gentleman why Japanese and Orientals in general are so smart. Learning their language alone makes me realize their intelligence. The man spoke no English all night but when asked this question he replied with a smile, "Because we're monkeys." Somehow, I shall never forget that. If the comment holds any significance whatsoever, it escapes me. However, Japanese have long subscribed to evolutionary theories before Darwin even existed!...

The Aomori Nebuta Festival and the dancing that went on all night.

Sapporo, by Train and Ferry
Sep 7, 1982

So, we were off! Equipped with backpacks (for clothes, etc.) we left Misawa by train bound for Aomori to take the 0:10 ferry (10 minutes after midnight) ferry to Hakodate. The station was absolutely packed with dreary Japanese. (Believe me, it took some fancy talking to get tickets...) While we were in line ready to board, one of my companions (the uncertain Kevin Hodge) was hungry and wanted to buy a snack before we left. He came back with what he thought to be a box of meat (jerky). Ah, but he couldn't read the box! I quickly deciphered *ika* as squid. They were squid crackers. But these were not flavored, they were shaped! You know as well as I do what the head of a squid looks like. We laughed. All of a sudden (with an old Japanese gentlemen staring at us and laughing), a whistle blew and this throng of people moved, should I say flew, to the ticket takers and on to the ferry. People that were dreary moments earlier, young and old, were now Olympic sprint champions. We shoved along with them and soon the ferry shoved off from Aomori. It was a sleepy ride because of the darkness. But everyone had a comfortable seat. Most of the older people stayed in the 'carpet' area, no seats, just partitioned mini-rooms for the traditional people. Somehow, four hours later, we arrived in Hokodate at 4am, not an envious time for three Americans in a strange Japanese town. As we exited the ferry we were greeted by a slight drizzle. What to do? We sat underneath a downtown overhang muttering how bad our trip had started out. Within a half-hour the drizzle had stopped and we walked to parts unknown. We saw a small dock and the rains came again. It was time to make a decision. Should we mope around and return or hope the wet weather would dissipate? We chose the latter and just a short while later the rain ceased. It was then that our adventure really started.

As a group, since we knew little of the town, we decided to walk and not stop until we found something interesting. It didn't take long. Actually, three policemen stopped and asked us for ID. And, we exchanged morning pleasantries. Continuing along, we stumbled across a curtain hanging outside a store (a symbol of an open restaurant). We went in finding a receptive owner and patron. It was a raw fish house. Squeamishly, I ordered eggs for the fish being served was sitting on the counter in front of our eyes. Eggs, it was, an egg cake wrapped in seaweed and free of charge were slivers of wild mountain ginger. I will think twice the next time that concoction is served to me. Jim Smith, not much of a food adventurer, didn't bite. My other companion did, and like me, wished he didn't. I never had a food that tasted like dishrags soaked in vinegar for six weeks. We all laughed and for a brief moment all of our carnivorous desires instantly came to mind... It was again time to ride, as it were, the general consensus being to hike to a distant mountain. What we found there! After a three- hour walk, nestled high above this charming port city of Hakodate was a veritable plethora of Christian churches. At least six or seven, and since it was Sunday, they were rather busy. We were awed. And, new churches under construction! I got the impression by the decay of the temples and shrines nearby, that Christianity had a firm hold of the southern Hokkaido village. What a stir that must have caused in the town's legislature! The entire tour with the long train and ferry rides and the rain had now been worth the trouble. I commented to my friends that if there were more interesting things to follow, I would be amazed.

We left the nestled-in-the-mountains city, boarding a train for one of Japan's most treasured cities, Sapporo. It was to be a three and one-half hour journey by train. Hokkaido is a very green place. Shortly after we left Hakodate, there were a few cities but after about 45 minutes the only thing that wasn't a forest, or rice paddy, or field was the railroad. Quite a sight, indeed! For almost all the ride... Soon we arrived in Sapporo bent on finding a hotel, finding McDonald's, and seeing some sights. All these we did in due haste. *Makudonarudozu* was especially exciting. It was located in an underground mall by the subway and I could read the entire menu! Boy, did we get stares! How did the food taste? How does the food taste in the States? Then, as we were roaming the Sapporo streets, I decided I could use a Japanese baseball cap (to make me look like a real tourist. I had wanted the Yomiuri/Tokyo Giants, somewhat of a national treasure and similar in success to the New York Yankees). Jokingly, I said to my buddies, "I wish there was a hat store so I could buy a hat" and Voila!! Two stores later a gigantic hat specialty store greeted us! I went in and snatched up a Giants cap while Jim bought a hat of his own. Kevin balked at hat buying. An amazing experience. I sure enjoyed asking the girl, "*Yakyu boshi ga arimasu ka?*" which is "Do you have baseball hats?"

We also probed the Sapporo TV tower, a mini-Eiffel located in a mini-park with the fountains and the proverbial statues of naked women and/or statesmen. Quite a pretty sight at night with street lights, etc.

Finally, it was time for sleep and we returned to our single hotel room with the thoughts that the next day we would explore more of the big city and then head back to Hokodate in the early evening. The rooms were Western and naturally curious, I probed into my dresser attempting to locate and read (ha!) Japanese religious material. I found a book on the teachings of Buddha in both languages, the Bible (not surprising) and in Japanese only, a biography of Ronald Reagan! I had no way of knowing the intent of that book (instructional or protest) but it was interesting.

We all enjoyed a restful sleep and awoke with new vigor. Somehow, breakfast was in Lotteria (fast food again). The other meals were strictly Japanese, but we had to satisfy curiosity. Armed with bulky backpacks we entered a gift shop, with a curiosity for Ainu artifacts. A bit of an aside on the Ainu. This is a people who, according to legend, were driven to Hokkaido by the Michinoku Wars, only one theory. But, the Ainu had very un-Japanese features for unknown reasons. They are hairy and still live in a primitive culture, much like the American Indian. In Hokkaido, there are supposedly a few villages where they dwell away from 20th century civilization. Gosh! This sure was a great store! Ainu wood carvings, t-shirts, postcards, etc. And we had heard of the cities the Ainu lived in and planned to visit them on the morrow, Kevin picked up a pack of postcards (100 yen, 40 cents) and bought it as we got ready to leave. The top card in the stack was a good action shot, an Ainu male in bear-skin jacket with bow and arrow poised yet...Jim noticed it first and laughingly said "Look closely at this picture!" Kevin and I stared and Jim repeated. "Look at his sleeves." Again, Kevin and I looked and I blurted out, "He's got a suit on underneath that bearskin!" What a commercialized farce! I had to respect their sense of humor and I thought that the picture was probably intentional. They probably wanted the public to think that they really were part of the Japanese culture instead of some act that made money. We were told on our return train trip that the Ainu look like Japanese and work in all facets of the society. However, they still did shows at specified times for those interested in paying and sold souvenirs all over Hokkaido. This information came from two Japanese lawyers. So much for Ainu. What a waste of time it would have been to see them...

From the gift shop we journeyed to the TV tower/Sapporo mini-park. What a nice time we had there! (Believe this: One of my dreams since I've been here is to have some Japanese girls ask to take a picture of me with them. Not for my looks. No. That wouldn't work. But, because I am a American and this would be a gesture of true friendship. International at that.) At the park, the dream was realized. About four college girls caught Jim Smith's blond hair (Why do you think I invited him?) and asked for a session. So many people in the photo yet no photographer. I asked another gentleman and he obliged. (Before we all gave him our cameras!) The photos were all made in front of the big fountain. Wow! We were all so happy. Questions of names and ages were exchanged, when the girls asked (trying so hard in English, little sweethearts, all 19) where blond Jim was from and he said California. The expression *waahh* was heard (Surprise, popular among females). We departed amid bye-byes and *kiyosukete* (Take care). It was all so pleasant.

Just a short while later we all heard an amplified male voice in all directions. It was very loud and the man seemed to be yelling. Finally, we saw the origins of that noise. Army trucks were parading around the streets with flags (no doubt related to Japan's recent military posture). It was a little frightening. Our journey continued and we spotted a small cable car and thought of visiting the Olympic village. This car would take us nowhere, merely to

122

shopping districts. The information was derived from a bevy of young females. I spotted them outside a hairdressing shop and they were politely asking people to come in for permanents. It was my big chance. I asked them in Japanese for directions to the Olympic village and got my answer in about two minutes. Most things were very hard to walk to, but buses...I spent the next 25 minutes conversing, making up stuff and wondering whether the original premise was directions or talking to cute, young ladies. One of the girls acted as spokesperson while the others stayed silent. After a while I said, "*Anata no tomodachi wa hazukashii ne!*" which meant "Your friends are shy, aren't they?" Immediately, the others brightened up and so did the scope of the conversation. My application is in for American Ambassador to Japan!

Soon, it became apparent that we must leave and we waltzed a few blocks towards the bus terminal. On the way I met a Canadian girl who was a student in Tokyo. I had to control my jealousy but was very happy for her. She was conversing rather fluently with Japanese friends. We finally made it to the bus terminal and stumbled across two tour services. We chose one with a nice three-hour tour to the Sapporo beer factory, ice-cream plant and rope-way cable car to the top of the city. It was smashing, especially the part where we had to be dragged away from the ice-cream tour guide because our bus was leaving. I now know what it's like to be in cable car with 40 hot and sweaty Japanese. I made a decision to follow two girls so we wouldn't get lost on the cable car. My friend, Jim Smith said he was going to be sick. I made gagging pantomimes and the girls could only laugh. Jim retained his sickness until the ferry back to Honshu; two hours in the bathroom for him. Anyway, the view from the mountain was beautiful. From there we spent the next day traveling back to Misawa. This time the ferry rode during the early afternoon and quite a sight it was we saw from the deck. The sights were mainly of Shimokita Peninsula, and we saw a submarine in Hakodate dock. I even recognized Wakinosawa, the quaint little fishing village. Of course, you know the old expression, there is no place like home. How true that was. It was good to be back despite the unbelievable trip.

Waiting for a cab at Misawa train station was a wino

mumbling something so slurred he probably didn't even know what he was saying. I felt sorry for him...A few minutes later I was nestled safely in my bed...

Twelve horrid days of work followed and then another break. This time I had decided to spend an entire day walking just to see how far I could go. My companion was irrepressible Thad Manning, my roommate and close friend. Armed with cameras and strong legs, we trekked the Japanese badlands. Shortly after we exited the base, we came across a kindly old lady at a country store. *Konnichi wa* "Hello," we said. She was so old and hunched back from working in the fields and she had one silver tooth, period. I had to seize upon this opportunity and asked Thad if he would agree with my plan. He did without hesitation, also impressed by the smiley lady. I asked her if we could take a picture of her with us. She quickly put her hand over her mouth and giggled. (a sign of shyness and embarrassment) Then, she began to comb her hair and asked the store shop lady how she looked. Two photos were taken. She was so delighted that she grabbed the both of us! It was all so charming. An aside: Ever since I've been here I've tried to think of myself as a goodwill ambassador. That sounds so haughty but so many G.I.'s spend their entire overseas tours making fools of themselves in the host country, for example, getting drunk, stealing, general rude behavior, total disrespect for the natives. Needless to say, I am solidly against this sort of attitude. It upsets me extremely to know that many of these nice people actually think that Americans are nothing but abrasive hellraisers. A shame...In Misawa, there is a bar that distributes markers so that the G.I.'s can go into the bathroom and write graffiti... I really think we made the old lady's day!

We continued on at least a mile and a half until we came across a coffee store. They sold unground coffee and all manner of machines including the Chemex beaker burners, that most of the fancy coffee shops here have. Believe me, coffee is an art, a science, and magical in the minds of the Japanese. As there was a cult of tea, coffee is now extremely popular. Coffee shops are everywhere. There are no city blocks without at least one, guaranteed. Ah, the furnishings in these places! Most often they are modeled after European designs. Some play jazz constantly. Some play pop or ballads. I have been to a million of these places and every one of them is immaculately clean. Most cups of coffee, whether they be Colombian, Blend, Kilimanjaro, Vienna, American about equal to $6.30 for a cup of coffee today but they are worth every penny. The atmosphere is always one of total relaxation. Studies have been made that the coffee shop in Japan is in direct contrast to the average businessman or worker. It is a perfect place to unwind. Anyway, Thad and I marveled at these machines and the memorabilia of the coffee store. Its name: Gondola. Our lady friend who explained how the beakers worked wasn't bad either. One tends to develop a coffee habit when the hostesses are so pretty...

The smell and thoughts of coffee lingered for a while until we decided to head to the beach. It was late in the season and mostly teasing, teenage couples could be found. We saw pigeons (or gulls) frolic nearby where the waves receded. In the distance we saw a house near the shore with breakers holding back the tide. As we approached we discovered it was a fishing resort with small boats and lots of hopeful people with their lines cast into the water. Young and old were fishing, so colorful were their boats and clothes. We couldn't help but notice a concrete wall that was attached to the breakers on the inside. On it was scrawled all manner of messages, love notes, and Japanese graffiti. Some of the vantage points were rather far from the shore yet the waves smashed up against them to shower the immediate vicinity. One wave, as we were standing on a perch, was so high that it showered a ton of water just in front of us and two Japanese gentlemen. I'm sure that we would have drowned or at least been blown off the edge into the water. I decided that it was time to go. After walking along the beach for a mile or so, we headed back to the base.

At my insistence, to my insistence, we stopped at a school where boys were playing baseball. They recognized my Giants hat and their game playing became much poorer. They were showing off in front of us, much to my delight. It was silly and we grinned, careful not to make fun of their game. One boy always gabbed as he hit the ball and didn't stop even when he made first base. When the next batter hit the ball "gabby" slid hard into second, capsizing another lad. I thought the second baseman would never get up. He finally did amid the taunts of "gabby." Another lad, the third baseman, had the curious habit of falling down trying to field a ground ball. At least four times the ball was hit to him and he flubbed it and tried to pick it up getting nothing but dirt in his mouth and on his uniform. I was so amused. Gabby called me "Mr. Giants" during our encounter. But, alas, even he became the butt of his teammates when he struck out just as a bunch of young girls were walking by. The kids screamed *baka* (fool) at Gabby. *Baka* is a word used by kids playfully but rarely used in public. To do so would mean to lose one's temper or "face" in public. In olden times, it would be honorable to commit suicide under the circumstances. However, that is not necessary today. Soon, it was time to depart playland and somehow we made it back to base. We later retraced our steps on a map and found that we had walked 13 miles...

The silliness and wonder of a trip to Sapporo.

The Venus
8 October 1981

In 1981, Thad Manning, Annie Holmquist, and I purchased tickets to a music concert in Hachinohe, Japan. The performers recycled 1950s-1960s American rock and roll tunes with mostly Japanese lyrics. Occasionally, English words filtered into the songs, however, their pronunciation of our language was so atrocious as to be amusing. This Japanese retro-band called themselves The Venus. Fronted by a female lead singer named Connie "Cute" Lane, all of the band members employed goofy American-sounding stage names like Nick Hopkins and Jimmy Brown. We had marveled at The Venus, having sampled their recent recordings "The Hit Parade" and "Love Potion No. 1." The latter recording jacket featured Connie Lane as a waitress peering out of a diner. Outside, the four male members of the band stared intensely through the glass, each swooning over Ms. Lane.

At 6:00pm we left the train and took a short hike through town to the hall. As we walked, Annie laughingly commented on the tickets, which depicted a cartoon illustration of The Venus cruising in an automobile. The concert was attended by hundreds-no thousands of high school girls in hoop skirts and pig tails. Leather-outfitted boys with slicked-back greasy hair complemented the girls. Motorcycle noise drowned out the giggles of the girls and I half-expected to see enormous two-toned vehicles with fins prowling nearby streets. With video cameras, balloons, and streamers being hustled into the building, we concluded that we were witnessing something akin to American Bandstand. The only person missing was Dick Clark. As Americans, we couldn't help recognizing that we were oddly out-of-place.

After the audience had settled into their seats, the house lights dimmed and a delay occurred to help the crowd anticipate the arrival of the talent. Guys and gals squirmed in their theatre-style folding chairs. Then, an English-speaking announcer appeared to introduce his mythical radio station KUPD and the band. Soon, Connie Lane appeared from behind a curtain with The Venus. She was dressed in a bright pink skirt with a ribbon in her hair. White bobby socks and pumps finished her lithe profile. Connie grabbed the microphone from its stand and screamed "1 2 3 4!" Piano, guitars and drums launched into the beat of "One Fine Day" and the frenzy began. As she sang, Connie sashayed from side to side, entrancing the crowd. The Venus were performing! My thoughts switched to Elvis, Buddy Holly, and Richie Valens. These dead rock legends weren't turning over in their graves, they were standing up and dancing to The Venus!

So infectious were the sounds that the normally-reserved Thad and I debated over joining the masses on the huge dance floor. We both were dying to see the band up close but neither of us wanted to venture first. Who knows, Thad and I might even meet some nice Japanese girls and go home with them! Right, and be eviscerated with samurai swords by their fathers! Annie demurred. I jumped up and gingerly stepped down the darkened stairs onto the dance floor. Thad followed. A feeling of reckless abandon overtook us as we bopped around amid the swirl of colorful, flashing skirts and super-combed hair. Admittedly, Thad and I were hardly a match for these rug-cutters. The guys seemed content to sweat nearly to death in their leather jackets before taking them off to reveal t-shirts. They were also adept at grinding their pointy-toed boots right into the waxed floor. The Japanese seemed reluctant to make eye contact with a couple of foreigners dressed rather inappropriately for the occasion. We spent most of the time staring at their retro-hair and designer clothes. Our bodies, almost uncontrollably, spasmodically lurched, twitched, and writhed in different directions. We were dancing, twisting, and shouting to The Venus!

A series of mind-numbing, time-warp excursions into Do-Wop and Rock followed including dead-on renditions of "Surfer Girl," "It's My Party," and "All I Have To Do Is Dream." The Venus' current smash single *Kiss wa meni shite*" or "Kiss my eye" caused wild screaming and clapping from the crowd. The music was based on a famous piano sonata by Beethoven, who unlike Mssrs. Presley and Holly, was probably rolling over in his grave. That is, if Mr. Beethoven could recognize its new, frenzied up-tempo and odd lyric "Kiss kiss fall in love." Later, the band attempted to vocalize a classic American standard. At the beginning of the song, Thad and I weren't quite sure what we were hearing. Connie and the boys were belting out "lucky lips" with thick accents.

Two sweat-drenched hours later, Thad and I staggered back to join Annie in our seats. The Venus played on into the night. We sat transfixed by the ambience of the moment yet exhausted by our non-stop dancing. Several encores later, red, white, and blue balloons floated down from the ceiling. Finally, the party was over.

Thousands of chattering bobby soxers and greasers boarded their rail cars to destinations unknown. All seemed as thrilled for the experience as we were. The sights and sounds of The Venus lingered in our heads on the way home, drowning out the incessant clickety-clack of the train.

Rocking and rolling in the Land of the Rising Sun.

I Was Karaoke When Karaoke Wasn't Cool
November 1981

In 1961, at four years old, several people in my family requested me to sing Elvis Presley's hit song "Can't Help Falling in Love." Sporting a crew-cut and short pants, I crooned *a cappella* to lyrics that I could not possibly have understood. My father's parents and uncle Ronald especially egged me on. In addition, my own parents thought my singing career to be "cute" and insisted I also entertain my mother's sisters Jeanne and Rose Marie.

Fast forward twenty years to 1981. Barbara Mandrell's signature #1 hit "I Was Country When Country Wasn't Cool"[10] ruled radio and jukeboxes. In that same year, while serving in Uncle Sam's Air Force in Japan, I learned about that country's national sport. Not golf. Not baseball. *Karaoke.*

Installed in every bar and club in The Land of the Rising Sun, a *karaoke* (pronounced "Ka Ra O Kay") system existed. Literally, the word meant "empty orchestra." Musical recordings of all types played through loudspeakers. However, the vocal tracks to these pieces remained deliberately absent. Enter audience members, or anyone else bold enough to sing. Thus, a club's nightly entertainment consisted of musical tracks and an amateur singer. After downing a few drinks, everyone sounded like a professional vocalist.

I had observed this mirthful practice in my favorite club, located in Noheji. A one-hour local train excursion was required to arrive in Noheji from Misawa Air Force Base. My roommate, Thad Manning and I ventured many times to this fishing village off-the-beaten path. We became friends with the proprietor, conversing haphazardly with him in our broken Japanese and his broken English. Shared notebook drawings and a small Japanese-English-Japanese dictionary proved essential to success. Thad and I learned about *karaoke* and its nuances while sipping on Kirin beer and

---

[10] In deference to the 1981 song by Barbara Mandell "I Was Country When Country Wasn't Cool." In that same year, I embarked on my karaoke journey, several years before the phenomenon hit the shores of America.

eating salty cuttlefish snacks. The proprietor, who referred to himself as *masutah* (master), pressed play on his cassette tape deck. As if by cue, an audience member hopped onto the small stage and began to sing. We later discovered that club patrons knew certain songs as their "own," and upon those first notes would be compelled to perform. Each new song drew applause and the clinking of glasses in toast. Everyone enjoyed themselves mightily. Thad and I could not help but notice the merriment. It didn't take long for our Japanese hosts to encourage us to try out *karaoke* for ourselves. At first, our attempts at singing must have sounded embarrassing. Thad tried some Elvis Presley. I opted for a few Beatles tunes. Thad was no Elvis. I was no Paul McCartney. But perhaps, these artists were not a good fit.

Over the next few visits, Thad and I brought in music on cassette more to our liking. *Masutah* lowered the vocal track as much as possible on his mixing board. We were in business! We practiced and practiced until we achieved a level of listenability. Sometimes, we sang a pop duet. I brought in two lively numbers from the Irish folk-rock band Horslips; "Trouble With a Capital T" and "Sword of Light." Both songs featured heavy flute and frenetic violin. Over the next few months, I sang Horslips dozens of times. When a few patrons danced to these Irish "jigs," I thought my heart would explode in joy. After a few months, Thad split off to visit his friends from another bar in town. I continued on at the same club, a fateful decision.

Although limited to a couple days a month due my work schedule, this singing business gave me much personal satisfaction. Mick Jagger could get no satisfaction, but I couldn't get enough. Singing, that is. The next logical step involved my attempt to sing in Japanese. A current favorite, receiving much notice at the time, was "Sachiko," a guitar heavy rock ballad. The pitch seemed about right for my voice. I'd heard this one numerous times at the club. One night, I asked *masutah* to play the artist version by a man performing under the name Nyc Nyusa. I listened carefully to the singer's phrasings. Why not go for it, I thought. When the crowd in the club thinned, I asked *masutah* to teach me the song. I am many things, but shy is not one of them. We sat together as I transcribed every syllable in the song in *romaji*. An hour later, he said *Dozo* (please), which meant I could go on to the stage. Like my four-old self singing "Can't Help Falling in Love," I did not know the lyrics' full meaning. I only understood that Sachiko was a girl's name. My delivery was clunky at first. But, by his request, I belted it out again and again. Feeling good, I gulped down my last beer of the night, preparing to make my way to the train station. I didn't know it at the time, but *Masutah* had other ideas.

As I put on my winter jacket, he said, "*Chotto matte, kudasai*," I knew this meant "Just a minute, please." He then asked me to accompany him to a wedding the next day. He had been catered to provide his audio equipment for the event. At first I thought, he wanted me to help haul his amp and speakers. I was wrong. *Masutah* would arrange me to sing "Sachiko" to the wedding guests, the song I was just learning! He invited me to sleep over at his house. Incredibly, without having to work the next day, I said, "Yes" to his plan.

That evening, I met his wife. His two kids were fast asleep. I was offered the top bunk in his kids' room and a pair of his pajamas. Somehow, I slept soundly, quite unaware of what the next day might bring. In the morning, his gracious wife offered a breakfast of fruit, eggs, toast, and coffee. Not wanting to appear rude, I partook. *Masutah*'s kids joined us with confused but wide-eyed smiles. Their parents explained the situation of a stranger in their midst. We soon packed his van with audio gear and were off. All five of us. At the venue, we were joined by another man, who helped set up the equipment at the venue. I could not believe the enormous size of the banquet hall, the stage, and the long tables displayed. This was an *onsen*, a traditional Japanese hot bath resort. While the audio gear was being put in place, I sat with his wife and kids at a table. Through rather hackneyed conversation, I asked her how many wedding guests were expected. She stated, to my astonishment, about 300. Really? I was scheduled to sing in a foreign language to this many people? The guests started to pour into the big hall, dressed in formal attire. The older women wore *kimono*, the men *hapi* coats. The younger crowd dressed in western formal wear, suits and ties. I must have stood out like a sore thumb.

In addition to being the only foreigner in the crowd, I was terribly underdressed for the occasion. I felt ridiculous in my blue jeans and cowboy-style shirt. My brain kept asking myself, "What on earth am I doing here?" The strangeness continued. I picked at my food and noted that corresponding to each guest under the table were large boxes, gift-wrapped. I asked *masutah*'s wife about them. She explained that those boxes were for *minasan*, everybody, gifts from the wedding couple to each guest.

As with most large events, a buzz floated through the air. Only, I could barely understand a word of it. When a gentleman stepped up to the microphone on stage, he announced the commencement of the activities. I picked up a few words here and there, "wedding" and "thank you" and "today." However, my heart fluttered a bit, when I discovered the name of the couple. Tetsuro was the groom. Sachiko was the bride. I would be crooning a ballad with its title the same name as the bride? Now, something akin to panic settled in. In short order, the entertainment began. A woman and a man sang *enka*, traditional Japanese folk music. Another seemingly recited poetry. I waited nervously for my turn, hoping beyond hope not to embarrass myself. More *enka* followed. Then, a man stepped up to the microphone and began an introduction. I could pick up "Washington, D.C." and knew all eyes would soon be on me. Six hundred eyes. "Tomu, stagie, come on!" That would be me. I lurched forward from my chair and made my way to the large stage. My mind raced. "Dear God, please…" I thought about older ladies in the audience whose sons may have perished in the war by American hands. I gripped the microphone in one hand and managed to wrap the chord around my other hand. My knees shook, but maybe it wasn't so noticeable in my jeans. With a prepared speech in Japanese, I read slowly, congratulating the couple on their special day, stating who I was and how I managed to be here on this day. The crowd applauded lightly, so they at least must have understood what I was saying. When finished, I nodded my head at the *masutah*. He pushed a button and the loud guitar wail wafted through the room. Somehow, someway, despite my being utterly petrified, I made it through the song's three verses, bowing after each of them. My rendition ended with an Indian whoop, something far bolder than for this restrained culture. As I made my final bows, the crowd applauded politely. I had survived! A string of young, gorgeous Japanese girls raced to the foot of the stage. They presented me with several envelopes and a dozen fresh roses. I quickly gathered them up and returned to my seat at the table. The *masutah*'s wife beckoned me to take them to the wedding couple. So, I walked the roses and the envelopes, filled with money, to Tetsuro and Sachiko. I couldn't help but notice their movie-star looks.

Apparently, I was the last act. After some changing of clothes by the couple, the lights were turned down in the banquet hall. The couple then emerged in western-style clothes and paraded slowly around the room to music and an announcer. A spotlight shone on them as they walked. At least twenty minutes elapsed until they departed. Upon their return, Tetsuro and Sachiko emerged in Japanese garb, conducting the same slow walk together with the spotlight, music, and announcer. A traditional wedding then commenced. A couple more hours went by, before finally, the ceremonies concluded. I assisted *masutah* and his friend in re-packing his audio equipment back into his van. He drove again with me riding shotgun. He dropped off his wife and kids back home and asked me to join him back at the club. I insisted to get back on the train and return to Misawa. However, *masutah* was not a man easy to persuade.

We returned to his club. By the time all of his gear was restored and re-set up, it was seven o'clock at night. He said he had a surprise. Without any knowledge of what he would do next, he said he had a video. "*Bideo arimasu*," he said. What? He then kerchunked a VHS tape into a player underneath a television behind the stage. The television roared into life. The entire wedding had been filmed, complete with yours truly. Aghast, I watched myself on video singing "Sachiko." My face turned beet red. *Masutah* plopped a beer and a plate of cuttlefish in front of me. After watching this, he again stated, "*Dozo, mo ichido*." It wasn't quite Casablanca, but I knew that meant, "please, one more time." Several people wandered into the club as I sang. The regulars knew me and expected this, but the proprietor explained to the first-timers that

134

we'd just completed an event at the *onsen*. I put away several more Kirins and then, to my amazement, another couple walked in. The *masutah* must planned this. Dressed to the nines, Tetsuro and Sachiko arrived. They sat on my left, she immediately next to me. The wedding couple thanked me for the song and asked several questions. After a few formalities, they insisted I sing again, live. When the electric guitar and bass opened up the music, I took the stage once more. By now, singing "Sachiko" became easy, especially to one so named.

For the next fourteen months of my assignment, "Sachiko" opened many doors. I probably sang the song at least forty more times, in Noheji, Misawa, Sendai, Hachinohe, and Aomori, to name a few. I had learned that Sachiko was one man's lament about an unrequited love. As my tour of Japan ebbed away, *masutah* invited me to the annual Cherry Blossom Festival in Noheji to sing for an outdoor gathering. Unfortunately, the timing was not right and I had to depart Japan before the event. Thanks to his generosity, *masutah* made a copy of the wedding. Today, a digital copy resides on my computer, playable for anyone who dares to watch it.

How to sing in a foreign country, in their language, and not lose your lunch.

Nama Kujira
December 1981

Call me Ishmael, too.

Years ago while serving an Air Force tour in the seaside town of Misawa, Japan, I decided to grab a couple buddies and head off base for a late night snack run. Our swing shift having ended at 11pm, four of us ventured where most American military men feared to tread. Our early morning hours would not be spent drowning our sorrows in a bar. Rather, we would seek the pleasures of Japanese sustenance.

I led the group into Kado, a restaurant that catered to bar patrons coming off a night of drinking. The life of a Japanese *salariman* involved late hours for which the company compensated by paying their workers to unwind with alcohol. This restaurant was a smallish place that featured about six stools, a countertop, a bleary-eyed *mamasan*, and little else.

Our party of four foreigners must have struck the proprietor as unusual. Nonetheless, she greeted us with a hearty Japanese welcome. As we climbed up on our high seats, we all noted the solitary patron dozing away comfortably with his face in an unidentifiable plate of food. In pidgin Japanese assisted by my trusty dictionary, I asked the *mamasan* if the patron was inebriated. She smiled politely and then responded that Mr. Sasaki was indeed *sutenko*. I surmised that he spent a good deal of his time in the restaurant in exactly this position. As I relayed the news to my three uni-lingual buddies, one of them stood up as if to leave.

"Sit down. We're just getting started." I said. "This is a night that we won't soon forget!"

The *mamasan* didn't seem to comprehend English. She soon grabbed a wet rag and tended to the business of the restaurant. I was intrigued, however. I asked my friends if they had any idea what comprised Mr. Sasaki's pillow. None of them knew and as another of my friends started to leave, I again motioned for him to sit down.

"*Sumimasen, kono sara wa nan desu ka?*" I then asked the *mamasan* to explain Mr. Sasaki's favorite dish, the one that he was currently sleeping in. She seemed a bit taken aback that I had now used a complete Japanese sentence.

Without using words, the lady placed one hand over her head and cupped it as if she were holding a pole. She then moved the hand up and down on her head while imitating a swooshing sound.

"*Nama*," the lady said. "*Nama kujira*."

I scrambled for my dictionary. I understood that "*nama*" meant raw or uncooked, having remembered the term from a drunken evening of exchanging English and Japanese tongue-twisters in a bar.

"*Nama mugi, name gome, nama tomago*," my Japanese friends insisted as I peppered them with "Sally sells seashells by the seashore."

What was *kujira*, I thought? Frantically turning the dog-eared pages of my little orange book, I finally spied the word. I thought of the *mamasan*'s funny hand gestures. She was imitating a blowhole. *Kujira* meant "whale." Mr. Sasaki had passed out in raw whale meat!

"Woah, that's Moby Dick, guys."

By now, my three so-called friends were attempting to depart en masse. I tried to reason with them by raising my voice.

"Hold on! This is history in the making, guys. The Japanese are only one of two countries in the world that still permit whaling. You'll never get another chance to do this again. You can tell your grandkids, for crying out loud!"

The lady seemed clearly upset by my untoward behavior and my soliloquy. The only way to keep my friends inside was to order the mysterious dish.

So we all stayed. In a few short minutes, the lady had retrieved about eight frozen briquettes of a rather pinkish meat and plopped them on four plates. Our collective throats let loose with nervous gulps.

This wouldn't be that difficult, actually. I had avenged those unfortunate swimmers in Amity Beach by devouring shark heads. Once in a club, an entire fish, eyeballs included, was placed in front of me, bought by a total stranger. There was no choice but to eat it all, or risk embarrassment over the giver's largess. (The eyeballs tasted like gelatin, by the way.) Octopus had stuck on the roof of my mouth, its staying power far stronger than peanut butter. And, I'd tried that most repulsive of seafood, squid, whose body part resembled a certain portion of male anatomy. The latter observation served as a sort of running joke in Japan. Actually, salty squid legs were quite good, washed down with Kirin beer. I couldn't speak for my buddies, but what was a little raw whale among friends? To not embarrass me, the GI's all took a delicate bite of their delicacy.

No one said it tasted like chicken.

Our departure was hasty. I paid the lady, said thank you, and waved *sayonara* to Mr. Sasaki. As we rushed back towards the base, two of the guys keeled over as if to vomit. Another guy shot me a dirty look, like he was about to harpoon me.

File under: you can't make this stuff up.

Tetsuko Comes to Misawa
6-8 Jan 1982

My social calendar is exploding with events. I have discovered another young lady, quite different from my nurse friend (that short-lived affair soured, I was faultless.) My new friend's name is Tetsuko, a sweet young thing with quite a desire to communicate. Unlike any other girl I've met, she is interested in speaking to me, being fascinated with America and Americans. I have yet to figure her out, though. I am still wondering whether or not her curiosity extends to my soul or I am merely a friend. Events in the past two days have only stabilized my position of doubt. Whatever the case may be however, she is still a sweetheart, easily one of the nicest and prettiest Japanese girls I've met. Tetsuko works in a French-named cake shop in Noheji called *Raguneau.* How's that for a classic love affair? American serviceman and Japanese cake-shop worker. Her cakes are sure sweet! Don't get the wrong impression. I haven't committed any sexual *faux pas* with her. Anyway, to date, we've seen each other about seven times and I invited her to see Matsuda Seiko with me. She accepted! I am blissful. Not only do I get to see the pop star of the planet but my date is a girl who is fast-developing into my girlfriend, if I may be so bold. I'm not betting, though.

Japanese people carry off these fascinating personalities. Due to social structure and deep-rooted family ties, the Japanese are very reluctant to talk about themselves. They feel they are always inferior to the person they speak with. This is also in bred into their personalities because of the "politeness disease" that permeates the country. It is quite remarkable. However, almost always a Japanese will act happy in public as it is embarrassing and impolite to do otherwise. This can lead to real problems, though. Especially for struggling foreigners like me who are ready to give their all to one of these wonderful people. I am becoming so enamored in the culture that sometimes I feel like saying "Don't come over here. You may never get back to the States." I actually believe that and fear for you. Back to stuff. The last two days were only GREAT! Only two of the better days in my life. Tetsuko and her lovely friend

Yukiko (which means Snow Child) visited me in Misawa and we subsequently made a double-date with my friend Barry. Some funny occurrences happened during this wonderful exchange. Yukiko and Tetsuko were trying to explain to me that Yukiko was also a nurse. This was understood, however, Yukiko kept pointing to her head and babbling on about sick people. My thoughts ranged from mental illness to lobotomy before I discovered that she actually worked as a brain surgeon (or at least assistant to one). Yes, actually removing tumors and stuff. Eccchhh. Then, there was the dorm incident. The three of us traveled to my quarters and immediately went to visit Barry. He was very surprised to see Tetsuko and as it turned out, quite happy to meet Yukiko also. After they left he talked about Yukiko a lot. Strangely enough, the next night I saw Tetsuko she mentioned that Yukiko liked Barry. So, on with the story...while the three of us were wandering into Barry's room to visit, Yukiko seized a pen and scrawled something all over some stranger's message board. The note was in Japanese. The next day I saw the same board with an additional note written in English. It said something to the effect of "What is this mess?" I laughed on that one...One other Japanese-American bizarreness. Tetsuko-bless her heart- knitted me a sweater, a belated Xmas present while her friend sewed the inspiration on the label MEDE IN TETSUKO. That is also funny as she meant to say MADE BY TETSUKO. However, it was an honest mistake. The Japanese post-preposition NI covers the English in, at, on, by, to, and other words.

A Japanese girlfriend?

Watering the Green
May 1982

Years ago in Japan I was coerced into signing up for an early-morning golf tournament. Though I enjoyed playing, I had learned from previous experiences to now avoid the game. I was an extraordinary liability to myself and anyone else who happened to be on the same course. Off the tee, my shots were so off-center that I made it a habit to not yell "Fore!" but warn the other golfers by screaming "FIVE!" The warning equated to the number of people, cars, or dogs that I could take out with one shot of my errant club. Sometimes, my warnings were directed at golfers on other holes. My balls spent more time in sand traps than camels. I splashed so many drives into water hazards that golf courses would routinely drain their ponds after one of my rounds. Birds would vacate their nests when they saw me striding up to the next hole. After one particularly bad tee-shot on a chip-and-putt course in Virginia, I found my ball, much like a squirrel finds an acorn, at the base of a tree. My only shot then was to blast the ball back onto the fairway. The idea was sound. My shot was not. After a hard swing, my sphere bounced off the trunk of the tree and ricocheted straight back towards my head, nearly cold-cocking me. Luckily, I managed to duck out of the way. Now, that would have been a unique obituary! Needless to say, this sort of play didn't exactly endear me to my friends who participated at a higher level. Subsequently, I was always searching for partners to play with.

The golf course, located in Misawa, Japan, bordered on the Pacific Ocean. That spring day the sky was azure and cloudless. Though it had rained the night before, temperatures hovered in the mid-sixties. Our Air Force-sponsored golf tournament would begin promptly at eight a.m. It was a best ball, closest-to-the-pin tourney, with ten teams of four men each competing. The tournament was unique in two facets. All the participants had just worked a midnight shift and there were two beer carts roaming the course.

Our team was comprised of Master Sergeant Richard Walasin, Tech Sergeant John Franklin, Senior Airman Barry Furnival, and myself. I had been persuaded to play at the last minute, despite my urging to the contrary. Chasing a little white ball around was good exercise, they said. Of the group, only TSgt. Franklin was an accomplished golfer. This was evident from the beginning when Furnival kerplunked his first tee-shot into the ocean and I followed him with a pathetic little dribbler. Walasin's effort sailed far and deep and...into a clump of trees. Franklin, however, unlike the duffer trio, drove his ball straight and true. Down the middle of the fairway went his ball, like the shots professionals make on television. We all knew then that we'd probably be using Franklin's ball for most of the morning.

Our foursome proceeded along in this manner. Furnival and I had paired up as had our sergeant teammates. Meanwhile, Furnival secured a golf cart, and sadistically enjoyed driving faster than the law allows. He'd careen a sharp left as we'd approach each tee. This invariably caused me to be thrown from the vehicle. Furnival was enjoying the fruits of the beer cart and even managed to dump himself out a few times. When I wasn't trying to straighten out my knees, I joined him in belly laughs. I'd also flagged down the beer cart driver and noticed that drinking actually improved my game. Walasin and Franklin contented themselves with quaffing their beers as they walked the fairways.

By the fourth tee, we were definitely feeling the effects of the alcohol. All except Franklin. Tsgt. Franklin again confidently drove his ball down the middle of the fairway. He then strolled along easily with his partner. With our rocket-powered golf cart, Furnival and I had reached the green much sooner than the sergeants. We waited while Walasin and Franklin putted out.

On the par-four fifth hole, Furnival again was kind enough to dump me out at the tee. Our team received a bit of a surprise when MSgt. Walasin outdrove Franklin for the best shot in the group. Extremely excited about his improving play, Walasin raced ahead of us and responded again by blasting his approach shot just off the lip of the green. Franklin, Furnival, and I watched puzzled as Walasin ran forward. He was fairly jumping with glee, like some kid at Christmas. Walasin seemed intent on shooting par all by himself. The rules of the best ball tournament had long since been defied, especially with a beer cart cavorting about the premises. As

Walasin set his feet for his baby chip shot, we strode up toward the green. We were still about one hundred yards away from our comrade when we noticed that Walasin had backed away. Though it was difficult to see, Walasin was relieving himself right there in front of God and everybody. He couldn't wait to get to the clubhouse. Unfortunately, where Walasin was standing was quite slippery and on the cusp of a hill. As we walked towards the green and joked about Walasin, we watched in horror as our Master Sergeant disappeared from view. He had apparently lost his balance and had fallen down the small hill. What we all did see, however, was a chaotic spray, like some untamed garden hose flailing in every direction.

Soon, we were to rescue our partner. When we reached Walasin, he was laying on the grass, wetter than a newborn baby. A crumpled, smelly mess, Walasin cursed the golf course, the tournament, and the very idea of a beer cart. However, in no time at all, he sprang to his feet. His clothes were sopping wet, but he righted himself, ever determined to make that elusive par. He smiled at us and then addressed his ball. Walasin's shot plopped onto the green and then rolled straight into the cup. It was the hardest-earned birdie anyone of us could ever remember.

A most dangerous game.

Final Train Excursion to Morioka and Sendai
13 February 1983

I am a bundle of energy, nerves, and joy. Soon comes the time of the great departure. The movers will be here in a couple of weeks and I am beginning to out-process on the base and say my final goodbyes to Japan - at least for a while. It has been wonderful, absolutely incredible and I plan to go out with a bang as I've mentioned before. Strangely enough, my entire tour has been spent in contemplation of what others would have thought had they been here. I don't know if they would have experienced the same joy and felt the same way about these people as I have. Many times I wanted to be a tour guide and show them the Japan that I know. But, alas, fate did not have it that way. I knew relatively nothing of the land when I came and know relatively little now, despite all the knowledge gained. Japan is brimming with mysteries and ways that Westerners can never hope to even imagine. But, despite all this, I feel as if I have gained from the experience of a lifetime. I am a bit older and believe that my life patterns have become ever so slightly Japanese.   That is, no longer have a harsh temper or readily condemn things I don't understand. Japan has taught me this. But you really deserve to be here. Everybody does, so that they can learn...

Now a word on eggs and parkas. A couple of days ago I went downtown with my good friend Mr. Manning to go coffee shopping - the zen art of total relaxation, coffee drinking and magazine reading in the unique atmosphere of a Japanese coffeeshop. I had bought a parka every year for the last two so why should this winter be any different? I spied a very nicely priced one before going upstairs to the shoppe so I bought it. It was *Makeru Hi* or sale day all over town. I really was getting a great bargain and as I handed the very cute girl cashier a ¥10,000 note ($42) she said "*chotto matte*" (just a minute) and ran off, I assumed, to get change. Wrong! She came back with a dozen eggs and stuffed them along with my parka, in a bag. Then, with the manager at her side, she asked both Thad and I if we liked to cook. We nodded yes and off she went again for a dozen more eggs, these for Mr. Manning.

144

I just had to laugh. We have no provisions for cooking in the dormitory. But that wasn't all. The manager brought over his calculator, whipped out some figures, and proceeded to hand me a pile of coupons. I just went in for a jacket, for Pete's sake! They bade us farewell so I needed some coffee to settle me down. After all, when was the last time you bought a jacket and the bag was fragile?

The next day I took a train ride to Morioka, a city south of Misawa known for its ancient Samurai ties. I boarded a train armed with a couple of changes of clothes, my mini-Sanyo cassette, lots of money *okane*, and a penchant for sightseeing. My original plans were to stay in Morioka one day and then travel south to the huge metropolis of Sendai. My local train was typical of my local train rides thus far (bunches of chattering schoolkids, the rickety ride I was accustomed to, packages of snack food scattered about and people with their *obento* lunches (*obento* is a collection of food packed in a thin wooden box usually reserved and associated with rail travel.) I was looking forward to my journey despite the fact that I was alone, but I knew I would find some good conversation later. The scenery was marvelous, so like the Japan I knew and loved. There were the endless packed-ever-so-tightly houses, old men and women walking the streets, playful youth going to and from school, and rice fields everywhere. Did I mention the nooks and crannies?

Four hours and a couple of Japanese music tapes later, I arrived at Morioka station. A grand structure, it also houses a shopping center on the basement and lower level and the *shinkansen* or bullet train on the top level. After a brief stroll through the mall gagging at the wares (and the girls), I went off looking for a hotel. It was 2pm. I decided to check down a few side streets for something more affordable and came across the *Won Won Hoteru*. I read the sign and was so proud of myself I went upstairs to the apparent location. No! This was someone's house so I decided not to knock. I went downstairs to a pet-shop that was apparently co-located with the hotel. I asked "*Won Won Hoteru Wa doko desu ka*?" Somewhat surprised, a gentlemen behind the counter answered in the affirmative. I began to feel a little embarrassed. The was a

145

lady nearby petting a cat and watching the proceedings. Then, like a bolt of lightning, it hit me. A long time ago in a wild night in Noheji, a bunch of Japanese people, Thad and I exchanged a game of animal sounds. In America cats "meow" but in Japan they "*neow*." Guess what dogs do? *WON WON!* To hide my embarrassment, I laughed and walked sheepishly out the door.

Soon afterward, I chanced upon an unusual meal in the same building. My food was normal enough (*katsu don*-pork cutlet with rice and eggs, seaweed soup, vegetables, green tea) but a couple within eyesight was gobbling up something very foreign to me. While a lady stood over them pouring an unidentified food into their bowls, they ate with an incredible vigor. Imagine the scene... Two young people wearing aprons that had some Japanese writing on it holding expensive lacquerware in front of them while another person dumped bowl after bowl of vegetables, meat, soba noodles, etc. into their bowls. It was timed like clockwork. The hostess had about 30 of these bowls in a tray in which to work with. I was quite astounded by the whole affair.

Filled to my stomach with my meal and filled to my eyes with the eating contest/ritual I decided to put my things in my hotel room (I had just acquired one) and wander around downtown Morioka. Last year I was there with a friend and we both wanted to see the park but never did. So this time I made it a point to see the park. After a sleepover in town, I walked there the next day and spent the better part of two hours in the almost empty park. It was a very cold day but most of the snow was gone from the city. Once inside the park, I saw a shrine, some birds, flowers, plants, and monuments. It was an exciting day despite the cold and desolation. I completed an entire round trip of the park and continued walking around until my afternoon train. I was bound for Sendai.

Once again the rickety rickety of the Japanese train system greeted me for the long ride to Sendai. At an unknown stop along the way I was greeted by some Japanese schoolkids across the tracks. I knew of only one way to communicate with them so I wrote down ROCK AND ROLL (in Japanese) and pressed it up against the window. They laughed and came over the bridge of the station so that we could communicate further. When they arrived I said, "Where are you going?" But, they replied with a hand gesture towards their ears. They couldn't hear one word I said. They were deaf. So, even the irony of my communication.

Sendai was amazing, too. However, I arrived at 6:30pm and had no hotel reservations. After asking a few questions a gentleman got me a room. That night I went to a bar near the station (I thought Morioka was big but this city was huge!) called Abbey Road. I enjoyed pleasant if not scattered conversation with a couple of gentlemen, one of whom was an architect whose company designed city hall in Misawa and many on base, he hesitated not to tell me about Buddhism being such an enlightening experience. I also got to speak briefly with Takako, the very pretty hostess, but by the time I left it was over $14! Then I wandered off to an all-night restaurant for *soba* and finally made it back to my hotel at 3am. It was really impossible to see Sendai though. This was really a huge metropolis and I felt really strange in such a big Japanese town. I did walk around long enough to see the computer buildings like NEC, Hitachi, and Fujitsu and notice some real hustle and bustle. It was here that I ran into my two record store friends and was helped onto the bullet train.

After returning to Misawa for two days, I was part of a bus tour to Hirosaki for the snow festival. Every winter Japanese towns hold these festivals to celebrate, what else? SNOW! The grandest in all the world is held in Sapporo where gigantic statues are carved out of snow and ice and displayed in the town's main area. This year, I tried very hard to make it but I ran into obstacle after obstacle. However, the main recreation center on base sponsored a bus trip to the Hirosaki *Yuki Matsuri*. This is a fair-sized town northwest that is the scene annually of the Cherry Blossom Festival. This time the park was the scene of a heavy snowfall, some very excited youngsters, sleighrides, cotton candy, and ice sculptures. We saw samurai warriors, Doraemon (cartoon cat), Cinderella's castle, slides made of ice for the kids, and lots of booths for food and drink. I had a wonderful time, camera-in-action, and just seeing those kids and the snow was a thrill. I know you'd have enjoyed it. Some of the Americans I met on the bus were pastry freaks and they took me downtown on a sweet tooth run. We were not disappointed.

147

A pastry shoppe we went into had every pastry known to man (and dentist!). On the bus ride back, we savored every morsel.

Today was most interesting. Despite the fact that I had no sweetheart, I still managed to buy a cake for a very special lady with the inscription "*Hapi Barentainzu Dai Tado to Tomu Yori*" (Happy Valentine's day from Thad and Tom).

We bought a cake in a cake shoppe and had a personalized message inscribed and presented to Kyoko-*san* in Noheji. She was very excited and it turned out to be a not so lonely day after all. Kyoko invited over our Noheji friends, Eiko and Seiko, the cute sisters. I like Eiko, as a friend, and often see her in Noheji. She makes the funniest faces; sometimes I can't help from laughing. Thad likes Seiko for reasons I can't explain though he says she always gives him the eye. It was a wild night. All of us ate the cake and made paper airplanes and flew them right in the bar. We all acted very silly. Imagine going to a place where women are summoned for you to help you enjoy this sort of madness!

After all I had read about the Japanese social structure about men and women; I have now experienced it firsthand. The experience shall remain entrenched in my mind. I'm sure you've heard about the long-time subservient nature of the Japanese female. This is what I observed: After returning to the ROCK WEST jeans shop (parka) to look around I got to talking with the manager about all sorts of subjects including the Washington Redskins, why Japanese-English is so bad on shirts and computers.

Thad then walked into the store and soon the both of us were invited to Towada city for spaghetti. We met the gentleman, Mr. Ogawa at the main gate and the invitation began with dinner at his house. We met his wife Keiko who served us fish, a carrot vegetable dish, tofu, potato soup, and tea. Ogawa talked of the worldwide tea connection; British, Chinese and Japanese. His explanation was quite fascinating. He explained how the Chinese use tea as medicine to help the body rid itself of impurities in food. Amazingly, Thad and I understood just enough of the 'gist'. He also spoke of the old things in Japan while a samurai show played on the TV. We sat on *tatami* mats in the small living room. Keiko said nothing as she was supposed to. Only when asked did she speak adding nothing to our conversation but a smile. She served the food, ate quickly, and then washed the dishes. (Everything that I had read about between men and women in the home and socially says that when the man and his friends gather the woman does not interrupt or even join in the merriment.) Soon afterward, we left for the spaghetti house (Ogawa insisted that it was a Japanese spaghetti house with over 50 kinds) with Ogawa-*san's* wife. She came in with us, sat down, and promptly picked up a magazine to get out of the way of our business. So, I had seen the drama played out and I felt saddened for this particular aspect of the people. Yet, to see these females display their graceful charm, when serving a simple cup of coffee or tea, made me long for living in this old, Japanese tradition. Hence, I am torn between two cultures in this aspect. It must be seen to be believed.

How I very nearly laid down with dogs and other adventures.

Fast Eddie:
A Special Interview with Ed Erkinger

Who is that man that lurks suspiciously behind the SMSS desk? Is it Humphrey Bogart? Is it Edward G. Robinson? No! He's not a criminal (or an actor) after all. He's Charlie Flight's own Ed Erkinger.

After a brief bit of reluctance, TSgt. Erkinger was more than happy to tell me about some of his experiences in Misawa. When first asked to reminisce on the years he replied, "Hell, I'd have to think back on that sucker."

TSgt. Erkinger is currently serving his fourth tour here. The first one started way back in 1960 before some of you reading this were born. (Not you, Cecil!) He's says he's spent 14 or 15 years in this quaint northern Japanese town.

Who else remembers the 6989th Radio Squadron Mobile? Who else remembers when the operations center was in the BX building? "Fast Eddie" Erkinger remembers.

Imagine this typical day watch years ago in TSgt. Erkinger's heyday. I was told so much information that I decided to reconstruct a day in the life of a Misawa airman years ago...

You are a struggling Airman First Class on your first tour in the Far East. It's 0430 on a cold and snowy wintry morning. You awake to a bloody alarm clock as your roommate complains of the time that you set. He wanted to wake up at 0500 to make the six to three day watch. So, you put on your robe and go into the showers, freezing to death because the hot water is slow to work. Disaster #2. As you get back to your room, you are just in time to see the Sergeant giving his periodic bed check. He determines that your sleepy roommate is not female and leaves.

You put on your clothes, chiding your roommate to get up, and telling him that you are not responsible if he gets to work late. He groans and buries his head in the pillow.

The chow hall is hardly consolation for the events of the day. You eat your eggs like a robot before hurrying off into the blizzard. The snow is really coming down. A thought crosses your weary brain, "Am I sure this isn't Alaska?"

Work is horrible. The same old stuff. Your supervisor tells you how worthless you are and the day drags on. At two p.m., everyone in the "gig" is informed of the severity of the storm. They are told they must work indefinitely. The shift continues. All you want to do is to get off work and grab a cold beer before going to bed. It is the only way you know to survive the whining of your roommate. Now, you are stuck at work. The Security Service can be cruel. Your mind starts to doze off. In your daydream, you write a letter home telling your mom how horrible Misawa is. You start to mumble aloud, "Mom, it's so bad here!" It is your supervisor who awakens you from your semiconscious state. A brief period of screaming follows. It all comes from one mouth and it isn't yours. What a day! You pray for the comforts of your room.

Hours later (or is it days?), the shift ends. You get back to your room before realizing that you just worked a 24-hr. shift. In the meantime, provisions have been made. The flight on break is called in to work your day watch so you don't have a thirty-three hour day. The Air Force is watching over you.

Wearily, you drag your body into bed, forgetting to shed your uniform. It is 0615 and there is a banging on the door. A Sergeant steps in to make another bed check. AAUUUGGH! Girls are the last thing on your mind. The sergeant reminds you that it is payday. You are to report to the Fire Dept. at 0700 to get your money for the month. Once again, you don your parka. Waiting in a blizzard after a 24-hour shift to get paid isn't exactly your idea of a good time.

A Sergeant calls your name, but you are slow to recognize. Your brain has deadened. Finally, you remember who you are. You stumble, walking into the Sergeant, falling face down in the snow. It is the ultimate human indignity; being embarrassed in public.

Years later, you relate this story to your friends and you can laugh at it all.

Isn't that how it was, Ed?

A brief fantasy based on an Air Force lifer. Originally appeared in Charlie's Midnight Express.

Let's Reading
(an explanation)

The romanization of Japanese characters is somewhat different as their sounds do not exactly match ours. However, this is the best guide to use:

A..as in father (AH)
I..as in female (EEE)
U..as in new (OOH)
E..as in pay (EH)
O..as in bone (OH)

I'm sure that all of you have been downtown and have noticed bizarre English (*eigo*) signs that are made by Japanese (*Nihonjin*). Have you ever wondered why there are shirts that say "Let's Swimming" or "Let's Eating?" (just two examples) Very strange *Eigo*. Isn't it (*Ne*)? Why (*naze*) is this? *Nihonjin* must study (*benkyoo*) our language for six years prior to college. Certainly, we as Americans (*Amerikajin*) don't slave for six years learning the Japanese language (*Nihongo*). Yet, despite all this *benjo*, uh *benkyoo*, the misunderstanding continues. *Nihongo-Eigo* high school books (*hon*) are filled with vocabulary words (*kotoba*) that our kids wouldn't know. Lessons are a bit undecipherable, too. So then, why does a phrase like "Let's Reading" surface? Let's (my favorite word) examine the facts. (Gee, I always sound like a scholar when I talk of examining and facts in the same sentence!)

In *Nihongo* sentence structure, the verb is always placed last. Of course, *Eigo* uses the subject/verb/object.

He hit the ball.
subj/verb/object

Simple. *Ne*? *Eigo* progresses in a logical pattern. (Then again, who told you that Japanese has to be logical?) The subject, most often a person, place, or thing, comes first followed by a verb. The verb can serve two purposes. It can be an "action word!" like something out of a Poccari Sweat commercial or it can be a passive verb. A passive verb is. Often, an object will be employed & a prepositional phrase or two. (Isn't that when he gives her the ring?) There's a lot more, but...I'm no *Eigo* teacher (*sensei*) and I'm boring you to death.

In *Nihongo*, as in *Eigo*, there are different verb forms to indicate tense. The *Nihongo kotoba* for eat is *taberu*. Drink is *nomu* and sit is *suwaru*. Conjugations appear with the verb themselves. If you wanted to say "Please Eat" then *tabete kudasai* would be the proper conjugation of *taberu*. *Kudasai* is the almost always used politeness imperative. On the other hand, *ikimashoo* would mean "let's go;" *iku* being the verb "to go" and *mashoo* a rough translation for "let's." *Mashoo* is the conjugation dependant on the verb *iku*. *Tabemashoo* is "let's eat" and *nomimashoo* would be...gurgle...gurgle..gurgle. Since *Nihonjin* are so interested in their leisure time, a.k.a. sports, etc., these phrases invariably find their way onto t-shirts and posters. "Let's ..." is only a result of *Nihongo* and incorrect *Eigo* verb conjugations. Someone has even come up with the term "Japlish" for all this mess.

Perhaps, this piece can be used as a warning. To call this anything but a genuine epidemic in *Nihon* is a lie. If the disease is caught by Americans, it could hinder communications, especially in the States. Imagine calling your friend (*tomodachi*) and saying over the phone, "Let's partying!" He's liable to think you've lost complete control of your *sensei* (an atrocious pun, forgive me.)

Hope this explains it. Now, as you look down at the pool of blood (*chi*) and slowly close your eyes (*me*)..... "Let's bleeding....." zzzzzz...

Explaining Japlish for the uninitiated. Originally appeared in Charlie's Midnight Express.

Angelos City
9 November 1982

The weather here is sweltering. Every day it is 90 degrees plus, the hottest temperatures I've been exposed to in some time. There are so many of those tropical trees and coconuts and Filipinos. These folks have very dark skin (no doubt due to the relentless heat) and black hair that seems to be baked on. They have similar builds to Japanese.

I arrive at the base to convert money into *piso*. The rate is about 8.2 to one US dollar. A lady hands me bills equaling about $30 with centavos coins. Since 1 *piso* is about 13 cents, these *centavos* are relatively worthless. I am handed a 5 *centavos* piece worth about 1/20 of 13 cents. The coin is octagonal. So much for tropical money.

The journey begins. I hail a base cab and he drives me $1.50 worth to Friendship Gate. It is a fast ride of about 50 MPH, a testament to the size of the base. A similar ride on Misawa Air Base would have pocketed the driver $6.00. In the heat, I am almost dying. I walk out the gate. I have been warned of the black market and street sellers. I give them several stern "no" messages. Hats, t-shirts, a shoe-shine (I am wearing leather. In Mexico I was wearing tennis shoes and approached by children who begged, even for a nickel) wooden carved items, paintings, etc. These people would try to sell you houses on the streets if they could carry them! Also present were three very strange transportation methods. There were jeepneys; nothing more than a jeep taxi. I was warned not to ask for the "special" ride. It was the same as the regular ride but more *piso* and you drive! Motorcycle sidecars were also present. But the strangest of all was the gaudy circus cars. These were jeeps with colorful designs on the side and loaded with riders in the back. I got the impression that these cars were really a status symbol. Family names were always painted on the back like "Santos Family." They were not for hire but the main thing to do was ride in these cars up and down the street to impress. What a way to spend a day! And to top it off, Angelos City roads were only about 4 or 5 blocks long and only three arteries at that! I had heard reports of $3.00 record stores so I decided to check. It was so. All new, all apparently not bootleg or excellent imitation, all made on Filipino pressings. These records were then baked in the sun! I didn't buy any. There were so many things to do yet it was so stifling hot. However, the Stanley Livingstone inside me escaped and I trudged on through the dust, forever greeted by honking jeepneys, and rot-teeth men saying, "I met you on the base, remember?" Another selling gimmick. I saw a two-man traveling band (drums and guitar). One gentleman sported only one leg and they were so old. I didn't bite. In a side street I heard a very loud "BAAA" and sure enough, around the corner, was a goat. The animal was tied but no owner was in sight. Probably because if the goat got loose in all those stores that sell hats...well...so much for Angelos City's economic fortunes.

Then I came across "Fantasy Island." What was it? There was no Mr. Rourke or Tatoo but it appeared to be a bamboo shack complete with garden. I had to investigate. Indeed, it was a fantasy, a wooden, open air restaurant. I could not help but stare as I wandered in. A man in a straw hat was cutting grass to ground level and a lady invited me to sit down. "San Miguel, please," I said and a tempting cold one was served & I savored every drop. All the while I was enjoying the interior design and the pretty hostesses. I was then handed a menu of highly versatile foods: king crab, steak filet, fried shrimp, etc. We struck up a conversation. I said I planned on returning in the nighttime. Until then, my entire impression of Angelos City had been one of uneasiness. I had been roaming the streets for nearly two hours but was rather perturbed at all the hawkers. "Fantasy Island" changed all that and I was beginning to feel better. As I departed I apologized for knowing only one Filipino word *magando*, using it to describe the hostess and the place. I even mispronounced it. It meant "beautiful."

I walked into a few more furniture stores and looked. Rattan, wood carvings, trinkets, etc., cheap or barter method. But after a while I was bored by all the "*papasan*" chairs (weaved bamboo) and I had to leave. I made a beeline for the Kobe steak House/Monkey Bar. A nurse had told me that there was a place that featured live monkeys as you ate and drank. I have not seen anything like it before or since. Behind the counter of the bar was a glass encasing that stretched about 30 feet. Enclosed with ample space were four rhesus monkeys. I ordered a coke and sat down to watch. The place was clean also. It was totally fascinating. Papa was checking baby for body lice while another peered on so attentively. I'm serious when I say he looked like a child at his first baseball game; eyes full of wonder. Momma monkey was so busy climbing about and eating that she had no time for this. Originally, I thought Papa was a Momma. They were all crouched so low on the perch that nothing was exposed. Then when Momma stood up and tugged on it for a second, I knew it was a Papa. Fortunately, I was the sole person besides the hostess in the place so I felt much more at home than in a crowded place with so much shouting. Undoubtedly there were have been some unkind words said about my four friends. I might have had to ask these beer-drinking, whiskey slinging buddies just exactly what are monkeys?...

First impressions of Angelos City, Philippines including the famous Monkey Bar.

Somewhere in the Philippines
November 1982

This Saturday I completed something that is akin to a safari. I decided to try one of the base tours, a $3 excursion to Pagnansan Falls. Somehow, my weary body dragged out of bed to make the 5:45 bus. It was to be a long ride but no one would really ever say. Two hours into the journey, we stopped at an American/Filipino WWII cemetery. (surely to warm our spirits) It reminded me of Arlington; the fields long and the graves laid out so straight and so precise. Naturally, there were war inscriptions everywhere and all so depressing and commercial. The only thing that things like that ever do for me is make me wonder why... there is war. But, it never stops and sometimes I think that the war moguls are proud of war so they can have a few more of these monuments. They are always well-planned whereas the beginnings of conflicts aren't. In all, there were over 17,000 young men that ultimately stayed young.

The tour pressed on. I was amazed at the highways. These were super-roads just like the ones in the States, complete with those familiar green day glow signs. (I hadn't seen one of those in almost 2 1/2 years.) Our bus didn't waste any time either, zipping along at speeds that I hadn't traveled in that long either. It was an instant trip back into the land I love and I was right here in the Philippines. Our tour guide was a Philippine gentleman who spoke not a word of intelligible English) Under the microphone, I understood about two of every ten words that he said. Perhaps he was telling us Philippine history as we passed through the towns but I'll never know. We stopped for *Po-Po* Pie (concoction of some wild fruit) and coconut wine (his joke was "It is said around the world that Mexican *tequila* has the kick of a mule, well, coconut wine has the kick of a water buffalo." Of course, I didn't partake. We also stopped at several roadside places that sold fruit, paintings, vegetables, all manner of cakes, pies, wood carvings, hats, shirts, ties, drums, guitars, pipes, and tobacco. A lot of items were sold by small girls with the saddest faces and eyes that you'd ever want to see. Somehow, I held fast and did not buy anything but I'll never forget those little girls.

Finally, we stopped at our final destination, the Pagnansan Falls Hotel. (3 1/2 hours later) We were to ride the rapids and see the falls. The hotel was nice enough, dining room, bar, restaurant, dining in "elegant splendor", etc. Our thirty-person party strutted in to buy our tickets for the boat ride and then we were free to do what we wanted for 4 1/2 hours. I must say that within the hotel I saw things that I hadn't seen before. Besides the normal entourage of beautiful ladies, there were so many others talking English, Bloody English! The place was loaded with Australians! I made it a point to accost several of them and marvel at their accent. Certainly, they must have thought me mad! With a friend, I purchased my ticket and left for the ride. (Aussies and Filipinos watching boxing on the telly didn't impress me). We walked down a set of stairs and were immediately greeted to cries of "cushions, only two *pisos* to keep you comfortable, sir" and life vests for five *pisos*. (Goodness, these people wanted you to get in a boat ride and then pay for your own safety!) I said no to all accounts and proceeded on. Somehow, my friend and I became very skeptical. I don't know why. It was only the dirtiest water that I have ever seen and our ride was to be in a four-man canoe (two drivers front and back). I was beginning to have second thoughts before I even went into the boat. Now, I get it. First, they whisk you into a hotel to buy the tickets to a boat ride before you ever see the boat, then try to sell you cushions for comfort and life jackets for safety. No wonder we weren't allowed to see the boats first! My only experience with canoes was nature shows about American Indians who must ride the boat almost flawlessly to stay afloat and show about rapids riding where it pays to learn when to tip over to avoid dangerous rocks! So, here I was, Filipino Nature Boy! NO lessons even! Both my friend and I almost tipped the boat just getting in and then had to sit face ahead and close to each other. Since he had more weight than I, we sat further back. The boatmen looked like Amazonians, for Pete's sake, some of the strongest arm and leg muscles that I have ever seen. You know, guys that could swim the English Channel and not even be winded. So, we started out with a serious disadvantage.

With quick instincts, I searched my surroundings. One the

other side of the small lake I saw a lady beating up her clothes with a piece of flat wood. I knew that she might be a threat so I kept a close eye on her. (The peasants lived alongside the river in wooden huts and washed their clothes in the murky water). Further down a group of small boys were swimming about naked in the water. (Actually, the boys were playing games like tough kid, touch the snake, and murk jerk). The canoe slowly rode away. Our boatmen first used paddles and then joined up with a group of about fifteen others attached to a small boat motor boat to take us a distance of the ride. Occasionally, a real fast gas-propelled vehicle would come by and the waves would nearly capsize our canoe. I guess the hotel didn't buy the whole river. The scenery was harsh, though. On both sides of the small waterway (100 yards across) were the villagers; all living in wooden shacks their parents and grandfathers probably built. It was a sad sight; pretty young girls doing chores, boys helping with the washing and the handiwork with father. An occasional water buffalo/*caballero* dipped into the water to stay cool. Dogs ran about aimlessly for the children to play with. Most of the houses on the banks of the river had boats that looked as old as their years. The vessels were equipped with fishing lines to catch a good portion of the villager's meals. It was a life without luxury, a life full of worry and survival into the next day. I couldn't help but notice these people; some of them must have spent whole days just watching the boat rides and riders. We were greeted with both indifference and waving arms. The slow ride wound into a series of ever-increasing shoreline and then the houses and the people began to disappear as if they weren't ever there at all. The banks of the river rode up and up, weeds changing into small trees, small trees changing into tall trees and monumental coconut vegetation. There was an occasional cliff with the trees that grew near rising higher than the eye could see. Every once in a while another canoe would go by in the opposite direction with personage that were Oriental but not Japanese. The guide informed me later that there was a Chinese, Australian, and Japanese entourage. I was amazed. Then, boat after boat, a pair of non-shirted Japanese gentlemen came by. I recognized them immediately by their unmistakable looks and one person's headband so I had to say hello. They said they were from Himeji, a city that houses one of Japan's most famous treasures, Himeji castle. Our small boat wound through the river. Finally, the long bus ride was worth it after all. This place was a godsend, a paradise the likes of which I had never seen. All was serene and tranquil. It was like had stopped and time had been sent back. The were no sounds at all, save for the whispers of the paddles through the water. We asked the boatman a few questions but after a while realized that it was futile to speak. The silence and the view were so awesome. We started going through the rapids, through because the riders literally carried us up through the upstream waters. These boatmen were sly. They stepped on rocks as if in some sort of choreography. Never was there a missed footfall or slip of the craft. However, water started seeping in the boat and we sat in a very nice slosh for the rest of the journey. (We all brought along a change of clothes for the ride.) Fourteen rapids we passed in- between the lazy stream ride; fourteen rapids the riders carried us over! Our scenery became muted to these eyes. I had seen the magnificence for all of an hour and I almost went into a dream because of it; so incredible was the beauty. Now it was time for the infamous raft ride, a journey inside a cave with a powerful waterfall closing on you. Luckily, that was another price and not included in the tour so I declined not to risk heart failure. We rested a few minutes as the small craft docked to watch the bravest of the brave and walk a tad. Backwards, or down the rapids as they say in show business, was a much faster trip. The water whisked us right through until we caught the motorboat and sped back. I was in awe; the trip had taken two and one-half hours. It was some of the best time that I had ever spent.

Getting out of the boat was a trip also. Oh, before I get out let me tell you about some of the passengers in the other boats. There were some gorgeous (*kawaii*) Japanese girls, some with dates. A few guys also floated by but I was amazed at the stately Chinese. They had a look of peacefulness about them; some of the older ladies had these hats that they wore making them look so prim. The Aussies had the look of anger on their faces; some went by having probably consumed a few too many San Miguel beers. A few of the younger Chinese almost made me want to jump out of my craft and swim over to meet them. So, we got out, again. I tipped the two boatmen, being so impressed with their hospitality and strength. Even got a picture of those two wonderful gentlemen. As we walked back upstairs to the hotel, we were greeted by most of the vendors selling canoe replicas, what else? As I entered the hotel, a very pretty girl handed me a photograph and said that it just fifteen pesos ($1.60). I couldn't believe it. Here was a picture of me and my friend taken in the boat! Color and everything! I couldn't resist so I bought one.

There was a wait of about an hour before the bus came. What to do? I went into the souvenir shop (did you think there wasn't one) and looked at the stuff so many gullible people will buy. I left. Outside, our tour group was greeted to a coconut demonstration. A young lad climbed a tree barefooted, procured some of the islands most famous fruit, and scampered back down. He then offered the fruit to all. Another gentleman cut the unclean fruit and we were off, drinking the inside and eating the soft "meat" as our guide put it. It was a different taste of coconuts I 'd ever eaten before and the water tasted less tangy. These were young coconuts, not the fibrous kind that are exported from here. So, since I paid for the tour, I decided to go whole hog on coconut. Coconuter or coconuttier I became? We'll just say that I drank a lot of juice. It was so much more natural with bugs in the cup! Our return trip produced more stops and a visit to McDonald's in Manila, the city that made the P.I. what it is today. It was the most crowded place that I had ever been to, and that includes Tokyo, Washington, D.C., my stopover in Mexico, Sapporo, New York, you name it. In Manila the traffic moves in waves, it doesn't bother to stop at stoplights, doesn't use turn signals, and never beeps its horn. In Manila the traffic is pedestrians. Automobiles that are stupid enough to go through, in, or around the place are not really interested in commuting. Gas vehicles stand still, such is the snarl. Believe me, I know. I was in a bus in all this madness. We were in the city just about an hour and a half just outside the ramp leading to freedom. As for the fast-food restaurant, I was quite pleased. The place was jammed. There were about four people ahead of me and it took all of two minutes.   After my order, a guy screamed above the din, "21.50." Instantly, my heart sank as I handed over the money. Before I could calculate about $2.33 of GI money, he handed back my change of 3.50 *piso*. The food was eaten on the bus, as tasty as McDonald's food ever was. It was only a few minutes before I had gotten the idea to give away something. To the side of the bus was a metal wall with kids looking out at our bus. Those sad, pitiful faces of the young girls I had seen of the roadside were haunting me, so I gave the kids my french fries. It certainly didn't atone for my guilt in not buying an item that was only a quarter (and worth a lot more in love) but it made me feel better.

As darkness approached, all of the weary riders were finally glad to be home. I asked the guide for a whole coconut and he obliged. They were gathered and placed in the back of the bus for all. I thanked our wonderful tour guide and patient bus driver. It was time for bed.

An all-day tour by bus and boat in the Philippines.

My Life as a Rocker (1970-1987)

I was the lead singer in five different rock bands boasting numerous recordings and a video. However, unlike most rock 'n' rollers, we did no drugs, had no groupies, received no press in *Rolling Stone* magazine, and never performed in front of live audiences. Wait. What? Defying all conventions, all five of these bands offered their audiences tremendous entertainment value. The only problem was that the audiences comprised only the band members. Silliness ruled.

My career started upon meeting Robert Thomas Karnes[11] in the Merrifield Village Apartments, Falls Church, Virginia in the fall of 1970. With several other kids, we waited patiently for the school bus to take us to our destination, Luther Jackson Middle School. Bob and I were starting eighth grade. What struck me upon that first day was Bob's non-conformity. He sported shoulder-length hair and seemingly never acted seriously. His personality, despite our shared dread of going to school, appeared to be mostly devoid of the moment. Bob preferred instead to treat every situation as an exercise in frivolity. When the bus came, we sat nearby and swapped tales of our lives. My existence and upbringing was the polar opposite; military brat, short hair, reserved in manner. In short order, I began to adapt to his ways, at least in his presence. After that first week of school, we met frequently in our respective apartments. After formalities of meeting each other's parents, Bob was introduced to my two younger sisters; Gina 5, and Beth not quite two-years old. Bob did not have any siblings. Within a month's time, at Bob's urging, we adopted a whole new conversational attitude in public. He dubbed us The British Insipids, a duo who spoke in *faux* British accents, with ridiculous mannerisms and absurdist humor, a la Monty Python. We'd go to sit-down pizza restaurants with our parents and carry on this way. In addition, we made up non-sensical words and phrases, employing them strategically so that no one else knew what we were saying.

---

[11] Some material culled from *The Holy Paragon*, Bob Karnes, Pocol Press, 2001. The book chronicles his days at Oakton High School, 1971-1975.

On all too many occasions, our parents would chide us for our ridiculousness, but then temper their own arguments with comments that we were "just being kids" that "would grow out of it."

From this spirit of madcap behavior, The Bonneville Follies were born. Starting in November 1970 and continuing intermittently until 1987, Bob and I recorded dozens and dozens of original songs on cassette tape, my father's old Wollensack reel-to-reel tape recorder, and Bob's four-track reel-to-reel tape deck. The songs were parceled into albums by Bob, who kept meticulous documentation of our efforts. Neither Bob nor I ever played instruments nor were musicians. We barely even possessed actual instruments, as someone might playing in school band or orchestra. That did not stop us, however, in the least. We employed pots and pans to bang on, tambourine, electric guitar sans amplifier, flute, and an assortment of children's toys such as a chord organ, numerous kazoos, slide whistle, xylophone, and a plastic "Dig That Sax" saxophone, so named by Bob. We cited rock, country, blues, gospel, bluegrass, jazz, soul, and pop influences in our musical meanderings. What transpired in our recording sessions amounted to caterwauling and a whole lot of cacophony. We recorded in empty apartments, basements, cars, shower stalls, and on a balcony. Although we both sang and wrote lyrics, I took the role of lead singer. Our goal was never a commercial enterprise, playing to crowds, fame, or engaging with record companies. Rather, the idea served to entertain ourselves. We recorded to enjoy the playback. In that regard, The Bonneville Follies were an overwhelming success.

Album and song titles are indicative of the band's output. In chronological order, album titles included Vomit Now! from 1971, Smackin' Crackin' on a Sunday, From Under a Log Jam, 1973's Fading Out with Glitter, and Bonneville Follies in the Dark, 1987. The titles of our songs also display the full wackiness of the band's makeup. To wit: "Hodgepodge and a Bit of Pewter," "Wicked People of the World," "Pickin' Your Nose," "What Am I Doin' (I Don't Know)," "Tweetsie Railroad," "Life in Pennsylvania," and "Downwind of a Thundergust," a paen to being trapped in a fog of unfriendly flatulence.

In its earliest days, The Follies also recorded our variations of national and local commercial jingles. Highlights included Utz Potato Chips and Herbie's Ford, a local dealer whose jingle contained a trumpet call, presumably a clarion call to the dealership. In addition, spur of the moment impromptu skits made their way onto cassette. The titles indicate where our 14-year old minds resided; "Guts Theatre," "Ode to the Commode," and "Gut Washterwong and his Pile of Army Sergeants," a recognition to the brave men fighting in Vietnam.

An offshoot of the Follies was Death By Hanging, a band whose first recording session occurred on my third floor apartment balcony. Although Keith Zarin and Bob Karnes formed the group, I appeared as guest vocalist on the album "Live at Margate." One can only imagine the reaction to three teens brandishing kazoos and wailing away for all to hear. We are forever grateful the police were not called.

In late 1973, my family and I moved to Punxsutawney, Pennsylvania. It was there, in my friend Tom Henry's house, we recorded an album on cassette called Football Frank in 1974. Unnamed at the time, I will now christen the band as Dicky Do and the Don'ts. The name was inspired by a multi-tracked concert experience recording we made for the record. Several imaginary bands are announced in a swirl of screams and excessive din. Among them was Tom's inspired "Dicky" band. Unlike previous musical forays, this one involved Tom Henry playing electric guitar. For the most part, this recording consisted mainly of three songs; the title track, "Met Her in a Hogtroft," and "Boogie Woogie." The first two numbers are laments. "Football Frank" concerns a retired football player, longing for that last roar of crowd noise related to his exploits on the field. "Met Her in a Hogtroft" starts off as a ballad and evolves into rock 'n' roll. The lyrics indicate a man who met the love of his life in a pig sty. "Boogie Woogie" can simply be described as a frenetic rocker.

In November 1980, Barry Furnival purchased a new Sony Video Cassette Recorder (VCR) in Misawa, Japan, where he, and three other Air Force buddies were stationed. Within a few weeks,

The Ugly Americans formed, a rock band based solely on a video production. Anchored by myself on vocals, Barry on saxophone, Mark Roe on guitar, and Dan Herrin on bass, The Ugly Americans did not employ a drummer, quite unusual in a rock band. Then again, there were no recordings either.

Barry filmed each of us in our dorms over several days talking about the band and its challenges. One of the members also filmed Barry. Another gentleman named Danny also found a slot in the video, serving as our manager. My interview occurred in my sleeping gym clothes, in which I complained about the intrusion and then stated, "switch to British accent," in which I completed the session. Barry slurred his words, making him appear as a moron. Mark and Dan went along with the game. In their interview, they sucked on cigarettes and downed whiskey from the bottle. Danny's manager interview became most memorable. Puffing away on a cigar, he pointed to a world map and droned on about the international concert dates scheduled for the band. Following these interviews, the video moved to the Security Hill Rec Center, a dilapidated empty hut containing a bar, stools, tables, and a few board games on a shelf. A friend named Jim became the videographer for this longer segment. Inside the Rec Center, the drinking, er interviews, commenced with the entire band present. Mark and Dan brought along their Jack Daniel's, Barry drank his Budweisers, while I appeared sans any smoking or alcoholic refreshment. Using The Beatles movies as inspiration, the band interview could be described as highly irreverent. We also assumed personalities based on our previous dorm interviews. The gangly six-foot-seven inch Barry played sax and "fell down a lot." Mark played lead guitar and "could really draw," being a comic book artist. Dan drank himself silly as "just Dan." Yours truly "likes to read," as evidenced by my more studious nature. After establishing our personalities, we ad-libbed ourselves into oblivion.

When all was said and done, Barry Furnival retreated to his dorm room and edited this nonsense into a one-hour film. A month later, we all watched The Ugly Americans eagerly and repeatedly, laughing heartily at ourselves.

The fifth and final band documented here is The Thermals.

Created in the winter of 1982, The Thermals existed only in a couple of pre-Photoshopped photographs. That's it. These photos displayed my Air Force roommate Thad Manning and myself dressed in thermal underwear and sunglasses. Heavy greased back hair and cigarettes dangling out of our mouths complete the look. Silhouettes of our torsos were cut out of another picture and grafted onto the snowy Japanese countryside, where we were stationed. A large gull flies overhead. The band's catch? We were to sing in Japanese and English, promoting the band with posters and videos all over the Far East. Our lyrics comprised English/Japanese puns. One such promo item involved the two of us walking across a Japanese street, in thermals, clogs, and holding jumbo shrimp. One of us was barefoot. Ebi Road was the title of this single, *ebi* being the word for shrimp. Another single was West Side Hitori wherein one of us posed in a leather jacket over top of our thermals. *Hitori* means alone. The Thermals' debut album, Eskimo Planet, would be released on BVD records and tapes. As with all the other bands, the main idea was simply self-entertainment.

Or, I could have devolved into a life of crime…

"Calling Mall Security!"

Following my four-year stint in the Air Force, I took a job at Sterling Optical in Tysons Corner Mall in McLean, Virginia. The year was 1985 and I needed to make a few bucks to help pay the rent. It wouldn't be so bad, helping people with their eyewear needs, right? Sterling Optical offered full eye care services such as exams by appointment; fittings; adjustments; and selling glasses, frames, and contact lenses. As an eager pupil, pun not intended, I learned the difference between an optician, optometrist, and ophthalmologist. The doctors and co-workers on the premises trusted each other and worked hard to satisfy their patients. In fact, unlike other stores in the mall, Sterling Optical did not have customers, and the medical professionals in the store emphasized that the staff call them patients. As a clerk, I could only read prescriptions, and pass them along to the doctors.

A typical day involved operating a cash register, suggesting glasses frames, and walking the floor at various times to see that everyone was properly helped. Underneath the counter, outside of the view of the patients, was a small heating unit filled with tiny beads. By request, workers could dip the plastic frames of patients in this solution and make it malleable for adjustments. Sometimes, patient glasses would become out of balance. With some practice, a little heat and finesse, and voila!...glass frames could be adjusted. It was one of the simplest parts of the job, but patients would often be effusive in their gratitude.

Sterling Optical stayed open seven days a week, including limited Sunday hours from 10am to 4pm. From Monday through Saturday, staff numbered about five or six people. However, on Sunday, the store switched to a single-man operation. The reasons for this will soon become apparent. Unbeknownst to me, the manager of the store scheduled me for a Sunday shift. I'd be alone as the store's sole representative. Keys to the front door's metal protection gate were passed along the night previous. One of the employees also pulled me aside and reminded me to grab a big sign and station it outside the entrance to the store. So far, so good. What could go wrong? The manager entrusted me with the keys to the

168

kingdom. However, I didn't know what the text on the sign meant, until later that day. I had to figure it out on my own.

Having arrived at about 10 minutes until ten on a Sunday morning, I opened the heavy metal sliding gate and let myself in. My first move was to switch on the lights and place the gate back down. Next, I set up the cash register and waited a few minutes before re-opening the gate. I grabbed the big sign which was just inside the gate and placed it in the mall concourse, just outside the store boundaries. Sterling Optical opened for business. But, for about an hour, no one entered. It looked like Sundays would be an exercise in fighting off boredom. After pacing around inside the store's selling floor, which contained the frame samples, I ventured outside to read the sign. The words read something to the effect of "Virginia State Law requires the presence of an optometrist for eye examination or the sale of, fitting, or adjustment of any optical device." So, according to this sign, my presence amounted to little less than the babysitter for the store. I must have needed an eye chart, so I read it again.

As I walked back into the store, a bit bewildered, a lady of about fifty years of age, entered the store. She stated she needed a new frame for her glasses. Unfortunately, all I could do was show her the display case. "Over here, on the wall," I said. She sauntered over and picked up a frame while I gulped.

"This one will do," she said, and reached into her handbag for her credit card. The lady did not even seem to care how much the frame cost.

"Can you get the glasses into a new frame today?" she asked.

"Aahh," I stammered. "The optometrist isn't in on Sundays and he'd need to do that."

I could only imagine what she'd say next. She blurted.

"What? You can't help me? Why are you open?" Her voice had become demonstrably louder.

I referred her to the sign outside the store, the sign that documented the legality of only being able to sell medical devices with a trained professional on the premises. Which we didn't have.

"Sonny Boy, don't get smart with me," she spat out. She

probably wasn't used to taking "No" for an answer. It's entirely possible that Sterling Optical served as the first stop in her day's shopping excursion. Perhaps, Nieman Marcus would be next.

"Ma'am, the sign," I reiterated. Then it occurred to me that the mall probably insisted in store leases that *all* their stores stay open, even on Sundays. Having a few stores closed looked odd.

"I'm going to call Mall Security," she huffed, and left.

If I could have ducked under the counter, I would have.

Incredibly, that same day, more people ventured into the store, eager to buy optical products. Each time, I had to explain our sign in the concourse. It got to the point where I memorized its language and could recite it verbatim. In monotone mode. I even looked up the phone number to Mall Security and when their name was invoked, I handed over the phone number and requested the patient to call. How many times did Security show up? Never, perhaps they became used to this shenanigan.

As the hours ticked away and my frustration mounted, a young gentleman came running in. "Come on, four o'clock," I desperately thought.

"Gotta have a frame, man," he cried frantically. When I intoned about the message on the sign, he came closer to me.

That's when I noticed his current frame. The lenses appeared normal inside their tortoise shell frames. However, the side bars that hold the glasses in place at the ears were *wood twigs*. This novel repair probably used super glue to keep it in place. I felt sorry for the young man and could only have imagined how his glasses became broken and his ensuing panic.

The incongruity of Sterling's policy of not employing a medical professional at all times and the mall's insistence on having all their stores open ended my employment. I gave my two-week's notice to resign and suffered through one more Sunday.

The vagaries of working at Sterling Optical.

"We Could Have Been a Shoe Store"

For a few years in the mid-1980s, I worked at Record World, located at the Fair Oaks Mall in Fairfax, Virginia. As with nearly all retail non-management positions, the compensation was low, especially for a man in his late-twenties. Despite this fact, I toiled on, buoyed by my love of music and my long-time friendship with Bob Karnes, who helped me gain the position.

Typical tasks at Record World involved unloading the truck in the morning and then filing "product;" CDs, cassettes, and the fading technology of vinyl albums. The shelves and racks then needed to be filled throughout the store. All product remained on the sales floor. Record World did not have some back room where it stored excess recordings. Other tasks included operating a cash register and waiting on customers. The company stressed customer service, emphasizing a mandatory verbal engagement from the employees to would-be consumers. Store managers mostly handled hiring and firing, and placing orders with the company warehouse.

As with all record shops, Record World played new and older music every minute of the store's operation. Rock, Classical, Jazz, New Age, Pop, Heavy Metal, Country, etc., all competed for "sound time," with employees being able to select their favorites from a sampling of opened product. Gaining customer's interest in these recordings increased sales. To further increase sales and provide an incentive, Record World offered its employees one free CD or cassette for every 25 "special orders" taken. Special orders could be notated on a postcard for recordings not currently in store stock. The fee would be the price of the recording plus one dollar. I probably earned over two dozen cassette tapes for my persuasive work in this area.

Making the job somewhat bearable were the interactions between co-workers and customers. Affable British-born Tony Jamie and Eric Blitz managed the store during my employment. During an out-of-hours Sunday employee meeting, Blitz uttered, "We could have been a shoe store." Although I've always been unsure what he actually meant, I believe it commented on the nature of American retail. Sell, sell, sell. I bonded with short-lived employee Tom Parker, who shared my interest in the Pittsburgh Pirates and the gravelly-voiced singer named Tom Waits. We both attended his concert at the Warner Theatre. A few others stood out, notably Jim McSweeney, an inveterate baseball fan, and Clint Mesle, a writer struggling to get his work published. I renewed ties with both individuals more than twenty years later.

"Paisley" was a nickname I gave to a man who always wore colorful shirts of that design. Painfully shy Greg, whose surname I've forgotten, probably had Obsessive Compulsive Disorder (OCD). Seemingly every half-hour Greg left the sales floor to go to a backroom and wash his hands with bleach. The habit showed when he returned with his extraordinary chapped, red hands.

Bob Karnes took the prize though for most interesting personality at Record World. Music-obsessed, Bob formally worked at Penguin Feather, a record and drug paraphernalia store in northern Virginia. Starting out as an employee, Bob was promoted to manager and later warehouse buyer. With two decades of experience in the business, Bob could easily rattle off rock bands, all their members and instruments, record album names, and stock numbers, all from memory. This amazing talent led me to sometimes play a practical joke on new employees. I'd ask them, "Do you see that guy over there?" They'd answer in the affirmative, then I'd ask the newbie to grab a random recording from the bin. "Shield the information from Bob and then ask him about the band." Uncanny Bob would then relay all the information without a miss.

During this time frame, one such music craze took hold. The genre was called New Age, a direct counterpoint to the current popular staple of Top-40 radio, Heavy Metal Hair Bands. New Age generally featured soft acoustic instrumentals geared toward classical and light jazz. Unlike its rival, doting on heavy guitars and blaring vocal histrionics, New Age could be described as thoughtful and contemplative. An entire record label named Windham Hill devoted itself to New Age. It featured a pianist named George Winston, a guitarist named Will Ackerman, and a Celtic jazz ensemble Nightnoise, among many others. The genre also produced Colors, a six CD series of new-age artists. Their standout recording was fantasy keyboardist Denis Haines' *The Listening Principle*.

Although I waited on thousands of people in my tenure, two particular individuals served as memorable examples. A rather ditzy high schooler approached me. At the time, I worked in the cassette tape area. Many tapes were stored in a large glass case and I had the key. The young lady asked if we had the new George Harrison cassette. A single called "When We Was Fab," climbed the music charts. As I opened the case and handed her the tape, I decided to engage in some sly, small talk. Without even asking, I predicted her answer. "Mr. Harrison used to be in another band," I said. "Really?" She seemed surprised. "They were called The Beatles. Have you ever heard of them?" Her expression turned puzzling. "No, but thank you very much." Excited, the girl skipped away, making a bee-line for the cashier.

Without question, an older gentleman provided me with one of my life's amazing conversations. Most all of the employees in the store knew nothing about classical music. My knowledge, although relatively minimal, probably eclipsed everyone else. A man walked straight up to me and asked, "Do you have any Strauss?" Again, I was working in the cassette tape section. "Right over here, sir. Are you interested in Johann or Richard?" I questioned. Without batting an eye, he exclaimed, "Why, Richard, of course. He sounds great in outer space!" I thought, am I waiting on a kook, or what? Thankfully, I held my tongue. Unlike, the George Harrison space cadet, there could not have been any way to prank this man. He then proceeded to explain the wonder of listening to "Also Sprach Zarathustra" from high above the earth. Further commentary included "You don't know what's it's like to have 30 million newtons of thrust up your ass." By now, my mouth was agape. He continued with several other space stories. Thankfully, he said next, "I'm Jake Garn, Senator from Utah, and I've just returned from the Space Shuttle." I knew that the Strauss recording he referenced was the theme from *2001: A Space Odyssey*. Ironically, both composers named Strauss' music appears in the film and on the soundtrack. Prominent also is "The Blue Danube Waltz" by Johann Strauss. I felt special having just waited on a Senator/Astronaut.

As my time in the job neared its close, the company staged

173

a contest among its staffers. Corporate headquarters in New York required all store managers to explain the contest. Due to the transition of CDs replacing vinyl albums, the name Record World seemed obsolete. The prize for the winning entry, as chosen by corporate, was a monetary amount. Enough to buy dozens of CDs or cassettes. I was enthusiastic for my entry. I chose "Cassidy's," which combined the two current music recording delivery systems. Alas, the announced winner, months later, was "Square Circle," a name which encompassed the round media inside its square packaging sleeve.

Selling musical recordings.

Maryland Renaissance Festival

In the mid-1980s, I discovered the Annual Maryland Renaissance Festival. For the record, the festival takes place in the fall time frame, in the woods of Crownsville. The grounds feature the created Revel Grove, during the reign of Henry VIII, in 16th century England. Suspension of belief isn't required, but highly encouraged. No transportation is provided at the event, and attendees must be willing to walk considerable distances to fully enjoy the festival. Over several years, I attended with friends Bob Karnes, Gaston Naranjo, Clint Mesle, and James McSweeney. My girlfriend and future wife accompanied on one occasion.

One was immediately drawn to several things; the vastness of the area, the organization of the event, and the colorful period costumes of the revelers. Many of those in natty, ancient attire were performers, and part of the show. These individuals roamed among the paid attendance, speaking in language of the era. The women sashayed about in long, flowing dresses with hair to match. The men cavorted with codpieces, displaying the source of their manly pride. Those in the paying crowd also arrived in period costume, knights and knaves, ladies-in-waiting and bedraggled beggars, befitting their status as subjects of the kingdom.

For carnivores and vegetarians alike, the aroma of food wafted over the grounds. Steak-on-a-stake tantalized those desiring red meat. Fresh, roasted corn on the cob was also plentiful with wondrous, mouth-watering bread concoctions. To satisfy the younger set, but infuriate parents with its stickiness, cotton candy was offered up. For the thirsty, mead, tea, and bottled water were available.

Staged mock events popped up everywhere. The performers hurled insults at each other, sometimes resulting in sword fights. Shakespearean plays were highlighted in excerpts. Dancers, expertly choreographed, twirled like whirling dervishes. A game of chess took center stage, with properly attired humans serving as the pieces. With the King and Queen trading witty barbs, and conducting moves from a perch above, the performers enacted a mock duel, resulting in a fatality. The vanquished were carted off

175

the board. Musical troubadours paraded around, playing ancient instruments like lyres, flutes, drums, guitars, even bagpipes. Others boisterously sang to their heart's content. Jousting tournaments employed rather brave lads on horses using long poles. Mock beheadings, elaborately staged, drew fake blood. To much applause. Happily, this time, the condemned walked away. Children delighted to their elephant and pony rides. But, highlighting the entire event was the appearance of the Queen and her considerable retinue. "Make way for the Queen of England!" bellowed a foot soldier, trumpets blaring, and leading her triumphant walk through the crowd. The Ren Fest, as it became to be known, never failed to entertain all ages, year after year.

As part of a special treat, female performers could be hired, unbeknownst to their marks. "Please sir (madam), can you spare…" In rags, these "wenches" would grovel at the feet of the victim, clutching at ankles, and begging for some small morsel or other such relief. The victim usually ended up being either highly bewildered, highly embarrassed, or both. In short order, crowds formed, laughing hysterically at the spectacle. Years later, friends and family probably still discuss the time that John or Mary, became victim to a groveler.

As a commercial enterprise, there were numerous vendors selling their wares and services on the grounds. Clothes, hats, books, period crafts, shoes, elaborate chess sets, games, flower bonnets for the ladies, music CDs, History Channel DVDs, all competed for reveler's dollars. One such vendor, fancily named The King's Armor, or a similar name, offered reproductions of swords, breastplates, family crests, and archery sets. Jim McSweeney and I ventured inside. Immediately, we spied all manner of imitation weaponry, including Japanese samurai swords, which seemed oddly out of place. Jim's eyes practically danced with glee, most determined to take home one of the pieces, regardless of the cost. When the salesman began his spiel, Jim interrupted, picking out a certain blade of his choice, propped by nails on the wall. "How much?" Jim asked, enamored with a sword that sported a handle of encrusted, fake jewels. I was unimpressed. An exorbitant fee was requested, and Jim, reached into his wallet for a handful of twenties. The salesman offered to wrap the item, but Jim demurred. For the rest of the festival, Jim proudly wore his sword, neatly in his scabbard, attached to his belt. When the two of us caught up with the two others in our party, Jim explained excitedly about his purchase, like an enthusiastic child at show-and-tell. We all shared a hearty laugh, clomping along like D'Artagnan and The Three Musketeers, plus one.

After walking some distance and much backslapping, I couldn't help but ask Jim, "What are you going to with your sword?"

He didn't hesitate, stating, "I'm going to use it for self defense."

My thoughts raced forward. "And, where are you going to keep it?" I asked.

With a straight face, Jim said, "Under my bed."
By this time, we all busted out another hearty guffaw.

I don't remember if I brought it up to the group's attention that keeping an imitation sword under one's bed wouldn't be much of a defense against a home intruder. At least not in the current century. After all, that pesky little invention of firearms might preclude Jim's heroic idea.

Two main events stood out. The ridiculously entertaining "Mud Show" featured a giant puddle of mud and dirty water. Hastily-made benches served as seating for the audience. A platform behind the puddle became the stage. Once the benches filled with spectators, three performers, two men and a woman, made their presence known. All dressed in little more than rags. "Ladies and gentleman," shouted the bearded man, "The Mud Show is about to begin!" Then, in a flash, he scurried among the seated crowd. Like a carnival barker, he shouted, "How much will you give for John here, to dip his head in the mud?" My girlfriend and my friend Gus and I were puzzled. What sort of entertainment was this? All the while, the female performer of the trio preened on stage, eliciting giggles for her overt overtures. The bearded man passed about a hat and the audience began placing quarters and dollar bills inside it. The bearded man kept up his ministrations. "How much?!" he bellowed. After a few minutes, he collected the hat and said,

"That's enough, John!" The performer named John, then dunked his head completely in the fetid, swampy water. A few seconds later, he pulled it out, a mucky mess of a face. And incredibly, we all applauded. This went on for several iterations, each more audacious than the last, and each time the same sequence of passing the hat and expecting larger and larger donations. After the head dunking, came a sit-down in the mud. More applause and raucous laughter. Each time the exhortations grew louder and the stunts more ridiculous. The sit-down became a full body immersion and then came this. "How much for the lady here to gargle swill?" When the hat was passed around, the barker grew impatient. He shouted, "That's not enough. Not worth our time!" A flood of money commenced, cementing the con. "That's enough," the bearded man shouted and sure enough, the young lady bent down, and placed her head in the mud with her mouth wide open. She captured a big gulp, cocked her head back, and gargled like the morning mouthwash. And we howled. Howled! The audience may have felt disgusted, but we were surely entertained by one of the most absurd excuses for silliness (and moneymaking) ever hoisted on an unsuspecting crowd. The *piece de resistance* followed, announced as the finale of the event. One by one, each of the "mudders" climbed a ladder and, after trolling for more cash, jumped into the puddle, in a full-body splashdown. A tidal wave of muddy muck cascaded into the audience, causing screams and gasps, and some other four-letter word expressions. Those in the audience, especially the front row, may have thought they were at a Gallagher show. This time, though, there was no plastic protection. As we filed out with the crowd, we wandered to other parts of the festival. A guilty pleasure? After much walking in a circle of the grounds, we chanced upon a new audience gathering for another performance. "Ladies and gentlemen, roll on up for The Mud Show."

Many people joke that one should never volunteer. But those arriving early often catch the eye of the entertainers, and this event proved the point. With a set of benches similar to the previously documented event, my girlfriend, friend Gus, and I arrived early for another performance. We sat in the front row as two mid-twenties jugglers plied their trade. The act was billed as Jugglery & Tom

Foolery. While practicing with their pins, they engaged in some small talk with our small group. Unfortunately for me, they found their mark. Slowly, but surely, a crowd formed filling up the seats. The show commenced with some nonsensical jokes. Then, the performance began, in earnest. With remarkable skill and precision, these two gentlemen juggled a variety of objects. First it was juggling pins, then balls, then bowling pins. They juggled alone and to each other, flinging their props quickly, accurately. We were mesmerized. Finally, unbelievably, they did something that no one should try at home. Yes, wait for it…they juggled chain saws! Operating chain saws that roared and belched out their gasoline. The crowd, not quite understanding what they were witnessing with their own eyes, broke out into sustained applause. What the audience did not know, was that this was just the warmup. The real show had not yet started. Only the jugglers knew what lie ahead.

Then, one of the jugglers pointed at me. "You there, you'd like to volunteer, help us out?" He was wrong on both counts. I wanted no part of this. But the crowd egged me on. They stomped their feet and within a flash, I was on the stage, which consisted of worn-out grass and dirt. After some more joking, they made me stand in the center. These two jugglers then walked about ten yards to my left and right and parallel to where I stood. Nothing could have prepared me for what happened next. Having reached into a box, the two jugglers each held their pins and proceeded to leisurely toss them over my head. This wasn't so bad, I thought. I'll look silly for a few minutes and it will all be over. The pins flew through the air, while I stood passively by. In an instant though, these same pins whizzed alternately in front of my nose and the back of my skull. If I leaned forward, my nose could be broken. Backward, a concussion awaited. I started to become nervous as the crowd amped up their reaction to the jugglers and the monkey in the middle. Me. Petrified with fear as I was, the pins zipped by, and their movements became faster and faster. I could hear the crowd in spasms of laughter. The more nervous I appeared, the more the humiliation. These guys were out to kill me! Hope they had insurance. I had come to the festival to see the shows, but not *be* the show. Just like that, the juggling stopped. I was ready to sit down, finally. But, one of them reached into a box behind me and to my right, and pulled out a 1920's-era leather football helmet. He tossed the helmet to the other man, who then proceeded to secure it to my head. The crowd again roared at my preposterous look. I couldn't see what they were doing at the box, but soon I discerned heat. These two jugglers now squarely held my life in their hands. Next, they lit torches. Moving about twenty yards away from me, the jugglers extraordinaire took up their paces and tossed these torches in front of and behind me. Within inches of my face! The torches zipped by, the awesome power of the flames seemingly stinging my eyebrows. My knees wanted to buckle. My heart pounded like a freight train. How much longer? If there was ever a time for an adult to have an excuse to soil their pants in public, this was it. Whoosh in front. Whoosh, from behind. Whoosh, whoosh, and the nervous wreck that was once myself began to slowly breathe again. The torches stayed in the juggler's hands. These two held up their flames high over their heads. One exclaimed, "Let's hear it for our volunteer!" I stumbled back to my seat, grateful for being alive, while the crowd clapped and clapped and clapped. I could only manage a wry smile for my friends. Thankfully, my fifteen minutes of fame was over.

Despite all the frivolity, the entirety of the Renaissance Festival belied the horrors of the age; rampant and extreme poverty, social strife, tortures or death for non-conformists, especially those who dared question the power of the King or Queen. Royalty afforded finery in clothing, shelter, entertainment, and exotic foods. The poor often begged for everything they had.

Nonetheless, over the years, the Maryland Renaissance Festival continues to grow in size and popularity, taking advantage of the romance and nostalgia of a bygone era. Critics may deem it a bloated mess, summoning the excesses of Henry VIII himself. However, in Maryland and several states which stage this event annually, paying customers often return, enjoying to escape their mundanity of modern life for the riches of merriment and mirth.

When in Rome…

Reaganomics on the Metro

On a blistering, typically muggy summer Sunday morning, a companion and I ventured forth into Washington's mass transit system. Entering at the orange end of the line stop in Vienna, we watched curiously as tourists and novices tried to use the farecard machine. These people appeared purposeless as flies buzzing about a favorite food. In actuality though, many of them did have a primary goal - to stop off at the National Mall entrance to the vast array of Smithsonian institutions and get some culture.

We walked through to the escalator, unable to help but notice the continuing confusion of the masses. Escalators have been around America and our planet for umpteen years and still people don't know how to use them? After a politely vertical push and shove, bump and grind, we entered the Metro train, settled into a seat, and waited.

In a few stops, a muffled announcement was heard and the train was boarded by three black boys and their female guardian. They were smartly dressed, one wearing a tie, but looked awkward in their Sunday clothes as children often do. The boys plopped into the plastic chairs nearby while the lady stood. Here, hurtling on a horizontal plane toward our very metropolitan city, was another slice of melting pot America. There were blacks and whites and Asians and Hispanics, short men, tall men, muscular machos, scrawny beings, obese men and women. Most were casually dressed, in a rainbow of colors. In the same car with us was the obligatory father and family with their brood of littles, on their way to gawk at dinosaur bones. On most of the faces, though, was that too familiar bored look of travelers in an urbanized environment. All except, for the animated black boys.

One didn't need to concentrate hard to hear the lively, innocent conversation of the boys. It perked up a stylish-looking woman, who broke into a gracious smile. Unlike the Metro train, seemingly following a straight line, the boys' talk took abrupt turns.

First, it was religious, possibly because the lads were on their way to Sunday school. "What if Paradise were free?" Then, it shifted to financial power; "If I had all the money in the world I'd buy 12 race cars and a rocket!" Soon, economics: "What if a penny were a nickel and a dime were a quarter?" Finally overheard as the boys were playing with their transfer tickets and posing them on their faces; "If I had two noses, I could smell everything!" The train slowed to a halt at the next station. The youngsters exited as quickly as they had come on, armed with a newer knowledge of the world. More passengers boarded and the train whisked us northward.

All this on a day when President Ronald Reagan haggled in Toronto at his last Financial Summit, a Pentagon defense scandal sizzled, and news of a date being set for night baseball at Wrigley Field in Chicago.

Impression on a train.

Joey

As the Ramones walked onto the stage to perform their driving, pounding brand of punk rock, it soon became evident that Joey Ramone commanded the most attention. He stood about six-foot six with his pock-marked face and sunglasses (which he wore inside the theatre). There appeared a mean streak in his mannerisms. Ramone sauntered over to the neck high microphone and adjusted it to his large frame. He wore dirty, ripped jeans, heavy boots, and a filthy jean jacket. The stare he gave the audience almost yelled aloud, "We're tough!" And before anyone could exclaim "gabba-gabba hey" (the band's recognizable chant claim to punk fame), Joey and the rest of the foursome plunged headlong into a robust, scintillating, pulsating act that defied description.

Slurring every word possible and making a mockery of the English language, Joey's voice boomed over a blaring guitar din to open this rock 'n' roll set. Ramone shouted, "You're a loudmouth, baby," the latter word being garbled to "ba." With this, the crowd tore the roof off the tiny theatre. The Ramones heated up.

Joey, never one to steal the show, gladly let the band play behind him. Accompanied by a bassist, lead guitarist, and drummer, Ramone contented himself with straightforward singing without sexual movements or obscene handling of the mic. And throughout the act, not once did Ramone smile. However, Joey enjoyed his notoriety as America's foremost punk lead vocalist. He danced with the band so excitedly that he gave the impression that he could not stay still. He sensed the audience reaction to be positive so he sang on with more enthusiasm and confidence.

The band rocked along, losing not an ounce of the energy they started with. While sweat poured from his face, Joey wiped off the perspiration with a dirty handkerchief that he pulled out of his back pocket. Ramone continued his slurred vocals, never missing a note. He remained a constant mass of moving excitement. Still, the act proceeded along, song after song. The band barely stopped between their two-minute numbers. The intervals lasted for all of about two seconds.

Then, in one of the more typical yet mellow of all Ramones

songs, Joey drawled, "I don't care." This described the general feeling amongst Joey and the entire band and genre of punk rock. He epitomized the punk message by those three simple lines. Joey maundered, "I don't care about this world, I don't care about that girl, I don't care about these words, I don't care, I don't care."

Following this piece, Ramone blasted away once again with an incredible display of high energy music. A policeman, who was guarding the theatre, walked by Ramone and Joey stared at him while singing. The audience howled at the cop to sit down but Joey just sang away seemingly saying, "You don't care about this world, why should we?" By now, the hands of the two guitarists bled visibly and Joey's face perspired so much that drops of sweat were falling from his face to the floor. As the final blaring guitar note ceased, Ramone calmly said, "thank you" and left the stage humbly with his mates. Three encores later; the crowd hollering throughout, Ramone finally said, "thank you and good evening." He walked offstage for the last time that night, leaving an impression on everyone in attendance. To the critics of punk, Ramone answered over and over. The songs he sang lashed out at all people, especially the "establishment." Unbeknownst to him, Joey Ramone did steal the show. Ramone not only sang punk rock but he *was* punk rock, and everyone who was there that night would agree.

Punk rock's Joey Ramone. RIP.

"Just Rest Yourself"

For a period of nearly 12 years, beginning in August 1988, I worked as a physical/electronic security guard at the MITRE Corporation in McLean, Virginia. The Physical Security component involved patrolling any one of the company's campus facilities by walking the halls and grounds carrying a hand-held walkie-talkie radio, answering alarm calls, driving a security vehicle looking for the unusual, escorting visitors, and pinch-hitting for receptionists at their desks while they went to lunch or the restroom. Electronic Security involved monitoring a few dozen entrances/exits on Closed Circuit Television (CCTV), answering phones, logging every task, and providing access/control to various locations in the buildings through a computer system. All of the Electronic Security occurred from the Security Control Room in the Hayes Building, the nerve center of MITRE's Security operation. Because MITRE employees accessed classified and sensitive information, strict protocols needed to be followed at all times. If this all sounds so very mundane and boring, one could make a strong case that it was precisely that. Even one of our managers, Joseph Verrett frequently stated, "Now you just sit down and rest yourself." Verrett, like many other employees in the department, didn't take the job very seriously.

Despite that generalized apathy, I treated my position with earnestness. I was diligent about my patrols and in time, I wrote the training manual that covered the entire dual physical and electronic security guard position. The manual included operation of each piece of equipment from the control room to the walkie-talkies. I briefed new employees entering the company about security procedures and proper care for and use of individual employee badges. The badges could access any of MITRE's doors outside of company main working hours by use of the badge and a Personal Identification Number (PIN).

While work was work and the number one priority, the job offered so much "down time" as to make tomfoolery an inevitability. Our collegial environment allowed for plenty of opportunities for nicknames and practical jokes and laughing at each other's habits. No one was spared, including managers who sometimes participated in the fun. Always silly. But, never malicious. To compensate for the daily boredom, we noted a certain gentleman named Jeff Krause. Mr. Krause's reputation for doing as little work as possible became known to all. One day a manager asked him to check something in the six-story Hayes building. Krause was ordered to the third floor. He complained, "Frank, you know I haven't been past the second floor in years!"

The practice of walking up and down hallways to ensure employee safety, building integrity, and making sure nothing appears out of the ordinary are the concepts behind security patrols. Security patrols are a solitary pursuit. Hour after hour of walking or driving a vehicle around company parking lots allows for endless contemplation. The mind wanders. I kept moving, and actually used this time to my advantage. Despite the danger of slipping into extreme boredom, always prevalent during patrols, I was able to compartmentalize and plan. I thought about the daily rendezvous with my wife, names for our unborn children, upcoming dinners, my love of reading and writing, and future family financial and retirement planning. When I had a chance, I scribbled down notes to use later. The walking patrols, to the cynical seen as time wasted, provided me the opposite impetus. It was always good exercise, challenges to body and mind.

Spending a shift working in the control room sometimes proved to be an exercise in the bizarre, especially when the phone rang. Ninety five percent of the calls concerned access control tasks. But occasionally, control room operators received some rather bizarre communications. It seemed as if MITRE Security was a clearinghouse for all manner of employee complaints. During the brief Gulf War in early 1991, someone called in to report an upside-down American flag flying on our premises. Some numbskull guard carelessly raised the flag in the morning. Unfortunately, the upside-down American flag is a distress signal. The caller started by questioning, "Is anything wrong?" I stated that I wasn't aware of a problem to which the caller explained the issue. From that point forward, I became the company expert on flag protocols. My assignment involved calling the Pentagon and obtaining proper training materials for flag displays. While that call was legitimate, others were not.

I received a call from a lady employee concerning a Canadian goose trapped in the bushes next to the flag pole. I did my best to suppress my laugh and tell the woman, "Whaddya think we are, the SPCA?" She explained that the "poor thing's wings were caught." Summoning every bit of tact learned from my father, I calmly stated that security would investigate. I dispatched a guard to call me in the control room. It was important that I explain the situation to an individual guard rather than blurt this over the radio where all patrolling guards and possibly other employees could hear. After a few minutes, the guard called me back to report that the complaint had been correct. I instructed the manager who tasked me to then call the local office for Animal Control. If that initial call was weird, the Animal Control response bordered on insanity. "The animal has to be boxed up first, before we'll pick 'em up." Wow, these people were really concerned about protecting the Canadian geese population. The manager requested the guard not touch the animal, but instead to shake the bushes a little. With that, our fine feathered friend was freed. But this would not be the only call received about Canadian geese. Another call involved a lady upset that someone appeared to be whacking a goose with a stick in the parking lot of a nearby MITRE building. When pressed for details, I discovered the culprit was a kid doing the damage, which she spied from her office window. The dispatched guard chased the fowl and fool away.

When Forest Gump uttered his famous line, "Life is like a box of chocolates / You never know what you're going to get," he could have been describing the next phone call. Answering "MITRE Security," the frantic caller then complained about a very loud noise just outside her sixth-floor office window. "I can't concentrate, there's a helicopter," she said. I paused and then asked her about the location of her room. I dispatched a guard. He reported back that indeed, a helicopter hovered nearby her window. An hour or so later, the news reported a fatal accident on the highway. The people flying the Traffic Chopper were doing their job. In the aftermath, it became difficult to process that phone call. A person had just lost their life on the road and this woman complained about noise. What exactly did she expect us to do?

Just outside the door from the control room was an unusual soda machine. When the Coca-Cola vendor came to MITRE, a security guard would be dispatched to escort him into the building to re-stock the machines. For reasons unknown, the 12-ounce cans went from 25 cents to 50 cents to 75 cents, all within the blink of an eye. This price gouge affected me, who habitually purchased one per day. Control room personnel, manned by two guards and the manager, frequently railed about the out-of-control soda machine prices.

It was my chance meeting with a twenty five-year old in an elevator that made soda prices irrelevant. At least for the long term. As I patrolled in MITRE's Reston facility, a gentleman who'd I'd only known to say hello to, starting talking about the company's retirement program. He asked me if I had enrolled in the plan. When I stated that I'd begun allocating a percentage of my salary, he shot back. "MITRE has one of the best plans in the United States. They offer company matching so you should max out. It's free money, man!" The elevator arrived at its destination and we stepped out. Continuing our conversation, he pointed out the company name. "Do you know what MITRE stands for?" "No," I responded, sheepishly. "Men Intending To Retire Early," he claimed. Although I knew that was not true, the phrase started me thinking. That night I went home to my wife and informed her of his comments. "Put some more of your money in," she said. Within a few days, I filled out paperwork to increase my retirement savings. This decision led to a lifetime of taking advantage of company retirement plans, greatly boosting my strategic income.

MITRE's cast of security characters involved several of the most interesting individuals ever encountered. At the top of this list was the rotund but genial Doug Moore. Possessing a gregarious laugh, Doug patrolled the hallways of MITRE with courtesy and a smile. Unfortunately, he suffered from obesity and was not shy in telling anyone who would listen. His clothes could not cover his large frame. For this reason, most security staffers did not appreciate Mr. Moore. I found him charming. But, unfortunately, staffers were right and it cost him his job. Doug Moore frequently worked night shifts until 11pm. He patrolled the hallways with 20 oz. bottles of soda in one hand and his radio in the other. After a visit to the doctor, Doug explained the doctor's advice to drink more liquids. Instead of interpreting that as water for weight reduction, Doug upped his game, now carrying one-liter bottles of soda with him. He consumed one of these every day he worked. Then came the rumors. MITRE employees complained that Doug Moore was "not professional." Doug explained that security management had warned him about his appearance. I felt bad for him, but indeed, he appeared slovenly. Under siege, Mr. Moore sealed his fate with his next perplexing act. One evening, while sitting at the front desk away from view, Doug tried to repair a rip in his pants. The tear occurred in his crotch area. I'm not sure why, but Doug's solution to the problem was to staple up the rip. After he finished, he continued his patrol of the building. So, someone noticed, complained to the security management, and Doug was told to depart the premises. I cannot imagine the consequences of his suffering, but Doug did this to himself.

Other memorable characters included Rocco Berry, Ellie and Brian Blackwell, Lester Brim, Rene Brooks, Frank Certo, Betty Danley, Michael Faison, Tom Perroni, Jim Spicer, and Betty Turley. To describe and collate all of the conversations with these people would be impossible. Suffice to say, though, I learned from all of them. Most remarkable were the coal mining growing-up heartbreaks of one Francis Certo, raised in the wilds of western Pennsylvania. Many conversations with Frank Certo could elicit tears after hearing his harrowing tales. Every year, without fail, the kind and generous Frank Certo gave Santa dollars at Christmas for the parents of children within the entire Security department. Santa dollars contained a drawing of Santa, deftly pasted in place on all dollar bills. When asked, Frank would exclaim they were legal tender, and indeed, they were.

Security employees did not have a monopoly on fascinating. There was a nurse on-site named Pat Dragonetti. Naturally, we all began to call her The Dragon Lady. Ms. Dragonetti was pleasant enough. Over the years, I went to her office about three times due to headaches and such. One time, however, when I showed up in her office, complaining of a neck ache, she responded with the phrase, "Well, you know, life is a terminal disease." That sound you hear is Florence Nightingale fainting.

Over the years, MITRE Security changed its organizational structure. Originally, at the time of my hire, the company performed all physical and electronic security functions. Later, our firm contracted out the patrolling tasks to another firm. MITRE employees would now be relegated to management and working in the control room. At least three separate contract entities came and went during my employment. Early twenty-something Kevin Vioral came aboard to work for one of these contract companies. His position afforded him a separate control room phone, where he barked out instructions for his troops. Kevin's communication style could not be missed by anyone around him. In every conversation, he'd repeat his "Kevinisms," with lines like "I'll hook you up," "I go out of my way for you," "You gonna be okay?" and so forth. This guy was a walking, talking cliché. Conversing with Kevin away from his phone calls to his company employees revealed his obsession with horse racing. He frequently played the ponies in Maryland, doting on an up-and-coming jockey named Kent Desormeaux. A wild idea for a practical joke on Kevin Vioral began forming in my head.

The plan needed time and accomplices. First, as a mild fan of the sport, especially the Triple Crown races, I talked up Kevin. I'd ask him questions about horses and jockeys and strategy. We'd discuss horse racing at every opportunity and he'd tell me about his betting experiences and Desormeaux. Ray Rybicki took over next. He explained to Kevin that he'd met a man on the fourth floor who was a big racing fan also. The MITRE employee could offer Kevin tips about picking winners. This part of the ruse took about three weeks. Then, Mike Arnold worked his magic. A burgeoning Macintosh graphic genius, Mike re-wrote a racing form following the design of the *Washington Post*. Unlike the actual racing form however, Mike substituted in horse names like Get You Squared Away, Hook You Up, and Security Kevin, playing off how the contractor answered his phone. All the names of the horses in the entire race were "Kevinisms." Mr. Vioral was not aware of the form nor the name of the man on the fourth floor. Upon Ray's insistence one day, he took Kevin to finally meet a fellow horse racing man. Ray had spoken to the man previously, also without Kevin's knowledge. When the two bettors met, the man handed Kevin a sealed envelope with betting tips inside. Unbeknownst to Kevin also was that the envelope contained Mike's brilliant *faux* racing form. With considerable glee, Kevin and Ray returned to the control room. Ray, Mike, and I waited excited to know about the tips. "Hey, maybe with these tips we could pick a winner, too, in off-track betting," exclaimed Ray. "Open it up," I said. The trap being set, Kevin took the bait. He tore into the envelope, tossing it on the floor. As he straightened out the paper in what he thought were tips, Kevin read for a few seconds and dropped the paper. "What does it say, Kev? Who does he pick for tonight's race at Pimlico?" Kevin let out a depressing groan, fully realizing the extent of the prank. He sighed, "You got me. You guys hooked me up!"

If the practical joke on Kevin Vioral wasn't enough, Ray, Mike, and I used our goofball talents together again to fool our boss. Calling Frank anything other than a fun-loving guy would be a disservice. He also loved Jeep automobiles and insisted we watch a promotional VHS tape on the glories of the vehicle. At the time, Jeeps were taking their lumps in the press with negative reportage about their safety record. Jeeps can roll over, screamed the headlines. As with Kevin Vioral, Ray, Mike, and I took advantage of this information to plan our next prank. In addition to these facts, Frank Thompson was frequently summoned upstairs to meet with his boss Frank Arndt. The day previous, Mike Arnold brought a blank VHS tape into the control room, keeping it hidden from Mr. Thompson. He then snuck into Frank's office desk, located in the same space as the control room. When the boss was away, Mike removed the original Jeep promo tape. Both tapes were encased in black plastic. Again, using his artistic skills, Mike carefully peeled the label from the original tape and stuck it on the blank VHS tape. He replaced the blank tape back into Frank's drawer while securing the original promo tape. Thankfully, Frank Thompson did not reach into his drawer for his Jeep promo tape to play. Over the next few days, very carefully, each of us chided Frank concerning his Jeep fetish. We explained the rollover danger and generally made fun of his vehicle choice. Coincidentally, Frank purchased a Jeep vehicle that same week. The more Frank gushed about his new car, the more we needled him. Another week passed. Frank could not possibly have known what was about to occur. While working at his desk, Frank poured over some security documents. In a flash, with the four of us in the room, Mike leaped from his chair. Yelling an anti-Jeep diatribe, Mike reached into Frank's drawer, grabbed the VHS, and slammed it to the carpeted floor. "We're tired of this seeing this video," Mike bellowed. Frank's jaw dropped. Mike then ranted and raved like a madman, stomping the VHS tape into oblivion. Mike's Oscar-worthy performance nearly caused poor Frank heart palpitations. To play along, Ray and I looked on as aghast as Frank. Still fuming, Mike went and sat down. Frank looked at him like he'd seen a ghost. Then, after about five minutes, we all busted out laughing. Mike slowly removed himself from his chair, retrieved the original video, and handed it to Frank. "Come on man, I didn't mean it. Let's watch it again!" When the promo tape started to play, Frank let out the loudest laugh we had ever heard, "You guys!" he said, as he shook his head with a wide grin on his face.

Without a boss like Frank, who understood the full power of relieving stress, we'd have surely all been fired. He liked a good laugh, as much as the next guy, even if the joke was on him. However, our next gambit pushed our employment to the brink. Especially mine. All of our dayshift control room staffers noted Frank Thompson's tardy arrivals and all-too-frequent absences. He was our shift manager, after all. But, we all simply knew the job tasks and performed them *without* a manager. Smooth as silk. More often than not, we'd take calls from the big boss Frank Arndt asking about Frank Thompson's whereabouts. It became embarrassing to respond that he had not yet arrived. Incredibly, Mr. Thompson's wife would call *three hours* into a shift and state that Frank was running late. Although he lived a considerable distance away in Baltimore, Mr. Thompson should be on the premises to manage his people. Neither Ray, nor Mike, nor I knew what his problem was, but we speculated some awful things. Unfortunately, my idea of a work ethic clashed dramatically with Mr. Thompson's. My father taught me consistency. Show up every day, head down, do your job, don't cause trouble. Well, at least I followed the first three of his maxims.

Due to the absurdity of the situation, I concocted an idea. Endorsed by teammates Mike Arnold and Ray Rybicki, we wrote down our prospective times for Frank's arrival. When the boss showed up, we'd jump out of our chairs and erase the information on the blackboard. One day, however, Mr. Thompson caught wind of my scheme. He asked Mike and Ray about the instigator. They pointed fingers at me. I would now be the Canada goose trapped in the bushes. In a private meeting with me, furious Frank explained that he did not appreciate this little game. Surely, I'd be relieved of my position at MITRE. I steeled myself for the inevitable. He then asked why. Without hesitation, I told the truth. I explained our frustration coming to work without the manager in charge. I told him the story of my father's advice. Finally, I brought up a current example of work ethic. Baltimore Orioles shortstop Cal Ripken had not missed playing a baseball a game in ten years. My honesty worked. Mr. Thompson calmed down and said, "OK, just don't do it again." With that, my fears of being fired evaporated.

For a period of three years beginning in January 1990 and ending in December 1992, I started an extra-curricular activity for MITRE Security employees. Informally, the events were called the Security Pig-Outs, wherein attendees gorged themselves after work once a month on Fridays. Nearly all of the 30 gatherings took place at Horn and Horn Smorgasbord in Annandale, Virginia. Judging by the way some tackled the assignment, the event took on numerous other names including Rumble Tummy; A Festival of Gluttony; Bacchanal; Food Kamikazes; A Roman Orgy of Wine, Women, and Song; Gorge Us; Feast in the East; Comrades in Arms; Hey You!; and the First Annual President Zachary Taylor Exhumation, Food Festival, and Memorial Sing-Along. I created and distributed promotional material for each event consisting of a graphic and some preposterous thoughts. The idea was to promote an *esprit de corps* among employees and attendees. And, that it certainly did! The restaurant manager and employees probably thought us an obnoxious bunch, because we definitely ate our money's worth. More so, we may have appeared as a group of riotous monkeys due to our joking around producing uproarious belly laughter. There were also frequent visits to the restroom to produce flatulence out of earshot of the rest of the group. Honestly, I laughed so hard during these events, tears sometimes formed in my eyes.

Horn and Horn offered more than adequate food and dessert varieties for carnivores and vegetarians alike. Usually, about ten people showed up. Once we took our seats and filled up our plates, the sustenance portion of the event proceeded earnestly. However, on or about meeting three, Doug Moore offered a memorable line. After consuming two giant platefuls of salad, roast beef, chicken, pork, vegetables, etc. Doug said, "Gentlemen, now let's get down to some serious eating!" Once far too much food was consumed, the real hilarity started. Someone would tell a story or a joke. Others offered nicknames for the participants, and we'd be off to the races. One employee relayed that fellow employee Sam Thornton's toupee flew off while patrolling the parking lot on a windy day. Another talked about Jim Robey's suspect golf game. Still another joked about Dan Chin's height, who was barely able to see over the dashboard of his Audi. Don Radabaugh, an Army veteran of the Korean War, spun his stories of days in the trenches overseas and his Revisionist History 101. But, despite his seriousness, the group always reverted to giant guffaws. John Hauser, MITRE employee Colleen's husband, never failed to provide riveting commentary on hi-jinks from his days in the service, contrasting with Don Radabaugh's serious lectures. As we'd all be laughing our heads off, Doug Moore would sneak up to the smorgasbord and bring back a plate full of ice. Puzzled, someone asked, "What is that for?" Moore's response, "Just wait and see." After a few minutes, Doug Moore walked back from the food tables with a plate full of soft-serve ice cream. When questioned again, he explained, "I was keeping my plate cold to keep it from melting." Looking back, it's highly doubtful anyone did not enjoy the MITRE Security Pig-Outs. What's better than sharing meals with family and friends followed by hearty cheer?

As Security offered the extracurricular activity of the

security pig-out, the company staged an annual Christmas party for the children of employees. During my time at MITRE, I married. Both my daughters were born during this time also and my wife graduated from George Mason University with a degree in Mathematics. The company Christmas party was a splendid event, completely free. It featured Santa and Mrs. Claus, live music, carol singing, face painting, crafts, treats for all the kids, and the opportunity for employee's families to meet each other. Although over five years apart in age, both my daughters attended the events to good cheer. Amelia bawled when Santa perched her upon his lap, but otherwise we shared a good time. Psst. Santa wasn't actually there. He was portrayed by future security manager Frank Ringel, whom I called Kris Kringle Ringel.

With my wife's college degree firmly in hand, she pressured me into finishing up a degree. I'd obtained an Associate Degree in General Studies from the Northern Virginia Community College in 1986. Unfortunately, our financial situation didn't seem to allow for my continuing studies. We strategized for weeks, planning to obtain part-time work, higher-paying jobs, but none of those options seemed tenable. If anything could be said about my wife, though, was that she did not give up easily. Nor did I. Enter the MITRE Institute. During my employment at MITRE, I'd heard about this organization within the company. They could offer monetary reimbursement to those employees completing advanced degree work. In addition, they taught various management and computer courses under their umbrella. I didn't need graduate work, however. My goal was the completion of a four-year bachelor's degree. Calling the Institute, I set up an interview with an administrator there named Mosetta Blackmon. Graciously, she offered me an opportunity to speak. When I began to explain my goal, she quickly stopped me in my tracks. "MITRE is an engineering firm," she intoned. "What degree are you seeking?" My interest was English, reading and writing. That suited me. Again, Ms. Blackmon stated, "We do engineering here." In response, I explained that I was the department trainer for equipment and trained new company employees in badge wearing and security matters. "I am the author of all of our security manuals concerning the same and I'd be happy to produce them for you." Ms. Blackmon likely noticed my persistence. She arranged for a meeting between the president of the MITRE Institute and myself. "You'll probably have to present him with a letter outlining just what you've said to me," she said. "All I ask for is a chance," I returned.

That night at home, I wrote my letter. My wife seemed excited. We both knew it was a longshot. A week later, I met the president of the Institute. He must have seemed impressed with my spiel and my confidence. He said, "OK, you know we've never done this for a non-engineer." He continued, "Go ahead and take one class and depending on your grade, A, B, or C, we'll reimburse. We'll see how we'd like to proceed going forward." I'd only asked for an opportunity. Now, with my meeting with the MITRE Institute president, that opportunity stared me in the face. I brought my first class home with an A. My first reimbursement followed. The next class was an A also. Subsequently, from January 1993 until my graduation, my coursework continued on a successful trajectory, earning me Summa Cum Laude honors. MITRE reimbursed me for over five years. Working full time, raising a daughter, writing a book, and attending college classes part-time kept me extremely busy. To my good fortune, I also fell into a midnight-shift position, which allowed me to study for college while I toiled on the slowest shift in the control room. In August 1998, I earned my undergraduate in English Non-Fiction Writing and Editing from George Mason University in Fairfax, Virginia. My determination, and my wife's prodding, paid off.

Ironically, the lady that called about the trapped goose later became a good friend. Sue Fuerst edited the monthly MITRE Matters corporate newsletter. This six-pager featured stories about company achievements, "attaboys" for staffers, birth announcements, necrologies, and human-interest articles. It was concerning the latter that I contacted Ms. Fuerst. Having just finished my first book entitled *MISFITS! The Cleveland Spiders in 1899*, I inquired about a feature article concerning my baseball book. I nervously explained that I was the security guard who took her call about the goose. Intrigued, she arranged an interview with me. I brought in my book, she took voluminous notes, snapped a few pictures of me holding a bat, and wrote the story. It would be an understatement to say I was pleased. Two or three months passed before I contacted her again. No wanting to seem pushy, I explained that I'd welcome an opportunity to write a human-interest article. Gaining further writing experience was important to me. However, I didn't ask her for a job. I simply wanted to research and write for the learning experience. Sue Fuerst, after asking her boss, agreed. She quickly gave me the opportunity to edit a story and write my own based on four assignments[12] piling up in her in-box. All MITRE Matters human-interest stories concerned MITRE employees and their outside work hobbies. The company also published a shorter companion newsletter entitled Centerspread.

From the name of the Centerspread came security's knockoff version entitled CenterDread, The Alternative Newsletter. I instigated and wrote all the material for the unsanctioned "Dread." The concept was fairly simple. It's tagline: Where You Dread to Be Read About. Employing light humor poking fun at other employees and myself, CenterDread featured two columns with graphics. A Rastafarian with dreadlocks served as the logo. Employing the cartoon artistry of Mike Arnold, CenterDread's material depended largely on inside jokes. Distribution was limited to about a dozen per issue. In effect, CenterDread stories were mini-versions of practical jokes. Short, pithy articles satirized someone's comment, or job performance, or other nonsense. CenterDread "published" from 1992-1994.

MITRE was hardly all fun and games. Blizzard conditions in two of the winters during my time there led to being on the premises around the clock. As we worked a day shift, the snow fell softly, but piled up frighteningly. The parking lot became inundated with the frozen powder in large drifts. Many company employees had departed early in anticipation of the snow. But, as the day shift slipped into evening, the security staff sheltered-in-place. Frank Thompson's generosity allowed for a massive pizza run at a nearby shopping center. A couple security staffers braved the elements to

---

[12] Two of those stories are included in this volume; *The Marathon King* and *Larry Kahn, Winks Champ*.

retrieve the food. One night I slept in the nurse's office. On another night, security night manager Ed Bulger invited me to stay at his house overnight. Mr. Bulger's lovely wife Carol, a heart transplant recipient, graciously prepared a meal, turned up the heat, and treated me like their own son. Thankfully, Mr. Bulger and I trudged through the snow to his nearby house.

These weather events subsided, but the fear surrounding a winter's day in January 1991 nearly shook MITRE to its core. Following the invasion of Kuwait by Iraqi forces, U.S. President George Bush issued his proclamation concerning a line in the sand. Saddam Hussein needed to withdraw his military from Kuwait or a coalition force, led by the United States, would eject them. These global tensions directly impacted us, company-wide. MITRE issued a memorandum explaining the seriousness of the situation, prohibiting employees from having unattended boxes, packages, or bags in its facilities. The threat of bombs was treated as a clear and present danger. Manning the control room one day, I noticed an unattended object in the rear door of our Westgate building. It was lunchtime and a security guard was posted there to help facilitate traffic. Immediately, I called Frank Thompson, my boss. He called upstairs to the main office. Within minutes, a command post was established. I was dispatched to the parking lot of the building to direct traffic. No cars were permitted to come into the premises, but they could leave. No one was permitted to enter the building. An alert went out to all employees to stay in their offices. The Fairfax County bomb squad was called to the scene. After some harrowing minutes, with walkie-talkie radio communications among security staffers increased, the word came back from the bomb squad. The unattended object proved to be a gym bag. A woman had decided to go jogging on her lunch break. Upon her return, she met the Fairfax County Bomb Squad. In the after-action report, security learned from the County that our radio transmissions could have triggered the bomb. As for the woman jogger, it's almost certain she received a rather unpleasant grilling from her boss. The lesson learned? Pay attention to company-wide communications.

To conclude, MITRE certainly lived up to its sterling and continuing reputation as one of the best places to work in the United

States. I'm most fortunate to have worked there after hearing about the company from Dan Chin. In my twelve years with the company, I married, fathered two children, obtained a college degree, published two books, met some fascinating people, and shared a lot of laughs. Although the work was steady, I never earned much money there, but was able to set a foundation for future employment as a government contractor. And I never followed Joe Verrett's advice to "Just rest yourself."

My twelve-year odyssey in MITRE Security.

The Marathon King

On February 5, 1995, Rex Wilson conquered Antarctica to become the first person in history to run a marathon on all seven of Earth's continents.

Twenty-five hundred years ago, Greek runner Pheidippides was dispatched from Marathon to Athens to report a military victory over the Persians. Traversing a distance of over twenty-six miles, the brave messenger ran without rest to deliver the news to the Athenian generals, after which the gallant runner collapsed from exhaustion and died. The ancient and modern Olympic Games commemorate this event.

Today, healthy people mimic the lonely Greek runner in marathon races all over the world. One such individual is Lead Engineer Dr. Rex Wilson of Fort Monmouth, New Jersey. Feeling overweight and out of shape in the summer of 1986, 45-year old Rex took up running to shed pounds and improve his cardiovascular system. At first, his jaunts were confined to a local high school track. Encouraged by a friend to run for distance, Rex paced himself and after five months of daily after-work training, decided to conquer the quarter-mile oval. Rex calculated that making 105 revolutions would be the equivalent of running a marathon. One November day, Rex "just did it" and completed his first "marathon," a solo run around and around the high school track.

Two months later, Rex entered and finished his first competitive marathon in Jacksonville, Florida. As he crossed the finish line (in just under four and one-half hours), a surge of emotion welled up inside him. Although he had never hoped to win a race, realizing that the real battle in distance racing comes from inside the runner's heart, Rex resolved to train harder and catch the emotion again.

Over the next several years Rex set running goals for himself far more ambitious than his original premise of losing weight. His marathons assumed a geographic flavor and earned him an exclusive fraternity of friends, all of whom share a special kinship to Pheidippides. Budgeting his money for travel, Rex soon boasted of having run marathons in every state in the nation, explored all the provinces and territories of Canada, and even took his running act to the Land Down Under, completing marathons in all the states and territories of Australia. Not satisfied with running in just English-speaking nations, Rex's athletic wanderlust extended to South Africa, Spain, Germany, France, Mexico, Argentina, Iceland, and Singapore. In each instance, the goal remained the same: running marathons despite sightseeing opportunities that would distract less dedicated world travelers. Every running presented different terrain and weather. Rex jogged on road surfaces, twisted his ankles on trails, huffed up and down hills, and slogged through mud. In Arkansas, he braved freezing rain. In the Two Oceans Ultramarathon in Cape Town, South Africa, Rex ran thirty-five miles. In Singapore, he sweltered in temperatures exceeding eighty degrees, twice the optimum 40-50 degrees usually encountered in North American races.

By the beginning of 1995, Rex's extraordinary perseverance had enabled him to run on all the continents of the planet except the one at the bottom of the world—Antarctica. Because of its extremely cold weather, political conditions, and environmental concerns, Antarctica had never hosted a sporting event of any kind. Enter Thom Gilligan of Marathon Tours and Travel in Boston, Massachusetts. Working in tandem with a scientific organization called Marine Expeditions, Inc., Marathon Tours sponsored an unusual excursion in which marathoners would compete on King George's Island, located in the South Shetland Islands of Antarctica. Billed in a travel itinerary as "The Last Marathon," the Antarctica trip was a nine-day combination sea voyage and distance race. Participants met in Argentina, boarding a chartered research vessel for the journey.

It was no ordinary cruise. While the travelers reveled in sightings of humpback whales, seals, and a variety of birds, much of the thirty-six hour journey involved perilous passage amid icebergs and choppy seas. As the ship approached the continent, a map detailed exotic local areas like Deception Island, Paradise Bay, and Penguin Island, named for its abundance of starry-eyed penguins perpetually dressed in their Sunday best. One tour stop included Pendulum Cove, where the marathoners relaxed by swimming in natural hot sulfur springs.

Laid out by all-terrain vehicles, the marathon course wound through territory controlled by China, Russia, Uruguay, and Chile. It traveled over natural pebbles, muddy roads between military camps, a landscape resembling the chalky whites of the moon, and streams and hills to test the world's best road racers.

The most difficult section of the course involved a one and a half mile stretch over treacherous glaciers, and many of Rex's fellow racers expressed fear of slipping or sinking into the ice. Adding to the danger was a wind that reached up to fifty miles an hour. Runners also had to concern themselves with predatory gull-like birds called skuas. These creatures, which feed on dead penguins, have attacked scientists working on the island. To prepare them for possible skua attacks, the runners were advised to hold up a fist to ward off the birds.

Eighty-four racers gathered at the starting line. Anticipating a difficult run, Rex donned heavy boots, running tights, a long-sleeved shirt, two pairs of socks, and mittens. At one point, Rex endured painful cramps in the near-freezing degree temperatures. In mid-race, Rex nearly overheated due to being overdressed. Despite his physical pain and the less-than-optimum conditions, Rex pressed on. Quitting such a race was unthinkable, especially considering the expense and the distance traveled. As the race wore on, however, many of his companions wore out. The winner crossed the line in just over three hours.

Rex was running in a pack of four men, all of whom were participating in their seventh continental marathon. To finish ahead of them would earn Rex the distinction of being the first man to complete marathons on all seven continents, and when he finally crossed the finish line, after five grueling hours, he had forged ahead. Again, Rex felt the ecstasy of the marathon.

For those in awe of running a distance of 26 miles and 385 yards, Rex offers the following advice: start with endurance walking. With the blessings of a doctor, wake up about 6:00 a.m. on a Sunday and walk until early afternoon. Chances are you'll have blisters, depending on the quality of your shoes, and you'll be extremely tired. Though the soreness will persist for a few days, you'll have walked a marathon.

NOTE: The Second Antarctic Marathon will take place in February 1997.

Concerning Rex Wilson and his global marathoning treks.
Originally appeared in Centerspread.

Larry Kahn, Winks Champ

Member of the Technical Staff Larry Kahn, an ocean engineer in MITRE's H050 division, specializes in a rare sport. Created in the late 1880's by a Londoner, this gentleman's game was all the rage in the England of Jack the Ripper, and over a hundred years after its conception, tiddlywinks occupies an elite band of dedicated fans. After a career spanning a quarter of a century, affable, modest Larry is recognized as the sport's avatar.

Not Just for Kids

Tournament tiddlywinks is not merely the child's game of snapping plastic disks into a cup. The playing field is a white felt mat measuring three by six feet. The disks, called "winks," are the size of dimes and nickels. Winks come in four colors, one for each player. "Squidgers" are used to snap the winks. Matches are often conducted at watering holes. So intense is match concentration that players and spectators sometimes fall into trances.

Rules, strategies and complexities of the game are less easy to describe. A "winker" can try to "pot" his winks, but most would rather make it impossible for opponents to pot theirs through the tactic of "squopping," or immobilizing an opponent's wink by landing one of your own on top of it. A referee officiates, often with a magnifying glass, and settles disputes on shot legality. Tournament winkers are sensitive about their game's flippant image. They especially resent the word "tiddlywinks," because like twiddling one's thumbs, "tiddlywinks" means "doing nothing." Call the game "winks" unless you want to be squopped!

The Goon Show

Modern tiddlywinks embraces the game's strong British-American rivalry. In 1955, as Americans were "Rocking Around the Clock," two students at Britain's Cambridge University formed the first club and published *The Science of Tiddlywinks*. After adding the concept of squopping, the players reveled in their new game, but interest waned. Three years later, a clever prank in the *London Spectator* created quite a stir when the newspaper questioned, DOES PRINCE PHILIP CHEAT AT TIDDLYWINKS? Although the queen's husband didn't even play the game, the spoof rippled through the royal household and the prince had to defend his honor when Cambridge challenged him to a match to clear his name. In March of 1958, the prince appointed radio comedians called "The Goons" (one of whom was movie star Peter Sellers) to play in his stead, and the Reverend E. A. Willis composed an anthem specifically for the event. Public interest swelled, and before six hundred curiosity seekers Cambridge easily defeated the Goons. Like a wink going airborne, clubs organized all over England. When a beaming Prince Philip later petitioned the International Olympic Committee for inclusion of the game, however, the IOC balked.

The Golden Age
     Despite the Olympic setback, the 1960s ushered in a golden age as tiddlywinks caught on at brainy universities in the United States and Canada. One zealous player analyzed the game with Hooke's Law, a scientific explanation on why winks fly. In 1962, Oxford toured the United States and waxed all challengers. In 1966, the North American Tiddlywinks Association (NATwA) was formed with the goals of sponsoring tournaments and promoting the sport, although their main mission may have been to snuff the British at their own game. Six years later the Americans achieved this goal when MIT defeated Southampton; since then, bloodless competitions have created numerous trans-Atlantic friendships.
     Larry began his winking career at the Massachusetts Institute of Technology. In the student handbook he noted "tiddlywinks" and in between his studies, Larry was soon practicing for hours with experienced players. He wasn't alone—the Boston area was a hotbed for winkers in the 1970s, and Cornell and Harvard also fielded teams. Due to his remarkable manual dexterity, Larry soon positioned himself as a master, winning several tournaments in his native country.
     Larry Kahn is a part of tiddly history, traveling to England yearly for world championships. Tournament finals can last for up ten hours a day, but the first time he "squidged-off" against the

British in the early 1980s Larry out-squopped, out-potted, and outlasted them. Larry's victory horrified the British. Though a television interview was scheduled with the winner, his American status so embarrassed them that the spot was canceled.

In Larry's winker career, he has collected 28 national and 20 world titles. Among his accomplishments are articles and air time from the *Washington Post* and WETA radio, and he is proud of his listing in the British Guinness Book of World Records. He is also the current secretary-general of NATwA. In late April, Larry defended his world singles and pairs championships in the United Kingdom.

Associate Department Head Richard Tucker is also a winker and the sport's unofficial historian. Rick's home serves as a repository for ancient tiddlywinks game sets and information, and two years ago he compiled a *Lexicon of Tiddlywinks*, which defines terms and strategies; Rick also defines tiddlywinks terminology like "piddle," "nurdle," and "gromp." Publications with punning titles such as *Newswink* and *My Winkly Reader* are documented, and player nicknames such as Sunshine, Mad Dog, and Larry's arch-rival Dragon, a.k.a. Dave Lockwood are listed (Larry's nickname is Horsemeat, but he prefers "just Larry").

An Uncertain Future

Sadly, interest in winking is waning. Fewer than two dozen players in the U.S. claim to be avid winkers, and NATwA has but sixty members despite their Latin motto, *fiat vincs ruat caelum* ("let winks be played, though the heavens crumble"). Recruiting attempts failed at local colleges and a MENSA meeting, and Larry laments that "MIT doesn't even have a team anymore, which really hurts."

There is cause for optimism, though. A promotional video may be in the offing and the game is now on the Internet. In the fall, Rick hopes to gain converts by presenting a paper at the American Game Collector's Association. Whatever its fate, tiddlywinks remains a quirky sport, but Larry and his dedicated colleagues don't seem to mind a bit.

Tiddlywink Terminology

PIDDLE - (U.S.) A delicate shot in which a squopped wink is gently freed. Also vt. (U.K.) Chip; carve out.

NURDLE, boondock, penhaligon - British drinking game based on counting.
    vt. - To shoot a wink to land in a nurdled position.
    adj. - Describing a wink that is very close to the pot, typically beneath the top rim of the pot and hence probably not easy to pot.

GROMP - n. A shot which moves a pile of winks to squop a wink.

AMIGOS - n. (U.K.) The act of swallowing a pint of whatever in one gulp.

SIDEWAYS AMIGOS - n. (U.K.) - The act of positioning a Mars bar transversely in the mouth prior to performing an amigos.

Lexicon of Tiddlywinks, Second ed. - November, 1993, Richard W. Tucker, editor

Meet Larry Kahn, a champion in a very odd sport. Originally appeared in Centerspread.

Minor Leaguer

On a crisp, late April evening, the Class-A Prince William Cannons hosted the Winston-Salem Spirits for a game of Carolina League ball. It had rained earlier, prompting many to wonder if the game would be played. Perhaps, many came inside due to the lure of the barbecue grill. However, the weather cleared and a fireworks display was promised. Young men in the late teens and twenties were following their American Dreams on the field. A nice crowd of three thousand chattered away, moved to their seats, and anticipated.

The contest featured a host of interesting moments. A right fielder lost a ball in the lights and the scoreboard lightheartedly read "It's foggy out there." The game was peppered with bad infield throws, missed batting opportunities, and strikeouts looking. On the outfield wall, the Marlboro Man appeared to be smoking when barbecue grill vapors wafted towards the outfield. Six lithe young ladies called the "Diamond Girls" danced for the crowd between innings. In short, it was single A baseball. With the score tied, and two out in the ninth inning, the home team hero stepped in and whacked the ball far out into the thick air of right field. The parabola was just right as the ball soared over the fence. One could almost expect the light tower to explode as in *The Natural*. It didn't. But, it sure seemed that way. In jubilation, the crowd all stood, applauded, and yelled. All the Cannons' players came pouring onto the field to congratulate the star of the game.

Shortly after, the stadium went dark. Screaming missiles of light shot up into the air from behind right field. For those that could see behind the outfield barrier, the explosives sent men scurrying about. "Oohs" and "ahhs" and "wows" were the shared communication of the thousands that stayed at the ballyard to watch the magic show. What's better than fireworks displays?

The highlight of the night, though, was my conversation with a small boy fan. Appearing to be all of ten years old, the lad made several humorous comments. He proudly proclaimed that he had been to every Cannons home game - yet he asked a short while later how many innings were in a game. A friend he was with piped in, "ten innings 'cause that's what the scoreboard says." The boy showed me an official Carolina League baseball he was keeping in his pocket and a miniature souvenir bat. On the ball were the autographs of some players and the Cannons team mascot. On the bat were the autographs of all six "Diamond Girls." When the girls were performing between innings, I whipped out my binoculars for a better look. As soon as the boy saw that I had magnifying power, he screamed, "Can I use those?" I obliged, but not before asking him if he was old enough. During a lull in the action, an object brushed me on the shoulder from behind. Before I could figure out what it was, the lad exclaimed, "Somebody threw something at you!" This seemed strange since I was sitting in the last row of the upper level of the stadium. It was a giant flying insect and it settled into an empty bleacher seat just below. Like an overprotective mother, the boy immediately snatched his bat and yelled, "Would you like it dead? Would you like it dead?" I said that it wasn't necessary.

So...within a few short hours, I had been entertained by baseball, barbecue, barbie dolls, and a curious little boy.

The wonders of minor League baseball and its quirky promotions.

First Born

All parents know of the incredible range of emotions swirling regarding the birth of their first child. Pride and promise. Anxiety and fear. Wondering whether or not they will be good parents. Hoping for the health of the baby and the mother. Could the parents agree on a name for the child? What would be the child's gender? Then there is the advice from family and friends and co-workers about their own experiences. It's easy for the mother and father to be overwhelmed and teeter between happiness and depressive thoughts.

For my wife and myself, and millions of others, the above emotions played out in real time. Additional complications surfaced, as my wife was a naturalized United States citizen, originally hailing from Seoul, South Korea. As an American father, together we felt the pressures of our own respective cultures. Would our child be raised as Korean and learn their language and customs? Would they be raised as an American? I firmly believed that our child be immersed in two cultures for the best of both worlds.

To prepare for the blessed day, my wife sought the expertise of a female Korean OB/GYN doctor in Northern Virginia. Our baby would be born in Fairfax Hospital. We met several times with the bi-lingual doctor. My wife coordinated all the preparations with the doctor in her native language. I was able to ask numerous questions in English. The gracious doctor answered them all with kindness and professionalism. I was thankful for this remarkably good choice by my wife. We both felt we were in good hands.

Despite living in Stafford, Virginia, over an hour away, we eagerly accepted the challenge of the long drive for preparation classes conducted by the doctor. As my wife grew bigger, it seemed as if the discomfort of her pregnancy melted away with her steely determination, her inner strength. I believe this determination to be a positive hallmark of Korean people. At the last class of preparation, I asked the doctor if I could bend her ear for a moment. My wife was in the Ladies Room and I needed to ask my question in private. "Doctor, you know I'll be there to support my wife throughout, but can you position me so I won't see the blood?" The doctor smiled and said, "Sure, sometimes husbands ask me that same question." As the days ticked away, with a false alarm or two, my wife began to become worried. Her due date had come and gone. She asked the doctor for the best course of action. "Come on in on Saturday and we'll induce you."

We checked into Fairfax Hospital in the early morning of July 3, 1993. My wife and I both knew this would likely be the day of the birth. As I sat in a chair by her bedside, the doctor's assistant administered an epidural shot to my wife to induce labor and mitigate pain. As the medicine worked its magic, I sat patiently wondering about the immense pain of childbirth. The hours passed. Slowly. I remembered a popular male comedian's thoughts about birth. "Gentlemen," he said. "Reach up and grab your lower lip, then, pull it over your nose. That's how my wife described the pain." Ouch, I thought. Men have it easy. Relatively. A television overhead displayed the finals of the women's Wimbledon tennis match final. I continued sitting in the chair as my wife held a couple of my fingers. My wife entered into the throes of labor many hours later. As she did so, her hands squeezed my fingers with such force, I was sure I'd soon be in an emergency room. Wasn't she supposed to be the one experiencing all the pain? Following the tennis match, I asked a nurse to switch over to the Orioles baseball game. Occasionally peeking at the baseball game, I realized the actions from the television, kept *me* from screaming out.

"Push, push!" the doctor said. By now, I assumed my pre-determined place in the room. I stood about ten feet away, to the left of my wife's bed. From my vantage point, I would not be able to see the birth. I deliberately stared off at a wall, afraid I might pass out. The doctor's assistant had brought in a large aluminum pan to catch the blood and the afterbirth. The doctor kept up her exhortations and my wife grunted along. "Push, push!" Just then, Orioles catcher Chris Hoiles knocked a home run over the fence. At nearly that exact moment, our new baby girl entered the world. My wife let out a sigh of relief. So did I. But, seconds later, the assistant dropped the aluminum pan. It clanged against the hospital room floor, causing my head to jerk towards the sound. My wife's warm blood spilled, causing an unbelievable mess. I saw it all, exactly the moment I had tried to avoid. Likely, I let out a demonstrably squeamish gasp. As the new mother recovered in bed, a nurse swooped in to cradle our brand new child and clean her up. Despite the pan mishap, the hospital staffers could not have been kinder. After a few minutes, our baby in a bassinette was greeted by her father. I tried to choke back tears, saying, "Alicia, hello, I'm your daddy. Welcome." My emotions also yielded an enormous sense of pride as a parent and the promise laying in the bassinette. My initial meeting took about a minute until the nurse gently placed our baby in her mother's loving arms. My wife offered her the lopsided smile of exhaustion and joy in that extremely special moment when mother meets child.

We stayed overnight in the hospital, comforting each other as baby spent her first night of life sleeping in a room with a dozen other newborns. The nurse swaddled her up. The ride back home to Stafford proved as maddening as any single driving event. After all, tiny precious cargo dozed away in the car seat, with mommy at her side. Taking extra precautions, I drove about five miles under the speed limit on I-95 South. An hour and a half later, Alicia, mommy, and I were home safe and sound.

Our children make us immortal.

"I'm Her!"

Barney. Sesame Street. Dudley the Dragon. Peanuts. Walt Disney. Totoro. Babe.

Alicia knows every one and can recognize nearly all of the characters and people involved in dozens of films, videos, coloring books, dolls, games, stuffed animals, toys relating to each of the above mentioned.

In Barney, there's the main star - a friendly and polite purple dinosaur that sings. There's BJ, a yellow kid dino who dresses in tennis shoes, and his little sister Baby Bop, who requires a nap now and again. Among the human tag-a-longs are Min, Jason, and Michael.

Sesame Street is the home to quite a collection of characters. Elmo, the red plush, ticklish boy. Big Bird, an overgrown yellow bird of an unidentifiable species. Bert and Ernie, the lovable roommates who get on each other's nerves. Oscar the Grouch, who lives in a trashcan. Mr. Snuffleupagus, an extremely large, dodo-bird-looking creature. Grover, a blue whatzit. Cookie Monster, who lives for his favorite confection. The Count, a lovable Transylvanian in a cape who doesn't feast on blood at all. He just loves to count. And, oh yes, there's Bob, whose been on the show so long, he's avuncular. But, he sings swell and Alicia and I saw him at Zany Brainy.

Dudley the Dragon is new to Alicia's viewing, so I'm not quite sure she knows all of them.

Charlie Brown and the Peanuts gang has always been a favorite. No reiteration of their characters are necessary here.

The empire of children is, of course, Walter Disney. Currently, we own Toy Story, The Lion King, Cinderella, Pocahontas, The Aristocats, and Snow White on video. Next will probably be The Hunchback of Notre Dame. And Alicia knows them all from John Smiff (as she calls him) to Buzz Lightyear to Simba to Sneezy to Dopey to the Fairy Godmother.

This is truly remarkable to contemplate that a child of three can have such an extraordinary memory. But she does. More amazingly, she can recognize all of their personalities as well. One of her favorite lines is "I'm her," to express her appreciation for a female character that she'd like to be like.

Next month is the Barney show at George Mason and tots will be taking over the campus for a weekend or so. Of course, we plan to go, despite the stiff admission. Barney's a harmless sort. Actually, he's quite good with children. He teaches them manners and respect and what foods to eat. Pre-schoolers delight. Sometimes, I'm sickened by the negative press that Barney gets. All those older kids (and parents) conspiring to kill him. Barney's OK and a fine role model for Alicia. That's why I mentioned him first.

We're glad that Alicia counts all these folks as her friends. And, although she knows they are not real, she holds a very special place in her little heart for each of them.

Alicia's friends.

A Purple Dinosaur

I must really love my daughter Alicia.

Let the record show that on 23 March, 1997, I stood in line for over an hour in 38-degree weather at George Mason University's box office to buy Barney tickets for my three and one-half year-old. The wait was both necessitated and tempered by several dozen other parental schmucks (and their young children) standing in line for the same reason. While in line, I noted the conversations taking place among the crowd.

One lady explained to another that they'd been to "Cats" the night before and that the lines for the Ladies rest room were unbelievable. "I thought there was going to be a riot." She then addressed a man and exclaimed, "That's one advantage you men have. You can go quickly."

Several of our brethren broke out in embarrassed grins.

As we inched our way in line, others complained about the prices that were being charged for the show, $26, $18.50 and $13.50. "For that you could buy two Barney videos and have him on demand," said another.

Several of the under four year-olds were frolicking next to a tree. The grounds were obscured by a layer of a green ivy-looking plant. The kids were rolling around in the ivy, dirtying up their Sunday best clothes. One incensed parent had seen enough of her child having fun. She snatched her youngster into her arms, admonishing the child, "There could be snakes in there, stay away!"

Despite the drudgery of waiting, I comforted myself with the newspaper advertisement I had carried along. "Barney's Big Surprise," it read. "With Baby Bop, BJ, Professor Tinkerputt and Mother Goose. Live and In Purple."

After about an hour, I and ten others were allowed to enter the building. Inside, we were all greeted by an employee overseeing this ticket purchasing event. "OK, all of you who are not the actual purchaser, please step out of line and stand over next to the wall. Have your cash or credit card ready. Give the teller the event, the price, and how many tickets you need. The Barney tickets are going on sale at all Ticketmaster outlets and by telephone, so if you want

215

seats for the weekend shows, please understand that they are half sold out."

Wow, I wondered, where did they get this guy, the gestapo? This is a Barney concert, not Treblinka.

Finally, it was my turn. "Tuesday the 29th, $18.50, 2 tickets," I confidently said, following Mr. Gestapo's instructions to the letter. The teller began to process my order in the computer explaining that I'd be sitting in the seats straight out front. Perfect for Alicia, I thought. Floor chairs were ruled out since my daughter would have to strain to look up to the stage. Just then, some of the ladies waiting behind me began to gab loudly. My teller's face registered anger. From behind the glass partition, the teller screamed for them to please be quiet. Selling Barney tickets is a stressful occupation.

The madness surrounding Barney.

Alicia's Cooking Adventures

She makes me breakfast, lunch, and dinner about seven or eight times a day.

And then expects me to eat it all.

Alicia rarely cleans up the residue of pots and pans and plates and silverware and dirty napkins and half-eaten food. And yet she goes on without fail making me meals she fully expects me to devour gladly. I smile and place the plastic food in my mouth, pretending to enjoy the chicken, hamburgers, hot dogs, french fries, eggs, ice cream, pizza, bacon, and cheese. To wash this all down, I'm served a cup of piping-hot coffee. Not quite as hot as McDonald's so there's no chance of a lawsuit, but hot coffee nonetheless. Another filling meal full of All American artery clogging favorites.

"What are you gonna make?" I ask.

"My dinner," she says matter-of-factly.

"What about mine?" I reiterate.

"OK, I make you something. Whatchoo want?"

Despite my cravings, Alicia is making what she wants to.

I catch a listen to her preparation:

"Corn with peas and french fries."

"I need that bacon!"

Children imitate everything their parents do. Today, our going-on-four year-old Alicia is imitating her mother make dinner with her plastic set of food. After spying a block in the food items, Alicia screams, "Hey, who put this in here?"

After some time, Alicia begins to make a new sort of dish. No one is sure where the concoction came from. We didn't tell her about it. But, she is very serious about this newfangled dish. I ask sheepishly what my new dinner is called.

"Banello!" cries Alicia.

My wife and I shake our heads. I guess that is sort of a cross between banana, vanilla, Jello and some other stuff. General Mills, are you listening? Where would this be marketed? In the third world?

It's certainly a good thing that I didn't eat all that food.

Alicia probably wouldn't have a father for long if I sampled all of her cooking. And, although she's not as good a cook as her mother, I love her to pieces for trying.

Daughter Alicia's sincerity shines on.

Valentine's Day

Ever since we've been married my wife (of six and one-half years) has insisted on me NOT buying her flowers. "They're a waste of money," she says. However, twice in that time frame I've defied her and tried to purchase a dozen roses. On both occasions, I called a florist directly across the street from her workplace. And, in both instances, the flowers were not delivered. Oh, well, perhaps it was not meant to be. I chewed one young clerk out two years ago. He was unfortunate enough to feel the wrath of my tongue. I exaggerate. I was very polite and simply asked if they could get a neighborhood stray cat or dog to walk them across the street. Or, a better idea was to actually hire someone off the street, perhaps a homeless man, and offer him ten bucks to travel two hundred yards to make the delivery. Hey, it wouldn't be FTD, but it would help turn a profit for the florist and ensure the homeless man another bottle of ripple. Am I being cynical? Perhaps. The only real truth in the story is the fact that my wife doesn't like flowers delivered. Maybe, it's just the fact that she's be embarrassed in the workplace? And, I'm such a pussycat, I couldn't conceive of cursing some poor sap out. At least not on the phone or in person. Had he some electronic eavesdropping equipment attached to my body or automobile, he would have heard a mouthful. But, that's as far as I ever go. It serves the same purpose and no one gets their feelings hurt.

Heavens! Whatever would St. Valentine's have thought of all this? And, what did he know about love anyway? Did he ever try to have flowers delivered to his sweetheart? Did he ever exchange those dopey valentine's in elementary school? I remember with fervent anticipation (probably akin to Charlie Brown's puppy-love for the little red-headed girl) receiving a valentine from a gal in 6th grade who could actually catch a baseball with a glove. Now, THAT was love!

Love is in the air.

The Human Heart

What is the sound the human heart makes? Is it da-dum, da-dum, da-dum? Or bum-bumm, bum-bumm, bum-bumm? Neither of these. Actually, according to the medical profession the sound is lub-dup, lub-dup, lub-dup. But, that's just the sound of the fully-formed heart. The embryonic three-month old heart offers a tantalizing "swoosh." At least that is the sound electronically-enhanced in a typical obstetrician's office.

My wife, as you have probably surmised, is expecting a baby. Our second. We're not sure if it is a boy or a girl and we don't want to know until the delivering doctor shows us. We're thrilled, especially for the reaction and learning experience for our first child, a four and one-half year old named Alicia. Never has there been such a more inquisitive, warm-hearted soul as this little girl. She's actually my best friend on this earth, my wife notwithstanding.

My wife and I have decided to start a family tradition. As Alicia is the first generation offspring of a Korean-American marriage (I play the part of the American), our children will all have names that start with "A." Alicia, or unborn Adrian's, Ansel's, or Annemarie's children should start with B. All of their progeny should start with C. And so on. That would make 26 generations, or ensure at least about 500+ years worth of lineage. This was really my wife's idea and I think it's fairly interesting. Convincing Alicia and everyone of the tradition will probably not be so easy. After I heard my wife explain this to me, I immediately thought of the Moody Blues' album title "To Our Children's Children's Children." And that's a lot of swooshing!

Alicia gears up for a new sibling.

By the Book

I love books. Always have. From the time I was a wee tyke when my mother and father read to me to the present, my love of books and reading defines who I am.

On one day in May 1998, however, this passion may have exceeded its limit. In the previous month, my father passed away from lung cancer. He died in Brookville, Pennsylvania and was buried in Punxsutawney, same state. As executor, I coordinated with my sisters for distributing items in his estate. Gina wanted our father's enormous collection of clocks. Beth sought the small porcelain figures, which were collected by my mother. I fancied the books, several hundreds of them, mostly non-fiction, which I dutifully packed in a few dozen boxes. The rest of the items, furniture and other knick-knacks, were made available to other family members such as my father's surviving brothers and my cousins.

My five-hour solo trip back home to Clifton, Virginia involved my small pick-up truck, stuffed with the haul of books. Upon arrival, I'd store these priceless gems in my home attic. But, "The best laid plans of mice and men oft go astray," wrote Scottish poet Robert Burns. No words could so perfectly capture what occurred upon my arrival.

My wife came to the front of the house as I entered. This door opened into the living room. My not yet five-year old daughter Alicia was playing with her seven-year old cousin Angela in the center of the room. Angela's mother had dropped off her daughter while she ran errands. My wife returned to her current chores in the rear of the house. I explained to Alicia that I'd be bringing in several boxes of books, some that included children's volumes. Access to the attic resided in the den, a room to the left of the living room. A drop-down ladder must be lowered for one to enter the attic. After pulling the chord and dropping down the spring-loaded ladder, I emphasized to the kids to stay out of the way. With this set-up, I walked back to my truck and began to unload. Some boxes were quite heavy, containing coffee table books. Lacking a dolly, I shlepped each box inside, up the ladder, and onto the floored surface. Only sections of the attic contained flooring. Otherwise, one had to traverse the area on the joists like a gymnast on a balance beam. And I was no gymnast. By some substantial effort, I had removed all of the boxes in the truck and placed them in the attic. One remained, substantially difficult due to its weight.

By this time, though, the tasking had worn me down. My legs ached. My arms ached even worse. Tiredness enveloped my physical being. With some effort, I managed to climb up the stairs with that one last box. I lifted the books onto the flooring before I wearily lifted myself. I straightened up standing and grabbed the box. Unfortunately, for all people in the house, including myself, I lost my balance. Within a second, I tumbled though two parallel joists, breaking the ceiling drywall, and causing the kids directly below to shriek. As the plaster rained down on the kids, in big chunks and small, I found myself, feet dangling through the ceiling, and wedged, arms outstretched, holding on for dear life. The ceiling stood about eight feet from the living room floor. "Are you two, okay?" I yelled to the kids. Instantly, my wife came running. She surveyed the scene and quickly moved the kids out of harm's way. Thank God, she raced up the ladder and managed to pull me up to safety. Had I fallen through onto those kids, I could have killed us all. Not exactly a good report for medical professionals.

By some miracle, no one was hurt. However, I suffered stinging abrasions to both sides of my torso as I slid through. The wounds did not require treatment other than lotion, lovingly applied by my wife. Within a week, the ceiling was repaired and flooring extended to fully one-half of the attic. In retrospect, my wife emerged the hero of the story and I played the fool.

The perils of owning too many books.

"Here's Your New Sister"

On the day she was born, November 5, 1998, my second daughter Amelia turned one year old. Wait. What? As my wife was native born in South Korea, Korean Age considers time spent in the womb as one year. Of course, in most places around the globe, the day of birth starts our personal chronological time. Thus, as Amelia was born in the United States, my wife and I agreed to adopt our standards of calculating age. As somewhat of a compromise, Amelia's middle name was Jisun, which means "Wise Immortal."

Nearly every detail concerning Amelia's birth differed from her older sister Alicia. Amelia began life in Arlington Hospital in Virginia, the same facility where my wife's father worked as a blood specialist. The birth attendees included five-year-old Alicia. Our oldest daughter's excitement and wonder surrounding the birth of a sibling cannot be overstated. She smiled from ear-to-ear and couldn't stop asking her sweet questions of when. "When mommy's ready, you'll have a new baby brother or baby sister," we both re-iterated. Although as parents, we'd done the birthing drill before, the presence of Alicia spurred our own sense of the miracle that is the human conception experience. It's impossible to explain to a child how a single sperm, swimming up the fallopian tube, merges with a woman's egg to cause mitotic cell division and eventually birth. Naturally, a child would further question more about sperm and their remarkable journey, and where they came from. Hence, the folk myth that a white stork delivers babies.

As with Alicia's birth, I stayed in the room. But, Amelia wasn't ready to make her grand appearance. My wife, God bless her, focused on the upcoming birth. I took care of Alicia. Deep into the night and into early morning, we waited. We both fell asleep in the chair provided, with tiny Alicia resting in my arms. Oblivious to the hullabaloo, my wife gave birth to our daughter Amelia, while father and daughter rested. The doctor came over and tapped me on the shoulder, waking me up. "Congratulations, Mr. Hetrick, you have a healthy new baby girl." My adrenaline kicked in. I nudged Alicia into the waking world and explained the situation. "Alicia, you've got a new baby sister." Alicia wiped her eyes and looked around. Her mother held baby Amelia, beaming in that motherly way, but thoroughly exhausted from the experience. I thanked the doctor and nurse as tears welled up in my eyes.

Now a family of four, we stayed in the hospital overnight. A nurse whisked Baby Amelia away to that room where newborns go. Over the next several hours, my wife's sisters and sister-in-law came to visit. The meetings were cordial and congratulatory. There were gifts of diapers and formula and baby clothes. To keep Alicia occupied, I took her on a tour of the facility. We walked the halls as I explained various hospital departments and procedures. We ate lunch and dinner in the cafeteria, alternating time with her mother. The excitement and exercise tired Alicia out and she dozed away, this time in the recovery room.

The next morning, as Alicia sat patiently in a chair, we presented her with a small, swaddling bundle of joy. "Here's your new sister, you can hold her," I said. Over a lifetime, one sees many things. Good, bad, and indifferent. However, few things can compare to Alicia's happiness upon holding her new sister. A snapshot preserves that beautiful moment. All that was good in the world reflected in Alicia's face.

When we arrived home in Clifton, Virginia, Alicia hardly acted the jealous child. She wanted to be in the same room for feedings, for diaper changes, even for sleeping. We told her in whispers to be quiet while Amelia slept. Alicia stared for hours at her new sister, nearly erasing the difficulties of parenting a newborn. Her thoughtful questions, answered to her five-year-old mind, further eased our struggle.

As time passed, baby Amelia grew into crawler, toddler, and terrible twos. Especially feisty for a couple of years, Amelia at two challenged her parents with willful disobedience. In time, her bad attitude waned. Alicia helped her sister every step of the way. Alicia taught Amelia to hold a crayon and draw on paper. Alicia assisted with changing her sister's clothes. Alicia trained Amelia to do the right things. She helped her sister with school and homework. All by her choice. In short, Alicia grew easily into a nurturer and caregiver. Her every task began and continued with the light of her smile.

In Korean mythology, dragons are considered to be helpful creatures. Alicia's middle name was Jiyong, translated as "Wise Dragon." Alicia has always been just that.

The Wise Dragon meets the Wise Immortal.

Amelia's Toys!

Like benevolent spirits, the toys of children linger long after they grow into adulthood.

My two daughters, Alicia and Amelia, five years apart, offer similar stories about their memory of and attachment to their toys. The impact of these playthings often last a lifetime.

At the age of four, Alicia doted on her favorite doll, Baby Talk. Battery-powered, the doll featured vocal utterances and a mouth that moved accordingly. She took the doll everywhere with her, dutifully performing motherly chores of caring for her baby. Alicia talked to, clothed, bathed, fed the doll, and tucked her in at night. During real mealtime, the doll ate with the family. It was heartwarming to observe the sincerity in which Alicia went about her daily tasks of parenting. Because Baby Talk was an integral member of the family, washing her outfit became too frequent for Alicia's mother. This resulted in the doll going *au natural*. During that summer, our family drove to Charlotte, North Carolina to visit my wife's sister Nichole. Naturally, Alicia brought along her doll. We enjoyed a pleasant visit for a few days. Nichole and her husband David were childless, but treated Alicia (and her doll) like a princess. The day before our return trip home to Virginia, the six of us went to a playground; Alicia and her doll riding the swings. No one noticed anything out of the ordinary as we spent a final night in Charlotte. Upon waking, we said our goodbyes and gathered up our belongings. Alicia started to cry inconsolably when she noticed her doll missing. In a panic, we searched all over the house. But, the doll was not to be found. I asked everyone to think about our previous movements. It didn't take long to realize that the doll may have been forgotten at the playground. Unfortunately, that did not calm Alicia. Her wailing broke our collective hearts. This was *her* child, *her Baby Talk*, and she was gone. Somehow, we strapped Alicia into her car seat and started on the trip back. She cried herself to sleep. A few miles later, we stopped at the playground. I jumped out of the car, as my wife stayed with our daughter. There, perfectly still sat the doll, on the swing set where she was left. Much relieved, I grabbed the doll and brought it back to Alicia, still dozing away. I carefully placed the doll into Alicia's arms and drove off. About an hour later, she awoke, as her mother now sat beside her in the back seat. As she opened her eyes and noticed her doll, safely returned, it was Alicia's parents turn to cry. Tears of joy.

But, this story is about Amelia's toys. My youngest daughter played with a wide variety of toys; from animals to make-believe to interactive to exercise. In a phone conversation, Amelia, now 22 years old, reminisced about the joys of her childhood. Certainly, parental and societal influences and school studies mold a child's personality. However, as they engage in playing with their siblings or on their own, toys must also be examined as influencers.

From earliest ages, most children learn that animals are cute and cuddly. This concept is reinforced in kid's picture books, visual media, and at zoos. Respecting animals, like people, remains part of animal curriculum. Amelia's animal toys reflected these principles. Before Amelia played with her own actual dog, she marveled at Robot Dog, a mechanical plastic version with a rather unsteady gait. Straight from the box, Robot Dog proved far easier to maintain than Fido. He was housebroken and did not eat anything at all. Elefun depicted an elephant with its truck in full trumpet mode. In operation, Elefun blew air from its trunk straight upward. In this blast of air, small pieces of cloth floated as butterflies for children to catch in a net. The good news about Elefun was its scaled-down size. A toy the size of Jumbo may have trouble fitting inside a standard house. Let's Go Fishin' featured tiny fishing poles and lures made with magnets. Kids tried to catch plastic fish, which also contained magnets in their mouths. Unlike real fishing, this toy did not involve the relaxation of the outdoors nor the realization that fishing is *not* about catching fish. Little Pet Shop afforded kids the opportunity to own their own business, replete with numerous animals for sale. Dogs, frogs, cats, and birds waited for new loving owners to take them home. Finally, an oddly purple stuffed animal named Doodle Bear came with a special marker. Children drew on the bear. When finished, Doodle Bear went right in with the laundry, erasing the doodles, and emerging fresh and clean again.

Dolls helped Amelia make-believe parenting. One such doll was Baby All Gone with her strange pear-shaped head. Complete

227

with her own milk bottle and baby food, Baby All Gone only ate cherries from her special spring-loaded spoon. That's not all. Baby All Gone talked and did what babies do after feeding, right into her diaper. Polly Pocket meant another mommy opportunity, complete with miniscule dolls and furniture inside their own carrying-case house.

Like other toys, interactive toys fueled a kid's imagination. Two classic examples are Slinky and Lite Brite. Slinky, first made of tightly-coiled thin metal and later plastic versions, walked down stairs on its own. Using gravity and spring propulsion, Slinky amused for hours on end. Unfortunately, as happened invariably, the metal bent when stepped on or dropped. Even the slightest change doomed the toy from an active marvel to a static paperweight. Slinky has been around since the early 1940s. The Lite Brite toy, c. 1967, allowed for children's creativity. A board contained a small light source. Colorful see-through plastic pins were placed on the board in shapes or designs. Because of its many small pieces, Lite Bright did not work well with infants and toddlers, who could mistake them for candy. Technology-wise, Pin Art stood apart from the competition, enjoyed by all ages. An eight-inch by four-inch box design, Pin Art utilized hundreds on tiny pins with dull tips. The entire device could then be placed on one's hand or face to create a 3-D bas-relief. Each pin's height would conform to the contours of the object. Once shaken, the pins would reset to their original position.

As a toddler, Amelia proudly exercised with Corn Popper. Like a hand-held lawn mower, Corn Popper contained a long handle and a globe filled with balls that popped when they landed on a powerful spring inside. The more the movement, the more the popping. In many aspects, this toy appealed to small fry. They could walk or run around with it, see the action of the balls, hear the sounds it made, and know that they controlled everything going on. The racket caused by this toy could drive any parent to drink. Corn Popper is over sixty years old. Dance Dance Revolution (DDR) capitalized on the dance craze. The game came with a dance mat with arrows and a cabinet for the hardware. Dancers listened to the music and moved around according to cues built into the system.

Like the Corn Popper for tikes, DDR served as a noisemaker for older kids and adults. Amelia's mother and sister enjoyed the music and the movements. I, however, departed to another room during DDR game play.

Based on anecdotal evidence, I believe any adult would respond favorably when asked about the toys they played with as youngsters. It might take awhile for the shyest among us, but toys being an integral part of growing up, likely spurs engaging conversation and a flood of fond memories.

What were your favorite toys as a child?

On the importance of children's toys.

Won Kyu Choi Starts a New Life in America

I conducted two interviews with Mr. Won Kyu Choi, a thirty five-year-old father of two young girls, who recently immigrated, with his family to the United States from Seoul, South Korea. Mr. Choi entered our country in search of a better life for his family. His study and profession involves television-programming production. As a slight interruption to his career, Mr. Choi served 32 months as an Air Force Police officer, following South Korea's mandatory conscription policy. Because of his excellent preparation and expertise in media, Mr. Choi related some demographics about his country. South Korea's 45 million people crowd an area of just under 62,000 square miles. Before engaging in serious dialogue, I fancied him a confident, upstanding Christian gentleman with positive family values.

At the start of our conversation, Mr. Choi informed me of his living situation on American soil. Typically, Korean households contain three and sometimes four generations sharing one roof. Mr. Choi resides in Fairfax, Virginia with his wife and daughters who share the home with Choi's mother and father. Thus, three generations live in the house. Although Mr. Choi pays the mortgage and has title to the house, his father occupies the top rung of decision making and authority. Choi's mother is second in command. Naturally, Choi is third with his wife and children comprising the base of the structure. This concept directly relates to long-standing Korean beliefs in Confucianism, a philosophic, patriarchal moral code originated from China. Confucianism, less a religion than a way of life, embodies strong principles of ancestor worship and filial piety. Because Choi's father is the eldest and most experienced member of the household, he's expected to provide strength and guidance in family matters. Sometimes, these ideas survive the death of the patriarch; a concept Choi calls the "spirit of the family." Largely due to Western influence, the collectivist Confucianist ideals may be eroding away with newer generations, who tend to think about themselves. This individualistic new generation not only makes Confucianism passé, but also can damage family reputations gained over long periods of

230

time.

Interestingly, Choi's family unit in the United States differs slightly from the same unit living in Korea. Here, family members solve problems more democratically; even the children can express their opinions. In Korean society, the social position of women usually falls far short of men, although this is slowly changing. Korean women also do not traditionally change their surnames upon marriage. However, Choi's wife changed her name in America for bureaucratic ease. The elderly in Korea rarely live alone, although some retirement homes have now been built. No social security blanket exists for elderly South Koreans. My curiosity peaked, I questioned Mr. Choi as to what would happen if he died. He related that his wife would assume house payments but would still answer to the senior Mr. Choi.

In the economic expansion of the 1970s and 1980s, work was more important than today. Incomes were smaller then, but 1990s Koreans enjoy more comforts. Without serious study, these advances would not have been possible. The current Korean educational system may have been adapted after the Japanese from the Occupation. However, over time, the Korean education system evolved its own teaching outlook. South Korean industrialization occurred by the hard study of engineers, scientists, doctors, and politicians. With a major cultural emphasis on globalization, Koreans often study abroad, depending on their field. Before their journey, language institutes help prepare Koreans. Art students might travel to Paris and Moscow. Music lovers go to Czechoslovakia. Film studies majors concentrate on Russia and the United States.

Although the spirit of Confucianism still pervades Korean culture, Choi explained that 40% of Koreans believe in Christianity with 23% ascribing to Buddhism. The interviewee could not provide an answer to my question about the inordinate percentage of Korean Christians.

We also discussed Korean politics. Mr. Choi unabashedly admitted little interest in the subject, conforming largely to young people's apathy of matters political. Generally, those under thirty years old consider politicians "stick-in-the-muds;" men who believe

231

in outmoded principles from forty years ago. However, the United States pays careful attention to democratic South Korean politics. From 1945-1948, the United States acted as "trustee" and ruled South Korea. Beginning in 1950, The Korean War began, which split the nation in half. Most importantly, for U.S. interests, South Korea's neighbors remain the Communist North Koreans. The United States and South Korea ally themselves against North Korea with millions of ground forces facing each other divided by the DMZ. Recent news reports, which Mr. Choi considers accurate, highlight severe North Korean food shortages and a desire to acquire nuclear weapons. The tense standoff continues, exacerbated by the fact that North Korea targets South Korea with missiles. As Choi explains, "The Korean War hasn't ended, it's just paused since 1953."

Mr. Choi illustrated examples of personal and mass communication in his country. Like the Japanese and Chinese, Korean society adheres to rigid, unwritten hierarchical rules, too complex to be analyzed here. On a personal level, Koreans recognize polite and informal requests. To be polite, older people will say to shop owners, "I'm looking for some Coca-Cola." The younger generation may ask for products in the negative. "You don't have Coke?" follows the assumption that the store should stock the product. Pleasantries can be exchanged but upon completion of the transaction, the clerk simply takes the money. "Thank you's" and smiles are not necessary. As a rule, Koreans generally do not smile. Nor do they use facial expressions or gestures. Unlike communicators here, who tend to elaborate, Koreans insult rather creatively by simply barking out, "Do!"

Despite it being his own profession, Mr. Choi takes exception to the vagaries of mass communications. In South Korea, he related, the media unfairly biases news reporting. He believes reporters should never act as commentators and influencers. Often, he complained, Korean newsmen don't report economic news truthfully. Choi sees the American media as far more powerful, but fairer in reportage of events. Last year, Mr. Choi worked for a local Korean radio station. According to Choi, the station operated solely for profit, caring nothing for their listeners. They rarely reported local news important to the 100,000 Koreans living in this area. Instead, the station broadcast outdated news feeds from Los Angeles that contained California traffic reports and news topical to Koreans residing on the west coast. The aim of these programs, he argued, was to promote products the station manager owned interest in. Choi quit the job after four days due to philosophical differences over business operations.

On evaluating his own culture, Mr. Choi's demeanor brightened. He seemed eager to answer, almost as if anticipating my asking. He described Koreans as unique and homogeneous. Westerners, in their Eurocentric ignorance, often confuse Chinese, Japanese, and Koreans as similar peoples. Anthropologically, Koreans descend from Mongolians. Five thousand years ago Korea established their own nation, complete with their own language and identity. Although they originally borrowed their written language from China, in 1443 a king named Sejong invented Hangul, the uniquely Korean writing system. Geographically, Korea is a peninsula, bordering with China in the north and the Sea of Japan from the south. Historically, the Chinese population, comprised of many peoples and languages, invaded Korea on numerous occasions, greatly influencing Korean sustenance and culture. Because of their geographic proximity, Korean served as conduit for culture transfer between China and other nations in Asia. As example, Buddhism, Confucianism, art, and politics entered Japan from China by way of Korea. Mr. Choi's less-than-positive opinions of Japan seem typical of Korean males I've encountered. With the government overthrow of Korea by Japan this century, who can blame him as describing the Japanese as "aggressive"? Japan's an island nation far less arable than topographically diverse China. Naturally, the Japanese depend far more on fishing industries. Unlike the other cultural transfers, Choi related that the Japanese "stole" Korean culture fifteen hundred years ago. A dynastic monarch named Paekche left behind Korean treasures and artifacts discovered in his grave.

Adapting to United States culture hasn't been easy. The language barrier slows down most new arrivals. Mr. Choi already speaks excellent English but sometimes has trouble articulating. To improve himself, he takes ESL classes. Unfortunately, two fears continue to disturb him. He's afraid of committing a mistake by uttering impolite words or misunderstanding an expression due to his ignorance. In Korea, for example, due to overcrowding, Koreans routinely bump into each other on the street. So-called "push men" are employed at subway station platforms to herd passengers into cars before automatic doors close. Yet, no one complains. Mr. Choi also fears the act of driving in the United States. The American transportation system, largely built around personal vehicles, offers a vast improvement over South Korea, designed for public transportation. Better roads, automobiles, and traffic than South Korea await drivers in the States. But, because Mr. Choi doesn't understand our "police tendencies" and feels uncomfortable arguing in English, he shudders every time he gets behind the wheel.

In conclusion, I was fortunate to have such a responsive subject. From the time I contacted him by phone, Mr. Choi conducted himself as a gentleman. On two occasions before the interview he called me to verify our meeting. If he may have been nervous, I did not detect such behavior. His discussions involving Korean families, group importance, communications, education, politics, and history greatly enlightened my perceptions of Korean culture. Mr. Choi even exposed his initial trepidation about our country and offered a fascinating example of unregulated mass media. Due to his courage to start a new life in the United States, I have little doubt that Mr. Choi shall soon find success in our diverse, "salad bowl" nation. Although my pre-interview expectations may have been correct about Mr. Choi, I refuse to take credit. Instead, I'll congratulate Korean society for producing such an insightful, thoughtful, and well-educated man.

An interview with a South Korean immigrant.

A Baseball Heckler
a speech about a speech

Four years ago this spring I presented a speech to promote my first book entitled *MISFITS! The Cleveland Spiders in 1899*. The speech took place at the local chapter of the Society for American Baseball Research. By coincidence, one month earlier, I received a call from the great-grandson of one of the ball players I studied. Naturally, I was excited and hopeful to meet him. Mr. Robert Harley was pleasant enough on the phone. He said that he was on a personal journey to discover the great-grandfather he never knew. Mr. Harley had been to the Baseball Hall of Fame in Cooperstown, New York and all over Philadelphia researching information about Dick Harley. When he mentioned that he'd like to show me an old ball jersey, I was flabbergasted. I decided to invite him to my first baseball speech.

As it turned out, not only did Mr. Harley come to the meeting, but he brought along a Mrs. Harley-Burns, the daughter of Dick Harley. Mrs. Harley-Burns was accompanied by her husband. The Harley clan arrived somewhat late to our baseball gathering, but in plenty of time for my presentation.

To say I was nervous would be an understatement. I nearly choked the podium. I stuck my hands in my pockets and rattled my keys. My heart was beating faster than a rookie pitcher with the bases loaded. To calm my anxiety, I opened with a trivia question asking "Who was the worst baseball team of all-time?" Several knowledgeable fans shouted out the answer. This ice-breaker complete, I inserted a graphic on an overhead projector. One of those players was Dick Harley.

As I introduced the drawings, a frail, silver-haired lady sprang from her seat like a centerfielder racing after a deep fly ball. She blurted, "That's not my father! That's not Dick Harley!" I was stunned. Not even five minutes into my public speaking career and I was dealing with my first heckler. As I wasn't the president of the United States, there were no handy Secret Service agents to hustle that woman out of the building. I tried to smooth over the situation by saying that this was just a drawing based on Dick Harley taken from an 1898 photograph. The audience, which numbered about 125 in a college lecture hall, began to elicit some laughter. Perhaps, they felt that this lady was a plant and that I was trying to make a joke out of this. I was dead serious. By golly, the Cleveland Spiders were pathetic. Their seasonal record was only 20 victories and 134 defeats. But, did I need this lady to stand up and quibble with me that a drawing of her father wasn't a good likeness?

With some fast thinking, I dispatched the angry lady. I simply made some awfully truthful jokes about this comical bunch. Like how the Spiders stopped playing home games after June because the management said they weren't drawing flies. Pun intended. Or about how they went a couple of months without being paid. My baseball audience howled. The lady returned to her seat and I continued on with the presentation.

During the course of the speech, I gave many examples of 19th century baseball. The game was violent and chaotic. The baseballs were as scuffed and dirty as the players. Often, many of the ball players were, shall we say, quite tipsy on the field. This contributed to much of their ineptitude. For example, Spiders' pitchers specialized in falling ass over tin cup on bunted balls. But, never once did I mention Dick Harley as among those drunk. In fact, he was a graduate of the class of 1896 at Georgetown University and was known as a gentleman; quite an honor in those early roughhouse days.

At the conclusion of my speech, the crowd applauded warmly. I sat down basking in the afterglow of my first public appearance. Within the hour, after the other speakers had made their presentations, I got to meet the Harley's during a break. We exchanged pleasantries. However, I felt rather uneasy chatting with them. After all, the elderly lady that had razzed me during my speech was standing right there. She was Mrs. Harley-Burns! Then, Robert Harley pulled a faded, woolen baseball jersey out of a box. I held my breath while I looked at the inscription on the jersey. In bold, script lettering the word "Detroit" stared back. This was Dick Harley's 1901 Tigers jersey!

Two weeks later, much to my surprise, I received a very terse letter from Mrs. Harley-Burns. The letter said that I had neglected several key elements of the book in my speech. I'd also intimated that her father was a drunk. At the same time, Mrs. Harley-Burns was praiseworthy of the book as a whole. She explained that it was a fine example of well-researched baseball history. The whole episode infuriated me so much that I zipped off a letter to Mrs. Harley-Burns. I wanted to write "You crotchety, old windbag! You missed a good speech!" However, like Dick Harley, I consider myself a gentleman. My rebuttal answered each of Mrs. Harley-Burns points in order and contained my presentation verbatim. I had tape recorded the entire event and transcribed it into the wee hours of the morning.

Mrs. Harley-Burns never wrote back. Though I had corresponded by letter with the great-grandson Harley, he never communicated with me again either.

What lessons did I learn? When writing, especially about real people, be prepared to fend off criticism, even from the most unexpected sources. Snappy comebacks are not sufficient for those offended. Top quality graphics aid in the presentation process. Poor quality illustrations can destroy a well-intentioned speech. Last but not least, always be aware and appreciative of your audience. A book about egregious losing, even one about a ball team that played nearly a hundred years ago, can be expected to open old wounds.

The perils of public speaking.

A Senators' Fan Remembers

Scott Campbell, long-suffering fan of the Washington Senators, still sits in his favorite ball park seats at Griffith Stadium, rooting for the perennial losers. A quarter century before, Washington's team relocated to Arlington, Texas, leaving a gaping hole in the hearts of many local ball cranks. For Campbell, a fifty-eight year old mental health professional, those frisky 1940s and 1950s ballplayers live on. He vividly recalls Senators' third baseman Eddie Yost drawing another base on balls, two-time batting champion Mickey Vernon, and 20-game winning pitcher Bob Porterfield. Alas, Washington baseball heroics were few and far between.

Born in 1939 to a career telephone man and a nurse, Scott Campbell's first exposure to baseball was at the Eastern Branch Boys Club in Washington, D.C., watching a small screen television in the library. Some time later, Campbell watched the 1947 World Series. After Billy Dick Thomas bragged about being one of the first in the neighborhood to own a television set, Campbell's friends stared wide-eyed at WTTG to see telecasts of the 1948 Senators. Those early tele-views were crude aerial camera shots, above and behind home plate. The batter and pitcher were visible, but when balls were smacked deep, blurry little men scurried from the outfield shadows creating impossible plays. Bob Wolff and Arch McDonald provided commentary. On rare Washington home runs, McDonald would gush, "There she goes, Mrs. Murphy," ostensibly warning a ball was coming their way. However, Scott's sweetest childhood memories involved listening to game accounts on a static-filled radio.

Hooked into baseball's sights and sounds, Campbell spent much of his childhood attending ball games at Griffith Stadium. Sitting with his father, who witnessed a Yankee named Ruth, and his brother Bob, the group would enter the park in the left field corner where bleacher tickets sold for less than a dollar. In those days, a thick haze of cigar smoke clouded the male-dominated surroundings. Most everyone, save for youngsters who sported ball caps, wore hats. Smallish capacity Griffith Stadium was rarely crowded, except perhaps when the Yankees were in town. "Those bleacher sets were my home inside the park." The Campbell's rarely strayed beyond their homely wooden slats. Once settled in, they marveled at the exploits of the great centerfielders like brothers Joe and Dom DiMaggio and the Senators' stalwart Jim Busby. Baseball souvenirs, courtesy of the batters, were quite rare in the centerfield area, as Griffith Stadium featured one of the most cavernous parks in the majors.

In high school, Scott Campbell played football, basketball and ran track. However, poor vision limited his baseball dreams. After graduation, Campbell played some more football at Montgomery Junior College, before dropping out. "I was a bit of a confused and troubled kid." Somehow, Griffith Stadium, now reduced to a quaint anachronism, beckoned Campbell. In the spring of 1961, at the age of twenty-two, he landed a job as a concessionaire. "I stuffed hot dogs into buns and filled boxes with soda pop." Luckily, the concession stand offered a clear view of the field for the workers. Concession manager Frank Nietzy often let his charges watch about three or four innings of the game in choice box seats. Campbell also remembered a touch football game organized by head groundskeeper, Joe Mooney.

That 1961 season was a home run heaven for New York sluggers Mickey Mantle and Roger Maris. During a pre-game Home Run Derby exhibition at Griffith Stadium, Mantle awed Washingtonians by depositing a half-dozen balls over the left-center field bleachers. Mantle's power display remined Washington fans of his 1953 shot against Senators' pitcher Chuck Stobbs. That blast, measured as well over 500 feet, ended up in someone's back yard. "Mantle's shot might have gone further had it not clipped off the National Bohemian beer sign in left-center," said Campbell. To commemorate the event, a baseball was painted on the sign. Campbell's concession job also allowed him to see baseball announcer Mel Allen, Yankees catcher Yogi Berra, Tiger first baseman Norm Cash, and many others, patrolling the hallways of Griffith Stadium.

Eventually Campbell did earn his college degree and ended up teaching Physical Education at Green Valley Elementary. In

1967, at the then-named D.C. Stadium on Safety Patrol Day, Campbell and his youngsters witnessed an astonishing home run from Washington behemoth Frank Howard. The ball left Howard's titanic bat and as Campbell described "had no sense of flight. It just crashed into the upper deck." Veteran Senators' trainer Doc Lentz said that Howard's smash was the hardest hit baseball he's ever seen.

From 1977-1990, Campbell worked part-time as an usher at the Capital Centre. He noticed that sports fans of the 1940s-1950s were more respectful and restrained than today's boosters.

Campbell's also been fortunate enough to visit many of baseball's holiest shrines; Fenway Park in Boston, Municipal Stadium in Cleveland, Yankee Stadium, the old Comiskey Park and Wrigley Field in Chicago, Tiger Stadium in Detroit, Memorial Stadium, and the sport's best new park that harkens back to a bygone era, Oriole Park at Camden Yards. "The old parks are like old friends. I go to the games to recapture the feeling of when I was younger," says a wistful Campbell.

These days, Campbell feels content with a camera in hand, wandering around ball parks and taking tons of photographs. He enjoys batting practice and the milieu that is unique to a ball park. With these multiple viewpoints, Campbell notices the eccentricities of certain fans who never cast their eye on the action, preferring instead to soak in the atmosphere of vendors hawking peanuts and beer, and the occasional crowd outburst for a strikeout or long hit. Campbell says, "The pace of baseball games makes watching easy and enjoyable."

In 1993, Campbell chanced upon a rare opportunity to get closer to his baseball roots. From a store in Waldorf, he purchased five attached seats from Griffith Stadium. Today these seats reside in a hallowed place in his recreation room. He eventually wants to build a step up to the seats with a wall with a memorabilia wall behind with photographs. So far, he's collected a 2- by 3-foot poster of the 1954 Washington Senators, a collage of the only World Championship Washington Club – the 1924 team, and hundreds of miscellaneous items.

Sadly, the Senators never finished in the first division for the years that Campbell followed their misfortunes. The 1960 squad fared well, forming the nucleus of a team that won the American League Championship in Minnesota five years later. One of his biggest regrets was not being able to attend the demolition of Griffith Stadium. After laying dormant four years, Griffith Stadium looked the part of a neglected bulk of metal and memories. In 1965, the park finally met the wrecking ball.

"There were circumstances in my life that prevented me from going, but I really wanted to be there for the end. It was a significant part of my life. I'll always remember the idyllic summer days I spent there with my father and brother, cheering on the hometown team."

Originally published in Nats News, *Winter 1998.*

The Old Glove

Thanks to old age and exposure to the elements, my baseball glove could be mistaken for an ancient relic in a museum. I purchased the "Bob Friend" signature model 493 on Easter Sunday twenty-nine years ago in a drug store in Northern Virginia. Up until last summer, it served as a workable, tangible link to my passion for baseball. After one particularly hard toss from a sinewy young man half my age, the friendly leather caught (or didn't catch) its final ball. The sphere entered into the glove's webbing and exited right through, as if the baseball were possessed by fire.

No wonder. The mitt looks as rustic and weather-beaten as a fan who remembers Mickey Mantle in his prime. Cracks abound in the brown leather, producing an intricate design not unlike swarming networks of capillaries. The glove is so worn with shedding flakes of leather that the name of the manufacturer cannot be read. The original stitching, loosened through overuse, has been re-knotted a million times. When the stitching started to disintegrate, I bound the glove together with shoestring and an occasional piece of coat hanger. The mysterious openings for the fingers are probably most inviting for cockroaches or other such crawlers of the night.

Today, even the ink markings I scratched into the leather read like some barely visible ancient hieroglyphs. These markings contained the uniform numbers of my three favorite players; #21 Roberto Clemente, right fielder of the Pittsburgh Pirates; #9 Ted Williams, the Boston Red Sox slugger of a generation past; and #33 Frank Howard, the gargantuan home run hitter for the Washington Senators. I'd lie to my buddies that all of these heroes had autographed my precious mitt. Naturally, Clemente's, Williams' and Howard's signature's had inspired me to legendary baseball feats, something quite impossible for a boy of my age.

As I matured into manhood, "Bob Friend" served me well, surviving nearly three decades of ball playing. I remember my one-year foray into Little League, hundreds of crisp games of catch with friends, herky-jerky pitch and catch with my father, sandlot softball games, and Air Force tours of duty overseas in Japan and the

Philippines. For a time, I stored the glove, some baseballs, and a bat in the trunk of my cars, despite only the remotest possibility of actually playing baseball on any given day. Like an athlete hanging on to the last vestiges of his career, I fiercely protected my glove. The mere thought of using another was sacrilege.

Unfortunately, the glove had now lost its functionality. No longer could I operate under the assumption that this antiquity could successfully trap thrown or batted baseballs, precisely what it was required to do. And, the aforementioned young man's throw was hardly the first that had passed straight through the webbing, hence the heroic measures employed to prolong its life. Retirement was the only answer. I carefully placed the relic on top of a bookshelf and said my thank you's for the tens of thousands of baseballs securely trapped over the years. Goodbye old friend.

The next day, I finally broke down. I went to a mega-athletic wear store to purchase a new glove. The new kid on the block resides next to my care-worn friend. He's a smallish black leather "Brett Butler" model. Maybe Butler can learn something from the old veteran Friend. One week after I forced the new and old leathers to "share lockers," I took Mr. Butler's namesake outside. The sun beat brightly off the bill of my black Pittsburgh Pirates cap. With all the intensity my 39-year old body could muster, I whipped the ball forward. The sphere sailed about twenty-five yards into the young man's glove. His leather cracked with that special vibrant sound. Then, he reared back and blistered his best fastball in the direction of my leather. I stuck out the "kid" with my arm and heard that unmistakable pop. Mr. Butler would do just fine.

Some thoughts concerning a very old baseball mitt.

Keeping Americans Safe

This generation's day of infamy began on a peaceful Tuesday morning, September 11, 2001. By its end, in New York; Washington, D.C; and Shanksville, PA, we all knew the horror of America under attack. One of our nation's largest industries, aviation, had been co-opted as weapons to destroy three thousand American souls. The devastation to our country's psyche cannot be overestimated.

The night before, by odd coincidence, I lay in bed clutching my back. An excruciating pain throbbed. I'd never experienced any back issues before. But, as my moans grew louder, I asked my wife to drive me to the emergency room. Weary from raising two kids and managing our household, she declined. So, I drove myself, slowly and painfully, to see a doctor in Fairfax, Virginia. After arriving and completing insurance formalities, I waited for over an hour. Finally, a doctor emerged, escorting me to an examination room. The visit resulted in some large "horse pills," which calmed my nerves and my pain. The doctor also ordered I take a couple days off work. At the time, I worked for a defense contractor as a systems analyst supporting the Federal Aviation Administration (FAA).

The next day and that Wednesday, I stayed at home with my stay-at-home wife. She expertly raised our precocious not-quite three-year-old daughter Amelia. Her sister Alicia attended Willow Springs Elementary School nearby. After breakfast, I plopped onto the couch and turned on the Today Show. I was in unfamiliar territory, annoyed due to being away from work. Amelia ran around the house. My wife joined me for a few moments to watch the news. We watched live as a plane rammed into one of the two Twin Towers at the World Trade Center. Shaken and fearful, we kept on watching, all day long and into the next day.

On Thursday, September 13, I returned to work, completely unaware of the pending assignment. Normally, I supported the FAA's Research Engineering Development Advisory Committee (REDAC) by attending their meetings and producing verbatim transcripts. The REDAC was made up of aviation officials, industry types, economists, technologists, and researchers. Our four-person team was comprised of Paul Murphy, Rebecca Ross, June Lidder, and myself. Collectively, our support extended to compiling, formatting, and editing the National Aviation Research Plan (NARP), delivered to Congress every year. On Thursday, however, all that work became secondary. The FAA summoned our team for an urgent assignment. Each of us suspected the meeting to involve our government's response to the 9/11 attack. Indeed, that is precisely what occurred.

Our federal FAA contact briefed us on our new assignments. To up the pressure, these tasks also included a Capability Maturity Model Integration (CMMI) component. The FAA piloted the concept following the attack, understanding its vital role in future mitigation. CMMI essentially meant that tasking should be precisely documented. The approach did not rely on individuals, who may take important knowledge away from an organization when they depart a position. Instead, it emphasized documentation, assurance for transitioning to others. In effect, proper CMMI implementation served as an insurance policy against organization brain drain. Mr. Murphy and Ms. Lidder received their assignment, the parameters of which escape me. Rebecca Ross and I partnered up on another task. The FAA wanted us to examine incoming proposals from industry, aviation technologists, scientists, private citizens, etc. and place them into "buckets" for further review. The ultimate goal was to prevent future attacks on the United States from the aviation industry's perspective. One bucket comprised internal airport security to screen passengers. Another concerned external, or perimeter, airport security. Others involved "hardening" the aircraft from explosives, arming the pilots, and creating more secure barriers in cockpit doors. In all, about fifteen buckets were identified. My job was to examine all the proposals, hundreds and hundreds of them, and place them into the pre-assigned buckets. Rebecca Ross created an airtight Excel spreadsheet that included proposal names, authors of proposals, buckets, a synopsis of the proposal, and points of contact. To satisfy the CMMI requirement, Rebecca and I documented every step to create a process document. The final "deliverable" included the spreadsheet with all of the data analyzed and the process document.

Overall, the assignment took about two months. Fortunately, I parlayed some of my Air Force experience and aviation interests into the assignment. The unique organizational skills of Ms. Ross contributed to the design of the spreadsheet and the process document. When all said and done, the final product amounted to over 700 separate entries.

Shortly after completion of the assignment, near the Thanksgiving holiday, the FAA summoned our team to produce our reports. Attendees were representatives of the FAA and the sponsors of the CMMI component from Carnegie Mellon University in Pittsburgh. To be clear, our team was on the hot seat. Mr. Murphy and Ms. Lidder's presentation of their findings went thud. Both the FAA and CMMI reps were sorely disappointed. This team had failed, leaving egg on the face of our contract. However, Rebecca Ross delivered a sterling presentation for the bucket team. She began by explaining our methodology, fully documented, and completed with a slide show of the data we compiled. The contrast could not have been starker. One of our teams failed, the other wildly exceeded expectations. As proof of our success, the FAA congratulated Ms. Ross and myself, as did the CMMI folks.

In my entire professional career in Air Force intel, as a technical writer and editor, a subject matter expert, documentation and process author, transcriptionist, systems analyst, and quality assurance manager, this task makes me most proud. The end result of Rebecca and my work contributed, if only slightly, to the creation of the Transportation Security Administration (TSA), arming pilots, hardening the aircraft, and other security and safety implementations. I'm ecstatic for all the opportunities provided by the United States of America.

Nothing brag, just fact.

Sledding and Snowmageddon

What's noticed is the stillness and the calm. Under just the right meteorological conditions, snow forms high in the atmosphere. When ready, the white powder falls to earth, tiny cold reminders of heaven. Each snowflake unique, as all of us mortal souls.

Over the years, I've cultivated a love/hate relationship with snow. As a wee child, using my Flexible Flyer sled to charge down the hill at my grandfather's house on 22 Lewis Street in Punxsutawney, Pennsylvania. Employing that same sled to fly down the mountainous Koch's Hill located on Mitchell Street in the same town. Later, stationed in Germany, as my father served in the U.S. Army in Stuttgart, my sled became my rocket ship to anywhere in the cosmos. When young, snow is magical, mystical, and perhaps a reason for the closure of schools. Cold, nah! Frostbite, nah! My mother bundled me up in long underwear, a sweater, a thick coat, boots, and a winter beanie. Off I went! Nothing could get in the way of the unbridled joy I felt riding my sled down a hill.

Sometimes, the snow in Germany raged into an unrelenting blizzard. My parents did not allow riding under these conditions. However, when the intensity subsided, my mother prepared me for the day's dangers. I simply grabbed my sled. Unfortunately, after such blizzard conditions, the thick, wet snow could be measured at 12-18 inches deep. With its low center of gravity and blades low to the ground, the Flexible Flyer could not handle this type of snow. It would easily bog down unable to plow through. Downtrodden, I cried to my father after such a sledding failure. Ever the fixer, my father offered an instant solution. Within a few days, I became the proud owner of a German toboggan. Made for deep snow, the toboggan's runner blades measured about a foot and a half from the riding surface. This was the perfect antidote for sledding in thicker, deeper snow. A brief physics lesson followed from my father. Overjoyed, I raced outside and tried said toboggan. Perfection! I was off again, braving the cold and the long trudges up the hill, to feel the exhilaration of the wind whipping in my face and my little form racing down the hill. Unlike the Flyer, the toboggan did not offer steering. Instead, turning in the toboggan utilized body shifting and boots scaping along the snow.

A few years later, our family moved back to the United States. Circa 1969, we were living in the Merrifield Village Apartments in Vienna, Virginia. One particular winter day would become my #1 fondest childhood memory. A heavy snow blanketed the area overnight. School was cancelled. That same morning, the neighborhood kids all congregated to a certain hill inside the apartment complex perimeter. It was "rough sledding" at first, the heaviness of the snow uncooperative. After many runs down the hill by the gang of kids, our snow flattened out, making conditions quite optimal. To this sledding party, I brought my toboggan, attached to a heavy chord to lug it around. The neighborhood kids, with their own Flexible Flyers and pizza pans, seemed puzzled at my toboggan's odd design. One by one they asked to ride using my unusual contraption. I obliged. We'd all slide down the hill, careful not to bump into each other at its bottom. On and on it went, each run taking a few seconds but the trudge back up the hill and the queue in line lasting over five minutes. In retrospect, was this my "Rosebud"? A few of the kids departed for lunch, based on their parents yelling for them. I stayed my ground, preferring the pleasure of the ride above all else. The day slipped into night, but we continued our sledding mania. Finally, when it became too dark, we all quietly trudged back to our respective homes, most satisfied. My apartment was a considerable walk. Upon entering the house, my mother looked at her tiny, frozen, human popsicle and gasped. Icicles had formed around my face. But, nothing a hot chocolate couldn't cure.

Many years later, in a land far away, the snow piled up so high it formed veritable tunnel walls once plowed away off the side of the road. The heavy winters at Lake Towada, in northern Japan, offered a most memorable car riding experience. Other snow memories include stopping on at least two occasions in blizzard conditions, helping motorists who'd driven into a ditch. Several "Snowmageddons" occurred when I lived on Pocol Drive in Clifton, Virginia. My two young daughters marveled at the deep snow, which needed shoveling to get to and drive our vehicle from our driveway. As my mother had before, my wife bundled up our kids with thick winter parkas and caps. On one occasion, driving to work, my car fishtailed in the snow and ice at Tysons Corner on Route 123 in Virginia. Only a miracle saved me from crashing into other vehicles. It's quite a sinking feeling when your car brakes lock up in that situation.

My all-time snow misery index hit near-panic levels on January 26, 2011. Travelling home from work in Alexandria, Virginia, I departed my job at precisely four o'clock in the afternoon. Normally, the commute took about an hour in the morning and up to an hour and a half on the return trip. As I hopped in my car, snow began to fall. I had assumed that despite the forecast calling for several inches, I could make it home before long. I was wrong, dead wrong. As I turned off King Street onto Route 123, the cold powder from the sky intensified. I had topped off my gas tank that morning, anticipating trouble. Once on 123, traffic began to slow considerably, but nonetheless, we creeped along. Rush Hour in the suburbs of the Nation's Capital often led to driving frustration. By the time I entered Annandale, it was unmistakable that this snow wasn't letting up. It crystallized into ice, slowing traffic not to a crawl, but to a stop. On a stretch of road that normally took five minutes, I spent five *hours*. Darkness started to fall. Traffic lights cycled without any movement detected from afar. I shut down my engine. Men and women stepped out of the cars and urinated while shaking in the frosty chill. Some people simply walked away from their vehicles. Snow fell at the rate of 2-3 inches an hour. Without food or drink in my car, I continued to brave the conditions. I could not believe what I was seeing and experiencing. In an attempt to maintain sanity, I turned on the radio. News reports flashed about the metropolitan area being hammered by a freakish winter storm. That was painfully obvious. However, a calm came over me when I tuned into a call-in talk show making fun of all the stranded motorists. The announcers, sitting inside a warm studio, mocked their call-in guests explaining their various predicaments. When the log jam finally broke in Annandale, I re-started my engine. The snow slowly began to taper off. At this point, even a paltry ten miles an hour, seemed like speeding around the track at

Indianapolis. Because of the icy conditions, I proceeded at this snail's pace all the way home. But, I was *moving*, through Fairfax and finally home to Clifton. Traffic had thinned considerably on the last five miles of the journey. When I finally walked into my house, at last, the clock read 12:30am. The commute totaled eight and one half hours.

My complicated relationship with snow.

Snakes and Mice, Oh My!

Cecil F. Alexander's Christian hymn begins "All things bright and beautiful/ All creatures great and small/ All things wise and wonderful/ The Lord God made them all." Every bit true and wondrously stated. But, I'm certain I don't want these creatures sharing my house.

In the fall of 1995, my wife, two-year old daughter Alicia, and I moved into a half-acre property at 6023 Pocol Drive in Clifton, Virginia. The house was located in a still rural section of Fairfax County. Clifton boasted exactly zero stoplights controlling traffic in the town. In late 1998, our family welcomed another daughter, Amelia.

As our family of three settled into the house in November 1995, my wife began to cook pasta on a crisp Saturday evening. She reached into a cupboard located underneath the stove for a large pot to boil water. Alicia played nearby in the living room. I worked on my writing on a computer in the den. Suddenly, I could hear my wife screaming and a cupboard door slamming. I raced into the kitchen. "What's wrong?" Petrified, my wife pointed to the cupboard and sat down at the table. Her body shook and she could no longer speak. Unaware of what to expect, I slowly opened the door. Inside the pot was a litter of about a half dozen mice. I grabbed the pot, opened the patio door behind me, and flung the mice outside. They flew through the air, and landed on the soft grass in our yard. Then, I placed the pot in the sink for cleaning. Not wanting a repeat, I used electrical tape to tape the cupboard doors shut. By now, young Alicia was crying, noting her mother's anguish. After considerable hugs, the situation calmed down. We piled into the car and drove to McDonald's.

Five years passed without creature incident. By the summer of 2003, my wife lovingly cared for a vegetable garden in the back yard. Beans and sprouts grew there. In addition, a few stake climbers helped the tomatoes. Alicia, Amelia, and their new dog Jake played in the house while I mowed the lawn. My wife was also indoors. At a point near the rear of the house, as I followed my mowing pattern, I stopped frozen in my tracks. I let go of the push lawnmower handle, discovering a two-foot long black snake with its head reared up. The snake did not move, remaining completely still, a foot in front of the mower's whirling blades. No situation had ever confronted me like this. I thought out my options. I could flee in fear, but that wouldn't solve anything. Should I run over the snake with the mower? Surely, it would be cut to ribbons. Perhaps, it could slither away. Would this try anger the reptile? Was it poisonous? The third option appeared right in front of me. I'd back up and walk slowly toward the shed. There, I could grab one of the thin, climbing stakes and return to the scene. Would the snake stay put? Because of my children and dog, I decided the snake must be destroyed. I chose option three. Moving deliberately, I approached the menacing creature armed with the stake. I'd have one chance, probably. Failure could result in a bite, not exactly my preference. Because my weapon was lightweight, I formulated a plan. The snake did not move, eying every movement of my muscles. Then, with all the violent force I could muster, I slammed the stake down just behind the head of the snake. In a flash, the snake suffered complete decapitation. Blood spilling from its head and torso, the reptile writhed for a second before expiring. Stake beats snake. Literally. The threat removed, I used the stake to lift its torso to the backyard and deposited it over my fence into an empty, wooded lot. I retrieved a garden scoop tool from the shed and did the same for the snake's head. The successful kill emboldened my sense of manhood. But, my feelings as a conquering hero lasted only a few days. When I returned to work, I relayed the story to a co-worker. "Sounds like a black rat snake," he said. "They kill mice, they actually help homeowners." I confirmed his analysis by searching the internet. The picture of the black snake perfectly matched the one in my yard. Although the snake was not poisonous, a bite could inflict damage on humans. Deflated, I kept the incident to myself, so as to not alarm the family.

A few weeks later, I walked down the driveway to check the mail. Something curious appeared unmoving in the grass. To my astonishment, it was another black rat snake. This snake, however, not only had its head severed, but its torso lay in numerous pieces, strewn about. I was used to the removal process by now. The next day, at work, I inquired again. My same co-worker indicated the high probability that this snake encountered a raccoon, its natural enemy. The battle royale probably occurred at night, raccoons being nocturnal. That evening, I had a nightmare about this natural fight to the death.

Thankfully, snakes stayed away from our house. During hardware shopping trips, we'd purchase old-fashioned mouse traps. Strategically placed along the wall where mice travel, we caught a couple a year. No major problems, or so we thought. In 2009, after nearly two decades of marriage, my wife and I divorced. We shared physical custody of the girls with two weeks on and two weeks off for each parent. Times were hard, but we all slowly adjusted to the new living arrangements. My wife moved out and I stayed on Pocol Drive. Unfortunately, the mice problem intensified. Instead of buying spring-loaded traps, I purchased glue traps and placed about a dozen of them around the house. Usually at night, I'd hear a small shriek indicating the capture of another mouse. Now, instead of twice a year, the glue traps caught about four a year. Once ensnared in the glue, the mice could not escape, unless they bit off their own feet, to get free of the glue. As they struggled, they sank deeper into the sticky mess. I hired an exterminator, who sprayed outside, and the situation somewhat abated.

One morning, in about 2012, while the kids were staying with their mother, I started to make some toast. Just as I placed the bread into the toaster, a tiny black snake poked its head out from inside the machine. Quickly, the baby, sensing danger, slithered away on the counter and behind the refrigerator. I never saw this snake again. However, it started to dawn on me, in a sinking feeling, that the snakes were here because the mice were here. These black rat snakes ate mice, who must have been frolicking around my house at night. I just wish they could complete nature's natural survival cycle out of doors. As the saying goes, "while the cat's away, the mice will play." The nursery rhyme doesn't mention snakes.

Two years later, my daughters were home with me. They were together in Alicia's room one summer evening. As is my habit, I was probably watching a movie. As did my wife years earlier,

Alicia screamed. She yelled "Daddy!" I ran to the rear of the house. Alicia lay on her bed. Amelia sat at a computer desk. The kids froze in place. A two-foot long black rat snake poised near the door. Fortunately for all of us, the snake barely moved. When it did, it continued to occupy the space around the door. What now? My daughters' safety being paramount, I thought about the ancient encounter. This maneuver would not work indoors. "Don't move," I said to the kids. I quickly searched for something resembling a pole. Finding a long, thin dowel used for craft projects, I attempted unsuccessfully to herd the snake into a large plastic tote. Minutes passed by. The stand-off continued. The only person or reptile in the room moving was me. If it was the last thing I did, I would remove that snake from the room. I asked Amelia to cell phone a neighbor boy who was her same age. Jake enjoyed being an amateur herpetologist, harboring several reptiles in his basement. The call went unheeded. Low on patience and ideas, I scrambled my brain to figure out what to do next. Alicia provided the answer. "Why don't you get some glue traps?" I stated that the traps only worked on very small animals, like mice. I thought about it, and decided to give it a try. Using a piece of cardboard, I placed several traps together. I secured the traps in a row with tape. I also secured the traps onto the cardboard. Then, very slowly, I slid the traps near the snake. With the dowel, I herded the snake toward the traps. Sensing danger, the snake arched over the glue. I used the dowel to carefully press the snake's torso onto the sticky mess. About thirty seconds later, the snake was ensnared. Its upper body, including the head, began to spin around like a top. With extreme deliberation, I guided the entire piece of cardboard and the snake into the tote. Then, I placed the lid of the tote on top. The tote was snapped shut. Secure inside the tote, I removed the tote and placed it in the back yard. The kids were safe. The next day, Amelia called her friend again. She asked him to visit and I told him the story of the snake in the room. By the time Jake arrived, the summer temperature reached into the 90s. Jake felt bad about the snake, which had suffocated and fried in the heat. Following my instruction, he tossed the snake over the rear fence and returned the tote to the back yard. I couldn't bear to look. For days, the tote stayed in the yard until my curiosity got the best of me. As I approached the tote, an overpowering smell wafted in front of me. The snake's residue remained.

In 2018, I retired from work, sold my house, and moved to Pennsylvania. While removing one of my bookcases from my den, I noted a horrific sight behind and underneath the shelving. A clump of house insulation, likely from the attic, appeared. Buried in the clump were two dead and decomposed baby mice. Somehow, these mice had taken up residence in this part of the house. They probably slept there during the day and scurried about at night, normally unbeknownst to the homeowner.

The critters on Pocol Drive.

Groundhog Day, 2020

For most of my life, I've been touting Groundhog Day, celebrated every February 2nd in my parents' hometown of Punxsutawney, Pennsylvania. Finally, after I retired to make my home in the small borough, my younger sister Beth and I attended in-person.

For the uninitiated, Groundhog Day in Punxsutawney traces its origins officially to 1887. Much earlier in time, in Germany, the Christian Festival of Candlemas and ancient lore used a badger as weather prognosticator.[13] If the weather was clear on this day, a prolonged winter lie ahead. Fast forward to America, where Germans settled the areas of western Pennsylvania, bringing and expanding upon ancient traditions. It began as an Elk's Club Lodge hunt for groundhog meat and morphed into the current Groundhog Club. The annual event took place at Gobbler's Knob, where hunters sometimes "consulted" with the groundhog, also known as chuck and whistlepig. Over subsequent decades, Groundhog Day became a ritualized but obscure event, attended by only a few thousand. The 1993 Hollywood film *Groundhog Day* changed all that, the event now drawing crowds numbering ten thousand and worldwide media coverage.[14] Clymer Freas, editor of the local *Spirit* newspaper, popularized the event.[15] Other champions of the cause include tireless promotor Sam Light, who appeared annually at the local high school. Light, dressed in top hat and tails, gave a rousing pep rally a few days before the event. Bill Anderson, another *Spirit* editor, a transplant to the town, wrote extensively about Groundhog Day beginning in the 1980s.

On the day previous, a Saturday, I had volunteered to work at the nearby Punxsutawney Area Historical and Genealogical Society (PAHGS). My shift was scheduled from 10am to 2pm, but I was unaware of my assignment. Shirley Sharp, who ran the daily

---

[13] Don Yoder. *Groundhog Day*. Stackpole Books, 2003.
[14] Peter Carlson. "His Moment in the Sun." *The Washington Post*. February 3, 2004.
[15] Don Yoder. *Groundhog Day*. Stackpole Books, 2003.

operation there, requested I serve as doorman to greet visitors into the small museum. The PAHGS was housed in a turn-of-the-century building known at the Lattimer House. It offered two back rooms housing groundhog memorabilia, a gift shop, a local genealogical library and research space, and upstairs comprised of four rooms with posters, artwork, maps, clothes, dolls, and toys all related to the town from days gone by. In addition, a guest sign-in book beckoned about ten feet from the door. PAHGS was part of a local tour of the town's landmarks, such as they were. My job was to steer visitors to the sign-in book and quickly explain attractions within. I dressed warmly for a February day in western Pennsylvania.

As the clock ticked to ten in the morning, a few visitors started to trickle in. In a friendly manner, I asked people where they were from. Over the years, I'd heard tales of visitors traveling from far-flung locations to experience Groundhog Day up close and personal. To pass the time, I kept a mental note of their answers. My mind game, kept entirely to myself, wondered about the furthest geographical distance visitors travelled for the extravaganza. Japan? Australia? Russia? Those locales certainly were worlds away.

After the first hour, I got a Phoenix, Arizona and a California, but nothing international. My greeting settled into a routine. How are you's, where are you all froms, enjoy your stays. Judging by their smiles, everyone seemed to be having a good time, going inside and as they departed the little museum. The people streamed in, parents and children of all ages. Many Pennsylvanians stopped by, from Pittsburgh, Altoona, Johnstown, and Philadelphia. During rare lulls, I'd step back to spy the guest book. In hour two, a group of Canadians stopped by. Wow, that's far away, I thought. About ten minutes later, a group numbering about six people made their way to the doors. They all appeared to be Americans, with one exception, a twenty-something young lady. After my instructions, they all signed in and proceeded upstairs. Once, out of their eyesight, I snuck over to the guest book to read their names. The young lady signed in as "Noriko." From my days serving overseas, I knew that name to be Japanese. The suffix "ko" always refers to a female, and it means "child" in their language. Careful not to disrupt the flow of visitors still arriving, I waited for this group to descend the stairs. Trying to be polite, I asked the young lady, in my rusty Japanese, if she was a native of that country. She returned my answer in Japanese and asked about my knowledge of her culture. I stated that I had served in the United States Air Force in Misawa nearly forty years earlier. Our all too brief conversation made my day. *Honto*!

Hour three flew by. The crowds entering did not abate in the slightest. Hundreds came through the door. I kept up my mental game, still searching for international visitors. Despite skipping breakfast and eschewing offers of coffee by PAHGS staffers, my adrenaline kept me upright. A group of four arrived, but with so many visitors, I sometimes did not have time to ask where they were coming from. This latest group aroused my suspicion. When I snuck back to the guest book, I noticed two names; Vladimir and Natasha. Oh my, they were probably from Russia! This foursome worked their way through the museum. Upon exiting, I wanted to say, *Dasvidaniya*, but held back. The word means "goodbye" in Russian. By the time the fourth and final volunteer hour arrived, I felt as if I was on autopilot. My relief doorman soon arrived. After he took over, I wandered back to the kitchen. Shirley Sharp, serving me a coffee, asked how I was doing. I responded I was happily exhausted and so grateful for the opportunity. With my coffee in hand, I headed to the back room containing groundhog memorabilia. For about ten minutes, I nursed my drink and just listened to the ambiance.

After the euphoria of being the greeting party at PAHGS, the next day was Groundhog Day. My sister Beth and I bundled up for the mid-twenties temperature, although the skies were clear. At 4:30 in the morning, we boarded one of the numerous shuttle buses bound for Gobbler's Knob. I made sure I was ready to brave standing outside for several hours by donning thermal underwear, a heavy jacket, and my trademark United States Air Force cap. The crowd on the bus was talkative and excited as were my sister and I. When we finally arrived through the fancy gate at the grounds, I noted masses of people gathering in the forest clearing. Gobbler's Knob is located about five minutes from the main thoroughfare through town. Due to limited parking at the site, shuttle buses from the school district transported the throngs of people. The "Knob" itself contains a newly refurbished meeting hall and a large swath of grass located on a hill. At the bottom of the hill is a small stage featuring a painting of Punxsutawney Phil. In the middle of the stage was a large wood stump. By the time we arrived, at before five in the morning, the crowds had already filled in front of the stage. We took our place near the top of the hill, next to a tree, with good sightlines to the stage, probably fifty yards away. The event was scheduled for just after 7:00 am. For two hours then, we watched the entertainment, comprised of local singers and dancers of all ages. A barbershop quartet crooned a few tunes, relics from an earlier era. As the time for the groundhog's appearance salted away, I noted a most festive group of people. To fight the biting cold, I hopped around in place, trying to keep my toes from freezing. My sister and I engaged in pleasant conversation and marveled at the crowd size, swelling with each passing minute.

Finally, the big moment arrived. We knew Phil's appearance was imminent. A dozen men in top hat and tails arrived on the stage. Several of the Inner Circle members spoke about the glories of the day, and sang the praises of the single groundhog, now housed within the confines of the hollow tree stump. Nearly everyone in the crowd knew the drill. If Phil saw his shadow, his weather prognostication skills indicated six more weeks of winter. If the groundhog did not see his shadow, an early spring was foretold. At about 7:20am, two scrolls were placed on top of the stump. One of the Inner Circle members whipped the crowd into a frenzy. In order for Punxsutawney Phil to appear, the crowd needed to chant, "Phil, Phil, Phil," over and over. With great vigor, the crowd did just that. Two members reached down into the front of the hollow stump and pulled out the animal. One Inner Circle member held Phil aloft, for all to see. Someone in the crowd shouted, "I love you, Phil!" Laughter rippled through the throng. After this display, Phil was placed on the stump. He picked one of the two scrolls, wrapped with a ribbon, and read the proclamation: "Hear ye, Hear ye…" This was important because only one member of the Inner Circle could understand "groundhogese" and speak on behalf of the groundhog. Phil did not see his shadow. An early spring was just around the corner. As the crowd erupted in mostly solid agreement, Phil was returned to his burrow. A light snow began to trickle from the heavens. Fireworks erupted over the treeline. As the day wore on, the snow blanketed the area, about six inches worth.

Just like that, the crowd disbursed. On the way out, Beth and I spied a man with a most ridiculous groundhog hat. We engaged him and he stated his name as Ryan Teti, from West Carlisle, Ohio. He was at the event for his twelfth consecutive year. Another man passing by said it was his 28th year and he was from Michigan. Beth received a cell phone call at the conclusion. It was from her son Sean, who had driven up from Virginia, some two hundred and fifty miles away. He said he was near the stage with a lady friend. Once we caught up with each other, we waited in the shuttle bus line for well over an hour. Glib, excited conversation followed. We were fortunate enough to meet an elderly couple who travelled from the Philadelphia suburbs to witness Groundhog Day. He was dressed in an old-fashioned suit and she played her part, in an ancient lace dress.

All in all, Groundhog Day, in fact the whole weekend, was a rousing success. Very few public events could compare. Our morning bus ride and wait at Gobbler's Knob had taken fully three hours. The main event lasted ten minutes. In order to understand the annual craziness in Punxsutawney, it's important to learn a bit about the town itself. The local high school features a groundhog for its mascot with the sports teams named the Punxsutawney Chucks. The downtown Chamber of Commerce sells groundhog trinkets; shirts, hats, postcards, posters, blankets, mugs, towels, all emblazoned with a smiling Phil. Annually, in addition to Groundhog Day, a Groundhog Parade and Groundhog Festival take place. Local businesses respond in kind, with numerous displays featuring the groundhog. Groundhog Plaza is the name of a local strip mall. The Inner Circle meets annually for a Groundhog Banquet. The Punxsutawney *Spirit* newspaper features Phil in its masthead. Although it can be observed that some residents of the town frown on the idea of Groundhog Day, there are numerous others that wholeheartedly support the effort. Above all, the event is meant to offer a slice of absurdity in a world far too accustomed to bad news. When one abandons oneself to the silliness, Groundhog Day can be embraced and savored. Thanks to bus records, over forty-two thousand souls attended in 2020, the largest crowd in the history of the event. I, for one, was most happy to be one of them.

Better than the movie.

Quintin White

In French, it's *joie de vivre* (buoyant enjoyment of life). In Yiddish, *l'chaim* (to life). The ancient Greeks emphasized *carpe diem* (seize the day). All of these words and phrases equate to toasts and the celebration of life. For an all-American three-year old boy named Quintin Liam White, like children everywhere, he celebrates his existence with joyful, precocious, reckless abandon.

Born on 21 December 2017 in New Orleans to his parents Parker and Emily White, Quintin seemingly began smiling upon his entrance into the world. He hasn't stopped since. As his great uncle, I've been fortunate to witness Quintin's amazing attitude on only four occasions. This is due mainly to geography. He lives with his parents and two older brothers on a military base in New Jersey while I reside in a small town in western Pennsylvania. Quintin is the offspring of my sister Beth's youngest daughter Emily. Although he doesn't know it yet, I've bought into his message of positivity.

The first time I met Quintin, he was two months shy of his second birthday. I drove my sister and I to New Jersey to visit his family. Like most boys his age, his boundless energy defined him. He ran around his house, never picked up his toys, made messes in his highchair when eating, tossed his snacks on the carpet, and generally created mayhem wherever he went. Like a tornado on two legs. Quintin's mother Emily and father Parker, attuned to his needs, allowed Quintin his space. On occasion, however, when he tossed his toys and dinner, Quintin received some mild "time-out" discipline. Fortunately for Quintin, his two older brothers Cammrick (12) and Deklan (8) kept little Q on the straight and narrow. Outside, while his brothers rode their bicycles and scooters, Quintin ran up and down the sidewalk. So, with this introduction to the Parker White family, I began my relationship with Quintin.

At first, he appeared standoffish. He'd run away from me, like boys unsure of a stranger. I kept my secret little boy weapon hidden from view until just the right time. Carefully observing the roughhouse wrestling his brothers engaged Quintin in, I noted the young lad possessed a common weakness. He loved, loved, loved to be tickled. As Cammrick and Deklan rolled around on the floor, they would lift up Quintin's t-shirt and tickle him. He'd squeal with delight. After the episode ended with all the boys exhausted, I grabbed Quintin. Lifting him high in the air, I commenced Operation Tickle Monster. He wiggled around like a greased pig. More squealing followed. At this moment, he warmed up to me. Then, for some reason, he began to climb all over my head. He'd giggle while using my hair to pull himself up. I'd feign discomfort, groaning a bit and he kept climbing and pulling my hair. Quintin basically re-arranged the skin on my chest, shoulders, and face. For twenty minutes this went on, until finally ole Mount Tom needed a break from Quintin's facial gymnastics. After Quintin's mother put him down for his daily nap, I closed my eyes also for a short catnap.

Upon waking, smiling and beaming Quintin came around again. He attempted his climb, but I decided on another activity. I asked Emily if Quintin possessed any books. "Of course," she said. "They are right over there in the toy box." I picked up an animal book, plopped Quintin down on my lap, and began to turn the pages. The book displayed about a dozen animals on each page. Quintin did not talk yet, but he knew each and every animal in that board book. I'd ask, "Where is the bear?" and he'd point to the bear. "Where is the monkey?" I queried and he'd smile and point to the monkey. Quintin's comprehension of all the animals in that book proved that his parents or his brothers spent considerable amounts of time teaching him about his animal brethren. Overall, I'd estimate his success rate at about 95%. I noted his incorrect responses and explained, "No, that's the pig," and so on. After the completion of the book, Quintin received a pop quiz of those animals he identified incorrectly. In that short period of time, he learned from all his mistakes. Guaranteed, Quintin now knows every animal in that book.

Over the next few days, the White Family, my sister and I ventured to the Six Flags amusement park, Johnson's Locust Hall Farm, and two events for his brothers. One was a soccer match and the other a school-sponsored running exercise. On each occasion, Quintin appeared ready for his close-up, starring in his own movie. At the amusement park, Quintin probably wowed everyone near him as he clomped around the park and rode the kiddie rides with his parents. When he wasn't on foot, Quintin enjoyed the comforts of his limousine stroller. Yup, he spilled his soda pop and managed to turn his face sticky with cotton candy. He pouted and cried like most "terrible twos," but overall he enjoyed himself.

On an azure blue sky day at the farm, however, Quintin's exuberance overflowed. Johnson's Locust Hall Farm, a short ride away in the White minivan, featured a playground, animals, a corn maze, a hayride excursion, a sunflower field and pick-your-own fruit trees. Naturally, the obligatory gift shop also stood on the immense acreage. In short, a child nature paradise. Quintin could not get enough of the place. His father Parker picked up his son to reach the apples, which he happily plopped down into his basket. Dad carefully advised Quintin of all the barnyard beasts. Father/son could get close enough to pet some of the creatures, close enough for their noses to process the awful smells. At the sunflower field portion of Johnson's, reachable only by hayride, Quintin rode in a wheelbarrow and posed on a large tractor. That winning smile never failed to follow Quintin's every step. When it came time to explore the corn maze, Quintin raced ahead of everyone in the group. He acted like some maniacal corn maze tour guide. This kid could have run off into oblivion. Our group, following behind, kept an eye on him so that he couldn't get lost. At certain parts of the maze, a plywood animal or plant appeared, allowing children to place their heads behind strategic holes. This resulted in numerous cute photographs of the three brothers.

Two months later Quintin celebrated his second birthday with dozens of family members at Grandpa and Grandma White's house in Juneau, Pennsylvania. After the obligatory blowing out of the candles, cake eating, and ice cream smears all over his face, Quintin was placed on a chair to open his presents in front of everyone. He flashed his gorgeous grin as he tore into the gifts, and looked at them briefly, while the crowd cheered him on. Cel phone cameras snapped dozens of photographs of the little boy. Then, when he opened a package containing clothes, he emphatically threw them down on the floor. Joyous laughter broke out in the room.

A couple months later, Emily brought Quintin and his brother Deklan back to Punxsutawney for a visit. Although my time with the kids was demonstrably shorter, I did manage to push him on a playground swing and try to keep up as he splashed in rain puddles. Young boys especially seem determined to dirty their clothes and themselves to the maximum extent possible. In that same visit, Emily, Deklan, Quintin, and I enjoyed an afternoon meal at a local Pizza Hut. Some of the food actually found its way into Quintin's mouth.

In July 2020, Emily again returned for a visit to her old hometown. This time the meeting took place outside in my backyard gazebo. Punxsutawney is known for its groundhogs. Unfortunately, they wreak havoc all over my yard, burrowing holes in the ground and even under my garage and shed. If you're not careful, you can twist an ankle walking over one of these holes. In addition to Emily, Deklan, and Quintin, my sister Beth and her husband Tom all gathered at the picnic tables under the gazebo. To keep the youngsters busy, I retrieved some balls and a wiffle ball bat. As the boys cavorted about the fenced-in back yard, we adults chatted. Twenty minutes or so passed until I called the youngsters over. By this time, smart little Quintin was talking and could understand everything his parents or brothers said. I asked Quintin to quietly sit on the picnic bench while I told him a story. Possibly remembering the animal book experience, he complied. I explained to two-and-one-half-year old Quintin that there was a groundhog hole behind me. I said to him, "Let me show you." Both boys followed me to the hole in the earth. "Be careful," I warned, in all seriousness. "You don't want to fall in."

They went back to playing ball briefly, being mindful not to go too near the hole. When they were tired out, both boys came over to their mother who said she had some snacks and drinks for them. They sat down to enjoy their sustenance. Unprompted, Quintin got up from his picnic bench, walked over to his grandma "Mimi" and his "Papa" Tom. Quintin said to each of them separately, with conviction, "Be careful. I don't want you to fall in the hole."

Despite these relatively rare meetings with the White family and Cammrick, Deklan, and Quintin, I've been treated again to the remarkable feeling of being around children. Experiencing their happiness, their energy, their ups and downs, their *learning and growing*. Each child is a precious gem, each a special gift from God. I offer this humble advice to the world. Let's treat them all that way.

My burgeoning friendship with a little boy.

Emery Elwin Hetrick (1904-1993)

Emery Elwin Hetrick was born in Munderf, Pennsylvania but grew up in the tiny town of Hamilton. He called his birth town "Blowtown." Little is known about Mr. Hetrick's early life, save for one rather captivating photograph. Somewhere around twenty one-years old, a black and white photo was taken of him, looking extremely dapper in a pin-striped suit. Mr. Hetrick is standing and grinning in front of a Ford Model T "Tin Lizzie" automobile. With him was a friend, but a third figure appears in the picture, visible only by the bottom part of two legs on the running board. High likelihood that the third person is a female.

Early in his marriage to Freda Hetrick, nee Miller, and after the birth of his first son Charles, Mr. Hetrick rode around in a motorcycle with wife and son aboard. Later, he bought a car.[16]

Beginning in 1935 and continuing for 32 years, proud and hard-working Emery Elwin Hetrick served in the Pennsylvania National Guard (PNG) on North Findlay Street in Punxsutawney, before retiring with his title as an Organizational Maintenance Supervisor, Chief and rank of First Sergeant (1SG). During this time, through World War II, Korea, and Vietnam, Hetrick never deployed overseas. He did, however, faithfully serve his country back on the home front, being the first full-time guardsman in the unit and hired by Walter Morris.[17] Hetrick's duties included taking care of the horses in the stable and managing the logistics of the unit. Tough training assignments were also part of Hetrick's never-ending duties. Military unit designations frequently change and the PNG was no exception. An original member of the Battery B, 229th Field Artillery (F.A.),[18] the unit transitioned in September 1940, sending all their horses away and acquiring artillery including the "Long Tom" 155mm gun howitzer.[19] Hetrick served as the

---

[16] Interview with Gina Hetrick Irving, December 9, 2019.
[17] Interview with Sergeant First Class, USA, Ret. Roger Steele, December 7, 2019.
[18] *Punxsutawney Spirit*. March 15, 1947.
[19] *Punxsutawney Spirit*. May 7, 1941.

caretaker for that big gun. At this time, the designation changed to Battery E 190th F.A.

Under this banner, with war raging in Europe, the unit mobilized for one-year training at Camp Shelby, Mississippi under the Selective Service and Training Act in March 1941.[20] Camp Shelby was no picnic with twelve hour days comprised of physical fitness and classroom instruction, punctuated by "mess", or meals.[21] Four-hour marching exercises sometimes took place in 115 degree heat, with soldiers wearing humping backpacks comprised of a blanket, half a tent, tent pole, mess gear, iron hat, raincoat, and an automatic pistol.[22] Although the military training was brutal on the men, the close bonds acquired during soldiering together also produced more than a few laughs. One scrawny local cow was captured by instigators. Stealthily, at night, the pranksters let loose said animal into a tent of five quiet sleeping trainees. One private jerked awake due to the unusual smell. Hilarity ensued.[23] Before the year of training ended, the war began in December 1941. The unit eventually took part in D-Day, the Battle of the Bulge, and other campaigns. After the war ended in 1945, Hetrick participated in a welcoming party for returning soldiers. In 1946, he studied as a supply sergeant.[24]

A few years later, Hetrick traveled to Indiantown Gap Military Reservation and brought back supplies of military equipment (clothing, field eqpt., office supplies, mount for .50 cal machine gun).[25] That same year, 1948, the group participated in a two-week intensive training course in Indiantown Gap, which included a bivouac and two-and-one half day marches. This time, Mr. Hetrick trained with his son Joseph.[26] Shortly after the start of the Korean War, two of Hetrick's sons, Joseph and Charles,

---

[20]*Punxsutawney Spirit.* March 15, 1941.

[21] *Punxsutawney Spirit.* March 15, 1941.

[22] *Punxsutawney Spirit.* June 16, 1941.

[23] *Punxsutawney Spirit.* April 5, 1941.

[24] *Punxsutawney Spirit.* July 22, 1946.

[25] *Punxsutawney Spirit.* April 14, 1948.

[26] *Punxsutawney Spirit.* August 4, 1948.

departed for Battery B, 28th Division combat training in Camp Atterbury, IN.[27] The story of the three men was covered in the local newspaper. Shortly thereafter, a third son named John Thomas joined the Pennsylvania National Guard, making Emery Hetrick the proud father of three sons who served in the PNG, Army Reserve, and United States Army.

Following his retirement from the National Guard, Emery continued to work deep into his seventies, always with enthusiasm, always with a sense of worth. Emery worked as a warden and dispatcher for the Punxsutawney Borough Police.[28] Who knows what exciting situations occurred there or how many drunks he might have thrown into the slammer? He also worked with the Stockdale Mine Supply, now called the Keystone Drill Services. He also kept meticulous genealogical records of his family, duly noting birth dates and locations, marriage records, and death information.

Later, he took up art, using his infinite patience and steady hand to create numerous paint-by-numbers pieces. Among them were DaVinci's Mona Lisa and The Last Supper, Blue Boy and Pinky, a naked woman, and a violin with musical notation. These paintings hung throughout his house on 22 Lewis Avenue. After his wife Freda's passing, the paintings were distributed to family members. Mr. Hetrick committed for years to Sunday drives taking the local pastor to church. Another hobby by Mr. Hetrick, especially is his later years, were frequent visits to cemeteries to "visit friends." With wife Freda, their cemetery hobbies were grave rubbings.

An expert storyteller and sometimes prankster, Emery held court on numerous occasions with family and friends. And once his storytelling began, interruptions were not tolerated. Ever. He'd chide those who'd dare to with a few seconds of silence. Then, he'd say, with indignation, "Are you telling the story?" No one ever answered in the affirmative and the story would continue. Quite often, at just the right moments, he'd speak about his days in the

---

[27] *Punxsutawney Spirit.* September 8, 1950.
[28] *Punxsutawney Pennsylvania Con Survey City Directory.* Mullin-Kille of Missouri, Inc. and Punxsutawney Spirit. 1967. p. 347.

service or comical events he'd been part of over the years. Once, a lady took a birds-eye-view photograph of Freda Hetrick sitting on the toilet. He'd break out and share this dog-eared photo with others, laughing in a manner similar to Barney Rubble.[29]

Mr. Hetrick loved to tell the story of a pesky, barking dog who kept him awake at night with untimely howling. After unsuccessful attempts to have the dog's owner and local magistrate listen to his disturbing the peace complaints, he decided on the most logical course of action. He simply made up his mind to outlive the dog. And, he did. After telling this particular dog story, Mr. Hetrick would wiggle his big ears, as if to laugh. He'd stay quiet, and then wait for the listener to laugh, which they always did.

In later years, he'd joke that he often felt so bad that he'd begin his morning by checking the obituaries. If he was not among those listed, it would be a good day, he'd say.

Mr. Hetrick was a member of the First English Lutheran Church and L.O.O. Moose in Punxsutawney.

For most of his adult life, Emery Hetrick resided on 22 Lewis Avenue, Punxsutawney, Pennsylvania.

But, without question, it was his family that Mr. Hetrick was most proud of. Life's responsibilities were fiercely taught to Mr. Hetrick's four sons and daughter. He was a man of loyalty, who'd take his son and grandson to Brookville for ice cream at the drop of a hat. Photographs of his children and grandchildren scattered about his house were testament to his long, fruitful life. In the mid-sixties, Mr. Hetrick flew with his wife to Germany to visit his two Army sons. While there, despite his initial reluctance, Mr. Hetrick actively participated in sightseeing visits, marveling at ancient German castles juxtaposed within modern technology. He relished home movies of his own children made in the 1940's. The setting for those crude, 16-millimeter movies? A water hole in Western Pennsylvania. He always had time for his grandchildren, easily able to mingle with babies and toddlers and teens. Young children could be held enthralled spying for birds and squirrels from his porch.

---

[29] Interview with Gina Hetrick Irving, December 9, 2019.

If the measure of a man is the number he leaves behind, Mr. Hetrick was quite successful. At his passing, Mr. Hetrick's progeny numbered twenty grandchildren and twenty great-grandchildren...and counting. No man ever loved his family more.

A short bio of my grandfather, the world's greatest storyteller.

Freda Miller Hetrick (1910-2001)

If anything could be said about Freda L. Hetrick, it was all about pleasing people, and this desire manifested itself in her expert cooking skills. At various times she worked as a waitress and cook at the Findley Hotel, located on 244 N. Findley Street, and in the Hetrick family restaurant. Her specialty involved baking pies and cookies, which she did with regularity and to much applause. This talent extended to baking pies for the original Star Lunch, owned and operated by Frank Mamolito. In family gatherings, her ubiquitous spaghetti and meatball dinners ruled the day. Freda didn't smile much, sometimes causing the misplaced ire of family members. But, she was more interested in doing, rather than putting up a phony demeanor.

With her husband of sixty-four years until his passing, Freda lovingly raised four boys and a girl; Charles Edgar, Joseph Streamer, John Thomas, Ronald Elwin, and Freda Yvonne. She doted on her family. Never once could Freda not find the time to share her boundless generosity with everyone she met. One particular event in her life stood out which defined her lifelong caring nature. This was a mid-1960s trip to visit two of her sons, Charles and Joseph, serving with the United States Army in Germany. While both of her boys were anxious to introduce her to the old country and to their military occupations, Mrs. Hetrick dutifully tagged along with her husband, never complaining of the long walks and exhaustive sightseeing. These forays included numerous historical landmarks, especially German castles, churches, and cemeteries.

Throughout her life, Freda's pleasures remained old-fashioned. When the grandkids visited her house on 22 Lewis Avenue in Punxsutawney, she'd immediately head to the basement to gather building blocks and dolls. When adult family members gathered, pleasant conversation ensued, but then Freda Hetrick would get up and move into the kitchen, where coffee and soft raisin cookies awaited. She also enjoyed quiet time alone or with others, knitting and crocheting. Parakeets screeched in the dining room for years. Lawrence Welk's music show paraded a bevy of clean-cut singers and dancers, seemingly always on television at the Hetrick household. Another television pleasure was Hee-Haw, the country version of Laugh-In. But the silly jokes on those shows could not compete with Freda's own sincere statement. After a family member asked her if she had watched the annual Westminster Dog Show, she stated "I caught the tail-end of it."

Freda also delighted in the wonderment of small gestures like gifted flowers from her kids. She appreciated when her adult children took out the trash and went grocery shopping for her. After her son Joseph won a year's supply of donuts, he realized that someone had to eat them and they were frequently brought into her house. Throughout the home were photographs of her children, lovingly displayed. On her kitchen windowsill rested several vases filled with cactii in the shape of ladies' heads. An organ took its rightful place in the dining room and the old Victrola rarely played, but these *objet d'art* were valued just for being there.

However, it was babies and their care that defined Freda Hetrick's existence. She adored the wee ones, baby-sitting for neighbors for decades, and earning a local reputation for motherly excellence. Dirty diapers and infant vomit deterred her not in the least. Freda also made sure pre-school kids got on their school buses safely. One couldn't help but notice the joy in Freda's face when these opportunities arose. As a gift, her son Joseph once bought her a porcelain baby doll, which Freda proudly displayed in its case.

In 1979, a 50th Anniversary Party was held for Emery and Freda. Family attendees and friends marveled at this rare event, coordinated at the Pantall Hotel. In the last year of her life, Freda Hetrick's family organized a surprise 90th birthday party. This party also took place in a ballroom at the historic Pantall Hotel. With dozens of family members in attendance, and Freda in a wheelchair, she began to cry, as did many of the attendees. The emotional gathering produced tears and well wishes. Just before the food and drink were served, two of Freda Hetrick's grandsons spoke. Frank Hetrick brought up her longevity and the numerous technological inventions that occurred since her birth in 1910. Joseph Thomas Hetrick stated somberly with his voice cracking that "Everyone in this room is here today because this lady was born."

Mrs. Hetrick was a member of the First English Lutheran Church and Loyal Order of Moose Auxiliary in Punxsutawney.

For nearly all her life, Freda Hetrick lived in Punxsutawney, Pennsylvania. The world is a sadder place without her.

A short bio of my grandmother.

Joseph Streamer Hetrick (1932-1998)

As a high schooler, Joseph Streamer Hetrick enjoyed the Hardy Boys but otherwise wasn't much for book learning. In fact, while attending Punxsutawney High, he was booted out of school.[30] The teacher had enough. "Go get your dad and bring him to school." But, Joseph disagreed and left his education behind. Father Emery Elwin Hetrick did not show up to be counseled about his son. Instead, the rebellious Joseph wanted to join the military. At fifteen, he enrolled in the Pennsylvania National Guard (PNG), to serve with his father, who'd been there for decades. Despite not being scholarly, Joseph exhibited natural ability in all things mechanical, a skill likely earned genetically and from his father's teaching aptitude. Hetrick also learned woodworking from his father. These abilities as a problem solver or "fixer" followed him throughout his life.

Joseph eventually earned a General Equivalency Diploma (GED) while in the United States Army.

As an enlisted soldier, Army life suited Joseph perfectly. Tours of duty included stops in Pennsylvania, Virginia, and overseas in Korea, Italy, Germany, and Vietnam. With wife Rachel, he raised three children; Tommy, Gina Marie, and Beth Ann. Sadly, another child named Marianne died shortly after birth. He utilized his mechanical knowledge at every turn but trained as a cook at, among other places, the fancy Willard Hotel, in Washington, D.C. In time, he was promoted to Mess Sergeant, eventually running the entire food operation at his various deployments. In Korea, one such operation occurred on a beach with a few dozen open spit grills. Upon command, the turkeys were all turned in synchronized fashion. All the soldiers enjoyed the bird that day. Being the Mess Sergeant also meant ordering and preparing in extreme bulk quantities in order to satisfy the troops, who ate in shifts. Cleaning as-you-go also informed Joseph's methodology as he trained hundreds of men to follow his instructions, culled from official

---

[30] Some information provided by Gina Hetrick Irving and Beth Simmers from an interview, December 16, 2019.

Army regulations. Because he was "boss man" at the Mess Hall, Hetrick underwent numerous inspections of his operations by Army officers, always keen to demean and find fault. Stateside assignments included Arlington Hall and Fort Meyer. During one memorable family-invited Thanksgiving around 1968, son Tommy came to learn the meaning of the word "cornucopia." The food seemed to be piled to the ceiling; all manner of delicious turkey, ham, potatoes, dressing, vegetables, breads, fruits, and nuts. The eleven year-old must have thought he died and went to heaven. And Tommy's father Joseph pulled it all off, effortlessly, without a hitch.

Joseph's cooking, cleaning, organizational, personal, and mechanical skills did not go unnoticed by the Army. These skills and his superior military bearing earned him an opportunity to serve two generals as their personal *aide-de-camp*. His duties included preparing and serving meals, laundry, driving, and any other task assigned. Joseph worked hand in glove for General Earle "Bus" Wheeler, Chairman of the Joint Chiefs of Staff during Vietnam, and later for Lieutenant General William Wilson "Buffalo Bill" Quinn. These two assignments, serving two highly-decorated officers, became the pinnacle of Joseph's military career.

In April 1972, after two tours in wartime Vietnam taking care of soldiers' bellies, Joseph was given a choice by his base commander. Sergeant First Class (SFC) Hetrick could deploy to Vietnam for a third time, or he could retire. He chose the latter. Overall, he served over 21 years in the Army and retired at the ripe old age of 39.

Following his time in the military, Joseph let his hair down a little bit. He kept his trademark crew-cut, but also grew a moustache. His family lovingly teased him about his choice of haircut and often wondered why he would not grow his hair longer. What was there to cut? Nonetheless, Joseph kept right on going to his regular barber "for a trim." He worked as a taxi driver, a locksmith, and as carpenter. He didn't really enjoy taxiing ungrateful people around. However, he did manage to have a taxi driver license photo snapped. Many family and friends said that he looked exactly like actor Dennis Weaver. Mr. Hetrick worked several years for his friend Earl Nuckols of Virginia Safe & Lock.

Although the work was challenging, Joseph could pick locks and solve delicate security problems with ease. Frequently, he worked on-call, responding to midnight phone calls to open car doors or homes and charging exorbitant fees from the company for this emergency service. In the construction business, however, Mr. Hetrick found his post-Army retirement niche. For this position, Joseph worked as a "punch-out" carpenter for new homes, which oversaw final aspects of the project. These tasks included creating and installing custom kitchen cabinetry.

To say that Joseph was a man of eccentricities would be an understatement. He'd snap off an endless series of jokes. Sometimes, these funny lines were off-color, but they were never malicious. Many times, his humor was self-deprecating. In the summertime, he'd frequently go shirtless, unashamed of what anyone might think. Parading around displaying his muscles became his comfort level. His parents hated this practice, especially when a family photo was snapped outside at 22 Lewis Street of the five adult children with parents Emery and Freda Hetrick. There was Joe, completely at ease without a shirt. Although he was a member of the SS. Cosmas & Damian Catholic Church in Punxsutawney, he did not attend, except for weddings and funerals, mostly the latter. His idea was to worship God outside of church, which he did. When purchasing small items, he always paid with $20 dollar bills. He'd stuff the change into his pocket and keep his automobiles filled with bills and coins that his children could use. Frequently, he'd drive his son Tommy around town. He'd insist on stopping at a movie theatre, and asking Tommy to go in and buy popcorn. "But, we're not watching the movie," Tommy pleaded. "I don't want to watch the movie. I just want some popcorn." Embarrassed Tommy would have to explain to theatre employees that he just wanted to buy popcorn, "for my dad, for the road." On many other occasions, he'd order his son to go inside a convenience store to buy cigarettes. Joseph would wait in the car. "Go inside and buy me a pack of smokes," he'd say. Kool was his preferred brand. Tommy would balk, claiming he was underage, but Joe always had a note ready for the clerk. After numerous successful tries, Tommy finally spoke up one day. "Dad, we're watching this film in school about the dangers of smoking. Please stop." Joseph finally did stop asking his son to buy cigarettes for him. However, he kept right on with his dangerous habit.

Then, there were the parlor tricks. Whenever the opportunity arose, at family gatherings or parties, or even in restaurants, he'd break out his science acts. Joe didn't mind being the center of attention. Securing a wine glass with a very thin rim, Joe would dip his finger into the wine and slowly rub the rim of the glass in a circular motion. If conditions were just right, a hi-pitched sound would be produced. Another effort involved an empty bottle that contained liquor. Joe would take a deep puff on his cigarette, and blow the smoke into the bottle. Observers could clearly see the thick smoke trapped inside the bottle. He'd then light a match and move it towards the bottle. Invariably, a loud POOF, small explosion occurred and instantly, the smoke would be gone from the bottle. Bystanders would gasp in amazement, and then applaud.

Mr. Hetrick participated in many hobbies over the years. In Germany, he began collecting clocks of all types, sizes, and shapes. These included hall clocks, wall clocks, ball clocks, grandfather clocks, cuckoo clocks, kitchen clocks, mantle clocks, tabletop clocks, floor clocks, pendulum clocks, tick-tock clocks, and alarm clocks. One particular clock, in extreme disrepair, was hand-made in Germany in 1887. This unusual piece featured a black marble base, and two dancing ladies on top. After several months, Mr. Hetrick restored the clock, meticulously sanding and grinding, spray painting, and fixing the innards to run once again. He called himself "a clock accumulator," always with his boyish grin. The floorboards in his living quarters strained under their weight. Many of the clocks did not tell time properly or were dormant. No matter to Joseph. He'd simply tinker with them in his home-made shop and spring them back to life. Sometimes, the fixing took minutes, other times it took weeks. This hobby included collecting elaborately-pictured books which described the technical details and histories of some of his timekeepers. And when the family moved, all the clocks were packed up and moved, too. No small operation this transfer of delicate mechanical machinery. For fun, on rare occasion, he'd set up the noisemakers to ring twelve bells at precisely the same time. Needless to say, for this cacophony, the neighbors in the apartments were none too pleased. Other hobbies included the regular maintenance of a miniature steam engine bought for his son Tommy by his grandfather. The toy blew steam with a shrill sound, powered by special power pellets. Mr. Hetrick explained construction of balsa wood gliders to son Tommy. Later, he taught his first grandson Sean how to construct intricate paper kit houses using hobby knives and glue. Projects included famous buildings like Notre Dame Cathedral. In addition to collecting clocks, Mr. Hetrick also collected National Geographic magazines. Some of the issues dated back to the 1910's, with fascinating advertisements for new automobiles. Books also became collectible items as Mr. Hetrick educated himself about American history, mechanical technologies, and even poetry.

While living in Punxsutawney later in life, his nephew Frank called him about a curious conundrum. "Joe, one of my tabletop clocks stopped running." Instantly, Mr. Hetrick hopped in his car, and traveled to Frank's house to investigate. Truth be told, Joe lived for these challenges. It thrilled him that Frank had called him to save the day. He arrived armed with his set of clock tools. After a quick inspection of the rear of the device, Joe put his theory of why the clock stopped to work. "Do you have a matchbook?" he asked. Frank puzzled to himself, "why does he need that?" Nonetheless, Frank, a non-smoker, located an old matchbook in a drawer in his kitchen. He handed it to Mr. Hetrick. Quickly, Hetrick tore off the top of the matchbook and placed the thin cardboard under one of the clock's legs. Then, he used his level tool to measure. Failure was not an option. "Wind 'er up," said Joseph. With that, Frank pulled out the clock key and wound it up from the rear of the device. Tick, tick, tick. The clock went right back into operation, as if it had never stopped in the first place. Astounded, Frank asked, "How'd you do that?" Mr. Hetrick smiled and said, "Simple, I looked to see if I could find where the clock was manufactured. When I discovered it was made in Germany, I understood the precision of balance necessary for these type of clocks. The matchbook re-balanced the clock's delicate mechanics, causing it to run again." Grateful for the fix, Frank offered Joe monetary compensation, but Joe would have none of it. "Have a nice evening," were the fixer's parting words.

In the fall 1997, Mr. Hetrick went to see a doctor, fully aware of his shortness of breath. After a checkup and tests performed over a few week's time, Joseph returned to see the doctor. The prognosis wasn't good. Joseph learned he had terminal lung cancer. He was given about six months to live. The lifetime of smoking cigarettes was catching up to him.

With no small amount of courage, he informed his children. They all got together to discuss his impending demise. Emotions could barely be contained in the meeting, but Mr. Hetrick held strong. "Tommy, I want you to be my Power of Attorney and Executor." Once all the crying ended, reality set in. Son Tommy was honored to perform these necessary tasks. He went to his local library in Virginia and researched the duties involved. Daughter Beth brought her father to live with her, to properly take care of him. After some time, Beth's burden became impossible.

Mr. Hetrick was hospitalized locally, and then at the Veteran's Administration hospital in Pittsburgh. During his care, he was transferred to numerous facilities in western Pennsylvania, before finally settling in at the Pennsylvania Memorial Home in Brookville.

During this time, son Tommy paid all of his father's bills, re-organized his finances, and took care of his personal belongings. Trips from Virginia to Pennsylvania were frequent and incredibly stressful. In February 1998, the two discussed matters. "I'm taking care of everything," Tommy said to his father. With his voice quivering, the elder Hetrick explained that he wanted three things before he passed into the great beyond. Joseph S. Hetrick requested last rites, performed by a priest. He asked for a military funeral with an American flag, and he requested that "Taps" be played on a bugle. Tommy swallowed hard, but said, "I'll do my best, dad."

What Joseph's son did not know at the time, was the difficulty fulfilling these requests. Two months went by before son Tommy received a phone call from Brookville. "It's about your dad," the caregiver said. "You might want to come up here," she said, her heart heavy. Son Tommy again drove the 250 miles to Brookville, but not before picking up his sister Beth, who did not drive. Gina had also arrived at the care home. The three children raced to their father's room. He lay on his back in bed, struggling to breathe, wheezing mightily. A nurse came by and said, "He's very close." The children all knew what that meant.

Tommy excused himself and raced out of the room. At the nursing station, he asked that they call a priest. Joseph S. seemed to be slipping away. Tommy then raced back to the room. No change. With his sisters crying, Tommy paced around feverishly. In between pacing, he went to his father and held his hand. The clock ticked away, inexorably. As no priest was forthcoming, Tommy again raced down the hall, frantically asking for a minister to attend his dying father. The call was made again to a local man of the cloth. Again, Tommy paced and grabbed his father's hand. "Hold on, dad," he said. But, the doorway to the room was clear. Only family were in the room. One last time, Tommy ran to the nurse's station. He begged for one more call, which was made to yet a third local minister. Again, Tommy repeated his ritual drama. Gina and Beth were bawling and alternated between sitting and standing and trying to comfort their father and themselves. Then, a man dressed in religious attire appeared at the door. "Are you Mr. Hetrick," he questioned. "I am, but that's my father over there." The man stood over Mr. Hetrick and softly uttered a few words. Then he turned away. Tommy followed him down the hallway, and saw him out the door. Incredibly, as he was saying thank you and goodbye, another pastor appeared and began heading down the hallway. He asked Tommy, "Where is Mr. Hetrick?" "Right this way," Tommy uttered. As the previous man had before him, the man bent down and offered words of prayer. Then, after a few seconds, he too ambled out of the room, Bible in hand. Tommy walked with him as previous, thanking him for his ministrations. Then, as if heaven sent and on cue, came the priest. As he walked down the hallway, he passed the other minister, exchanging pleasantries. "Son, are you Mr. Hetrick?" "Come right in, father," said Tommy. As he led the priest into the room, he noted the crying had stopped. The priest uttered Latin, performing the Last Rites of the Catholic Church.

After a minute or so, the priest departed. Tommy walked him down the hall toward the door. The first dying request from Joseph S. Hetrick had been fulfilled, in *triplicate*! Armed with this knowledge, Tommy again went to squeeze his father's hand, now noticeably weaker. "It's OK, you can let go…" Tommy softly said. Gina departed after group hugs. Beth wanted to be driven home to take care of her returning schoolchildren. And so, after begging her to stay, Tommy left too with his sister.

The two entered the car, but Tommy knew it would be one of the hardest commutes he'd ever make. Just outside Brookville, a traffic jam formed, due to road construction. Tommy said, "Turn on the radio" thinking it would help alleviate their pain. A minute passed, then another and the cars continued to be stationary. Gloria Gaynor, a disco queen from the late seventies, roared into action. "I will survive," she bellowed out her famous hit. Tommy asked his sister to note the time. "3:47, why?" "You'll see," he said. Somehow, Tommy knew. The Gaynor song was significant because Mr. Hetrick used to play the song over and over again in tribute after his wife of thirty-two years had passed away.

An hour later the siblings arrived at Beth's house. Just as they entered the door, the telephone rang. "Let me get it," exclaimed Tommy. It was the care facility. "Is this Tommy? We regret to inform you that your father just passed." Tommy gulped and dropped his eyes toward the floor. Through tears he asked, "May I ask what was the time of death?" The nurse, a woman with all the experience in the world at these terrible types of conversations, softly replied, "Pronounced at 3:47."

A few days previous, Tommy called local Pennsylvania veteran's groups to inquire about a military burial service and the playing of "Taps." Having veterans present the flag wouldn't be difficult, but finding a bugler was becoming quite a mountain to climb. Tommy made several frantic phone calls to a veteran's group, but each time the answer was something like, "Jimmy died, and he was our last bugler. He could blow 'Taps' though."

The day for the funeral came and Tommy thought he failed his father. The wake occurred at the Pifer Funeral Home in Punxsutawney. Tommy proffered the story of Frank's dead clock, which defined Joseph Hetrick's expertise and personality. Following this eulogy, there wasn't a dry eye in the house. Especially touching was Joseph's 88-year old mother Freda, who cried as she looked on at her son in his coffin. Then came the funeral at SSCD. The family tried to hold together, but the tears rained down all their faces in buckets. There was one more stop before final goodbyes. As promised, several honorable veterans came to the burial site for a man none of them knew. The somber service took place in a large mausoleum at Calvary Cemetery. An American flag draped over the casket. As next of kin, Tommy received the gift of the folded flag, honoring his dad's service in the United States Army. Father Joseph Riccardo presided, offering as much comfort as possible. When his words concluded, the gathering slowly made their way outside.

Incredibly, the notes signifying the death of a soldier sounded through the haze of mourners. Tommy thought, "It was Taps!, Who? How?" His spirits saddened but simultaneously uplifted by the music, Tommy saw a young girl posed with her bugle, blowing the sweetest twenty-four notes ever composed. He approached the girl and asked, "Who are you? How did you get here? I...I..." The high schooler explained, "I learned this last night. One of those men asked me to come." Tommy's heart nearly burst with joy. He hugged the girl and whispered "Thank you." Joseph S. Hetrick's final three wishes had been satisfied.

Concerning the miraculous life and death of my father, my hero.

Rachel Ann Perri Hetrick (1930-1987)

Rachel Ann Perri Hetrick's childhood was difficult, to say the least. Raised in an Italian Catholic family with six sisters (Pauline, Mary, Theresa, Jeanne, Rose Marie, Louise) and a brother (Frank), Rachel Perri was born on 240 Pine Street in Punxsutawney. Her mother Mary died in 1950 and her taskmaster father and sisters teased her unmercifully. Indeed, her childhood nickname was "Ninny", which stuck with her throughout her life. Despite being somewhat of a favorite child by her father, he nonetheless became concerned when she went roller skating as a teenager at the local rink. Mr. Perri believed that Rachel could injure herself, and thus become unavailable for work in the family business, Perri's Dry Cleaners.[31] In Catholic school, the teasing continued. When one of the teaching nuns asked if she was chewing gum in class, Rachel initially tried to hide the forbidden practice. She then was forced to blow a giant bubble with the gum, place it on her nose, and parade in front of all the other students in the school.

Rachel was a 1948 graduate of the SS. Cosmas & Damian (SSCD) Catholic High School in Punxsutawney, Pennsylvania. If she learned anything there, it was the now forgotten practice of penmanship. Rachel's cursive writing was so stylish and beautiful, that it could be an art form in itself.

In 1955, she became engaged to Joseph Streamer Hetrick, a soldier in the United States Army. It was Rachel who eventually proposed to him, securing a $1000 dowry from her father Gennaro Perri. Mr. Hetrick was also forced to show his future father-in-law the engagement ring to prove his sincerity. The couple eventually eloped to Arlington, Virginia, where they married in October of that year. The event was attended by only her husband's military friends, but no family on the Perri side. A military newsletter published after her marriage described the newlyweds as "well-known in social circles."

Silly stories and incidents abound regarding Rachel. It's

---

[31] Some information in this biography provided by Gina Hetrick Irving. Interview with subject 16 December, 2019.

hard to understand precisely why because she was a sincere, kindly, gentle spirit who always thought of others before herself. It's possible that some were due to her stern household upbringing or lack of experience in worldly matters. Nonetheless, a few of them will be documented here. While out for a drive with her future husband, Rachel spied an equine animal clopping along the side of the road. She exclaimed, "Look at that big dog!" Her date had to explain that it was a horse. Two other stories manifested themselves in the local grocery store. She saw a television ad announcing a sale on cat food. Happily buying ten cans of the stuff, she explained her good fortune when her husband came home from work. "That's great," he said. "But, we don't own a cat." On another occasion, Rachel asked the clerk for "Nauseous Cheese Doritos", unaware that the first word was actually "Nacho." Family outings allowed for other silly adventures. In a wooded resort called Shannondale in West Virginia, she hopped into a boat with daughter Gina and a family friend. After rowing out into the lake, for some reason, Rachel stood up, and the boat capsized. After a trip to a park with her husband, Rachel lost one shoe. When her husband asked her about it, she didn't realize it was missing. Another time she slipped on the ice. When concern arose from her husband that she might have sprained an ankle, Rachel stated, "I genuflected." She became quite a good cook. After cooking up a delicious roast one day, she waited for her husband to arrive home from his military job. The aromas of the meat overpowered the kitchen and tempted her to pick at the dish all day. By the time her husband arrived home, nearly all the meat had disappeared. Husband Joseph also gave her an off-the-books driving lesson one day. But, it didn't go that well, as Rachel nearly steered the car into a lake. Following that incident, she never drove again and never possessed a driver's license.

Although she was often the butt of jokes, Rachel forgave all. On one such memorable occasion, the family went to visit in Punxsutawney. Teenage Tommy stayed behind, being the proud owner of a new Super 8 movie camera. Calling up a couple of friends including Bob Karnes, Rusty Gibson, and Peter Brichant, Tommy invited them all over to the apartment in Fairfax for some fun with filming. Although not having a solid plan at the time, Peter

Brichant soon asked to see the parent's clothes closet. He discovered a cool black dress, some pumps, and a wig. After a few minutes in the bathroom, Peter emerged looking like one hot mama. Peter then grabbed a purse and the game was on. The pranksters went outside with their new *femme fatale* and Tommy started filming. Hollywood would be jealous. Peter vamped around the neighborhood and it was all caught on film. A minute of fame and glory. The family arrived back home that Sunday night with Rachel asking Tommy, "Did you boys have a good weekend?" Tommy didn't let on, saying, "Yeah, uh huh, mom." After the film was developed a few days later, Tommy invited the family to a special movie night. He made a bucket of popcorn and all were served soda pop. "You've got to see this," said Tommy to mom Rachel, dad Joseph, sister Gina, and little sister Beth. The projector clicked and clacked to life. In the darkened room, there appeared Peter, sashaying around, as Rachel screamed, "That's my dress!" Joseph broke out in a guffaw. Rachel and everyone else laughed like crazy. And, the film was played over and over again that night to everyone's amusement.

On and off, Rachel worked at Kann's Department Store, Ben Franklin, Dart Drug, Bradlees, and T. J. Maxx. Most of these jobs involved stocking. However, no matter how much money she made, she did not splurge on fancy dresses for herself. Instead, all of her earnings went back into the family, buying clothes for her three kids; Tommy, Gina, and Beth. She also worked with her daughter Gina at a hair salon.

Above all, Rachel valued children. Babies and toddlers and kids under ten and tweens. It didn't matter what age. She'd want to spend the day with anyone's kids, including her own. Perhaps, it was due to her simplistic nature or innocence of young people. Rachel related with kids. She'd play games with them, laugh with them, cook for them, comb their hair, play dolls or build blocks with them. This love affair with children happened wherever she went, with kids of all ages, colors, and creeds. Once, with her daughter Gina, she made a doll out of pantyhose stuffed with cotton. The doll looked realistic enough when dressed up and a picture was taken of her caressing the doll. Husband Joseph, upon seeing the photograph,

286

exclaimed, "Whose baby is this?" When her first and only grandchild in her lifetime was born, she took great delight in changing Sean's diapers and singing him to sleep. It's impossible to say, but one could only imagine what she'd think of the grandchildren she never knew; namesake Rachel, Emily, Alicia, Amelia, Sarah, Nicholas, and Katie. That thought could break one's heart.

Being married to a soldier wasn't always roses. In fact, it was often a singular pursuit. Sometimes, she'd request in her loneliness that her own children miss school to spend time with her. "What can I get into?" she'd ask her daughter Gina. Unfortunately, she often identified as a "bored housewife." However, in Fairfax, in the late seventies and eighties, she met Anita Spain Axford, a neighbor and accomplished pianist. The two women became instant friends, occasionally conversing in Italian and reliving the olden days.

With her husband serving in the Army overseas on multiple occasions, Rachel traveled with him and the family to Germany and Italy. Germany was the land of ancient castles and modern industry. Rachel tolerated these 1960s assignments, making a half-hearted attempt to learn a few German words and mingle with the local population, when the occasion called for it. However, the Italian experience proved far more interesting as the country of her parents' birth. Husband Joseph was under the impression that his wife could speak fluent Italian. In a restaurant, Rachel looked at the menu and ordered a plate of pasta. The waiter brought back plain pasta only, without sauce. Rachel was disappointed. Joseph was so embarrassed, that for his order he just pointed to a nearby patron, and stated, "I want what he's having, over there." The waiter could not understand English, but soon figured everything out. At a military Bingo Night in 1961, Rachel won the spectacular prize of a Fiat automobile. Rachel, not being able to drive, sold the car shortly thereafter to a serviceman. Not a bad haul though for the Hetricks, for a game that cost probably a dime to play. At about that same time, her only son Tommy was enrolled in the local *asilo*, an Italian nursery school. Not being able to speak Italian, with the Italian children not being able to speak English, nonetheless, the class would not start until their beloved Tommy had arrived. Rachel told this story *ad nauseum* to anyone and everyone. Two other Tommy tales emerged during this era in Italy. On a paddle boat ride in the Adriatic, mother and son drifted too far off shore, and had to be rescued by Italian authorities. During a tour of St. Peter's Square in Vatican City, Rachel explained to her charge that it is customary to kiss the feet of the large statue of St. Peter. Little Tommy did so, dutifully following his mother's advice. Unfortunately, he straightened up with a bloody lip, proclaiming to his mom, "Don't they ever cut his toenails?"

Over twenty years later as her son Tommy was serving overseas at Misawa Air Force Base, Japan, in the United States Air Force, Rachel decided on a visit. A well-off relative had died and money was willed to Rachel. With this news and her new fortune, Rachel called her son. He answered but quickly cut-off her plan. "I'm in the military, always working. Besides, you can't come for a month. That's crazy." Rachel, however, would not be deterred. Determined to see her son, she summoned up the courage, obtained a passport, and was ready to fly. That evening, son Tommy oft-handedly mentioned this dilemma to a fellow worker. Without hesitation, Sgt. David Chapmon said to the young airman, "She can stay at my house. No problem." "But Dave," said A1C Tommy. "You have a wife and besides, a brand new baby!" "I'll make it happen," the sergeant stated emphatically. Chapmon even made arrangements with the Lieutenant Colonel to grant the airman time off to see his mom. And with that, the adventure began. Rachel was told of the arrangement by her son, was on a plane, and arrived at the local Misawa, Japan airport after a stopover in Tokyo to change planes. Sgt. Chapmon even drove Tommy there to pick his mother up. First thing was a meal in a Japanese restaurant, which Chapmon paid for. She settled in at his house off-base that evening. The next day, Rachel walked to the local train station while son Tommy hopped a bus from his quarters to the main gate. He then walked into Japan proper and met his mom halfway. For the next month, the two traveled all over the countryside, using taxis and trains. Rachel could not speak Japanese, but her son taught her a few words to get by. Rachel learned to eat some of the local dishes, and developed a few favorites. Her son also took her to nightclubs, singing *karaoke* to her in a foreign tongue. In Noheji, Tommy introduced him to his "other mother", a *mamasan* in a club called *Karoru*, or Snack Carol. By nightfall, following like a curfew, Tommy deposited his mom right back at the local train station where she could walk to Sgt. Chapmon's home. And, this is how things went day after day, for a full month. Had Sgt. Chapmon not offered his home, it's doubtful that Rachel could afford to stay at Japanese hotels for one month. There were no such accommodations on the base. After thirty days of beaming smiles, uproarious laughter, tortured translations, and tons of new friends, the time came for Rachel to return to the States. Son Tommy would later brag that he never saw his mother happier.

Mom...forever.

ABOUT THE AUTHOR

J. Thomas Hetrick is a baseball writer fascinated by profoundly thorough research and totally lost causes. Following the publication of his critically acclaimed book, *MISFITS! The Cleveland Spiders in 1899*, an in-depth study of major league baseball's worst-ever team, Tom turned his attention to documenting the tragicomic rise and fall of the owner of a 19th century baseball team in *Chris Von der Ahe and the St. Louis Browns*. His baseball biography became a Finalist for the Seymour Medal, an annual award given to the best book of baseball history or biography. It also earned him an invitation to speak about the story at the National Baseball Hall of Fame and Museum in Cooperstown, New York.

Born an "army brat" in Fort Belvoir, Arlington, VA, Hetrick comes from a family of military servicemen who've logged over 125 years over three generations. He proudly served in the United States Air Force, graduated from George Mason University, and worked as a contractor for numerous U.S. government agencies. Hetrick retired to the wilds of western Pennsylvania. He is an active member of SABR (the Society for American Baseball Research) and has presented numerous research papers at regional and national meetings.

Gratitude is Hetrick's third book.

www.ingramcontent.com/pod-product-compliance
Lightning Source LLC
Chambersburg PA
CBHW060250100426
42742CB00011B/1697